LADY'S HANDS, LION'S HEART

A Midwife's Saga

LADY'S HANDS, LION'S HEART

A MIDWIFE'S SAGA

By

Carol Leonard
Bad Beaver Publishing
Hopkinton, NH

Bad Beaver Publishing
585 Hopkinton Road
Hopkinton, NH 03229
603.224.4596
www.badbeaverfarm.com

Library of Congress Cataloging-in-Publication Data
Leonard, Carol
Lady's hands, lion's heart, a midwife's saga / Carol Leonard.
p.cm
Includes glossary.
ISBN 978-0-615-19550-6

First Printing

ALSO BY CAROL LEONARD
The Circle of Life (co-authored with Elizabeth Davis)
Women of the Thirteenth Moon, A Baby Boomer's Survival Guide to Menopause
"Medea" (short story)
The Beauty Girls
"The Making of Bad Beaver Farm" (*Downeast* Magazine)

I would like to thank Dr. Gerald Hamilton, FACOG, for so patiently doing the medical edit of this book. Gerry has been my backup and my dear friend for over thirty years. I also want to thank my editor and colleague, Jane Hunter Munson, for her fabulous nit-picky eye.

CONTENTS

Author's Note

The names and some identifying facts of clients have been changed to protect the privacy of the individuals. Many births are composites of several melded together to make a whole. Otherwise, all stories are true to my experience.

Carol Leonard
Hopkinton, NH
2008

DEDICATION

My lifelong gratitude to the thirteen midwives
who sat in the pew directly behind me on February 15, 1987:

Susan Bartlett, RN, NHCM; Deborah Black, CNM;
Molly Connelly; Robin Cornell; Valerie Gonzales Dowling Morcom;
Cindy Dunleavy, NHCM; Laurie Foster, NHCM/CNM;
Cindall Morrison, CNM; Valerie Jacques, RN, NHCM;
Deb Keith, CNM; Mari Patkelly, RN, NHCM; Ruth Roper, CPM;
Brenda Sanborn, CNM; and Lauren Savage.

You are my sisters.

CHAPTER ONE

MILAN'S BIRTH, SPRING, 1975

So, it begins. I lie awake in the dark; the first firm squeezing of my uterus has wakened me. I lie in bed with my heart pounding. Labor has taken me by surprise; it is a full week early. I am astounded. Another squeeze comes. I look at the clock. Twenty minutes apart. I get up quietly and walk around to see if the contractions stop. I pace around our bedroom loft. I look out the window to the trees, shadowy in the soft moonlight. I am tingling with anticipation. Today I will meet my child.

I lie back down and try to sleep. I try to ignore my excitement and the strong squeezing. John is curled up on his side, facing away from me. I feel my belly mound in rhythmic waves. I lay my hands over the stretched, paper-thin skin of my abdomen. My child within stretches his foot out to deliberately push my hand aside. This is his game. I manage to grab his foot through my skin; he immediately jerks his foot away and rolls to the other side. He tentatively sticks his foot out in the new spot, teasing me. I pinch it again. He retreats quickly. This makes me smile. I am so in love with this child and I haven't even seen him yet.

In mid-afternoon I drive through a late-spring snow into town to my ob-gyn's office to be checked. I know the prenatal nurses

whisper about my appearance. Sanctimonious wenches. It has
been a long, harsh winter in the backwoods of New Hampshire,
and we heat our home with a wood stove. I am wearing my heavy
winter boots and smell like gasoline from the chainsaw. I notice
I have wood chips in my hair. I see they have written "Mountain
Woman" on the front of my chart. This makes me grin.

I hoist myself up into the cold metal stirrups, and I lie with
my legs splayed. One of the bitchy nurses snaps on a pair of
latex gloves, squirts on some K-Y Jelly, and prepares to examine
my cervix. She doesn't speak and does not bother to warm her
hands. She plunges her fingers into me, and her eyes widen in
surprise. She says I am already five centimeters dilated and wants
me to go straight to the hospital because of the bad weather. I
decline. I opt to go back home.

I go back home because I don't really want to hang around
in a sterile institution, waiting for labor to kick in. I also go
home because tonight we are having a fabulous dinner party
for the men who helped us build our new house. I love these
guys. They are all committed bachelors and very baby-phobic.
But they are incredibly hardworking, funny, intelligent friends.
Together, we all have built a beautiful handmade home in the
New Hampshire woods.

The dinner party is frankly ridiculous. The contractions
shift gears and are now coming every five minutes. I try to be
nonchalant and charming. Every five minutes I tense, catch
my breath, and try to fake a sickly smile. I begin squirming
uncomfortably in my chair, as I feel that my bottom could—very
possibly and at any minute—turn shockingly inside out. I try
to breathe unobtrusively, but my nostrils are flaring. I grit my
teeth, and my eyes start to water.

Every five minutes, the guys stop eating and hold their
collective breath. They stare at me in horror. Robert looks as if
he may retch.

Michael says, "Shouldn't we boil water or something?"

I go upstairs and call my neighbor, Talie. Talie has had three babies, all born at home with a local doctor. I don't know about the home-birth part, that seems kind of sketchy to me, but she's a pro at childbirth. Talie tells me to lie down and concentrate on the intensity and that I will intuitively know when it is time to go. I lie down. I throw up green beans and roast chicken. Now I know. Definitely time to go.

John and I fairly fly out of the house, leaving the guys standing there helplessly. Their eyes are wide, and their mouths are dropped open.

"Good luck," they mutter.

"Do the dishes!" I shout victoriously as our car careens down the driveway.

Thirty minutes later, when we can see the lights of Merrimack Valley Hospital in the distance from the highway, I get my first real wave of serious labor. That sucker hurts. Without warning, the contractions begin coming every minute. This is no longer fun, nor funny. I am gripping the dashboard of the Peugeot. I find I am panting like a dog. Yup, this is *serious* pain. Not pain, like if you broke your leg, or pain without a pattern to it, but real, genuine pain nonetheless. The insides of my nostrils are getting hot from panting. Beads of sweat drip from my forehead. I am seriously wondering how I am going to get out of the car once we get there.

John and I manage to make it to the receptionist in the lobby of the hospital, although John has to drag me the last half of the way from the car. The receptionist informs us that because it is still a half-hour until midnight, we will have to pay for a full day. John and I look at each other. We don't have medical coverage. I decide that I'll be damned if I'm going up to the maternity ward before midnight and get billed for it. I stay in the lobby. I huff and puff and pace, waiting for the clock to tick away. I begin to get tremendous pressure in my butt. I groan and squat down, pretty unconscious of my actions at this point. The other lobbyists peer over their magazines in abject fear. At 12:01 AM, I accept the offered wheelchair and am escorted up to Merrimack Valley Hospital's maternity ward.

A night nurse wheels me down a long, beige-tiled hall and into a large, beige-tiled room with several curtained-off, high-railed hospital beds. I catch a glimpse through a crack in the curtain of the woman in labor next to me.

"*Jesus, Joseph, and Mary! This is all your fault!*" the woman yells over and over, like a litany.

I am about to make a snide comment on the woman's catholic choice of labor-coping mantras when I am engulfed in the worst pain known to womankind.

"*Holy crap!*" I yell.

When I can breathe again, I find myself repeating my own personalized mantra during contractions.

"*Oh, shit! Oh, dear! Oh, shit! Oh, dear!*" I wail.

"*Jesus! Joseph and Mary!*" screams from the other side of the curtain.

This proves to have a strangely comforting effect, a technique not commonly taught in Lamaze class.

I am ordered to hoist my rock-hard belly up onto the rock-hard bed and to spread my legs in order to be "prepped". Prepping consists of shaving off all my pubic hair and giving me a high enema so that "we" will be "clean" for the doctor, as the labor nurse so delicately puts it. The labor nurse is an older woman, and she is chewing gum. The old nurse examines me and looks quite pleased. She announces that I am already eight centimeters dilated. "Only two more to go! Good work, young lady!"

She instructs me to use the adjoining bathroom, if I need it. *If?* With seven gallons of hot, soapy water in my rectum? She's kidding, right? She says to be careful not to soil the bed sheets and leaves the room and closes the door.

Within minutes the enema is becoming unavoidably insistent.

I try my best to make it to the loo without leakage, shuffling in between whopping contractions. I am semi-successful. Now, I am sitting on the throne, reassessing my predicament.

Here I am, panting on a rusty toilet in a harshly lit, drab, concrete room, shitting my brains out.

I am thirsty, very hot and sweaty, kind of dizzy, and I am all alone.

There is a woman shouting desperately to the Holy Ghost in the next room.

I am about to experience one of the most profound and meaningful acts possible in my entire lifetime.

What the hell is wrong with this picture?

And how come no one has even checked the baby? Maybe because it's late at night and they are short-staffed? And what if my baby is born in this jailhouse toilet with nobody else in here? Then what?

Labor certainly is an interesting process. I am in awe that my body knows exactly what to do; it is functioning like a finely tuned machine. I am feeling pretty proud of myself, but with the next contraction, I do believe my bottom is history. My yoni is excruciating, on fire. This is impetus enough for me to drag myself out of there and back up onto the scaffolding of the bed. The Jesus woman has been taken away.

Now the pain is overwhelming. I can't move. I can't even swear. Forget the breathing, Jesus. I lie here as wave after wave of crushing spasms wash over me. I gape at the ceiling. Oh, my god. I can't handle this. This is truly unbearable. Then ... a remarkable thing happens. I separate from myself. I realize that I can give my life to bring my child through, that I will willingly die to be his gateway to this world—my love for him is that strong. I stop struggling. I feel myself surrender and open up. I start to push. I push in big, involuntary, moose-call pushes. The old nurse runs back in. John is allowed in after filling out all the necessary payment forms.

Pushing is unbelievably powerful, and I am unbelievably vocal. I am not prepared for this. Either I really am being that loud, or it just sounds that way inside my head. The old obstetrics nurse is pleasantly perched between my legs, snapping her gum. She gives me a thumbs-up and an ongoing progress report on the visibility of my child's head.

"I can see a dime. Yup, now I can see a nickel," she reports. "Hell, I can see a quarter!"

I like her. In between straining, I ask her if she can just deliver my baby right here in the bed. Maybe tell the doctor it was born too fast to make it to the delivery room. Her face creases with a huge smile but she shakes her head no. The doctor on call would have all hell to pay if she failed to wake him up in time. Especially because it is Dr. Easey.

Dr. Easey! Damn. I hadn't thought about this. The obstetrics practice I go to is a group of five men. They are secretly referred to as "Fifty Fingers" by their women patients. Easey is the doctor I like the least. I see him as a cold, steely man with mocking, ice blue eyes. Now, he is the obstetrician on call. Shit, Murphy's Law.

John sees my momentary distress and attempts to comfort me by placing a cold washcloth on my forehead. Just at this moment the strongest bearing-down urge hits my butt. I angrily wing the washcloth across the room. I tell him not to touch me—as a matter of fact, to never touch me again, *ever.* John retreats to the safety of a chair in the corner of the room to wait it out. He hides his face in his hands.

An hour and a half later, a lot of Milan's head is visible; it no longer retreats between pushes. I can see bald wrinkles. Then all hell breaks loose. The doctor makes his cameo appearance. He is grumpy and rumpled with sleep. He takes one look at my efforts and grunts something unintelligible and turns to the delivery room to scrub up. Some orderlies appear from nowhere. They slide my contorting and pushing body onto a

high, narrow gurney and rush me down the hall at high speed
to the delivery room.

Once there, I am moved again onto the even higher delivery
table, all the while with a head between my legs. I am made to lie
flat on my back with my legs up in the air in metal braces, like
a June bug stuck helplessly on its back. The table is divided in
half with the lower part removed, so my butt is now suspended
in midair. Because I have had no drugs, I am allowed to watch
the proceedings in a standup mirror. I see myself being painted
from navel to kneecaps with orangey-brown Betadine.

Now Milan's head really starts to crown. The stretching is
merciless. I feel as if my fragile labial tissues are splintering like
a thousand shards of glass. Nobody is paying any attention; they
are all getting ready to do their assigned jobs. My butt is still
hanging in midair and my poor expanding yoni is *burning*. I do
the natural thing; I reach down to soothe the fiery skin around
my child's emerging head.

Dr. Easey sees me do this. He flips out. Totally and irrationally.
He is irate that I have the audacity to touch myself in front of him.
He slaps my hand away. He shouts that I have contaminated his
sterile field! Godammit! He gives orders for me to be restrained,
for my hands to be strapped down. He continues ranting as
though I am a disgusting, wild beast. The nurse ties my hands
securely with leather handcuffs that are built into the table; they
look like the wrist restraints found on electric chairs. I watch as
Dr. Easey cuts a huge midline episiotomy in my vagina. Milan's
head is born.

It *is* a miracle! As Milan's body slides out of me, he kicks me
one last time. The doctor puts him in a clear-plastic warming cart
across the room. I am straining to see what my son looks like.
All I can see is one pudgy leg stretched up, tentatively testing
the air with his toes. How sweet! I want to hold and inspect that
chubby thing.

"Please give me my baby," I say politely.

Nobody pays any attention to me, so I say it louder:
"Please give me my baby!"

On the third try I fairly shout for my child. *"Give me my damn baby!"*

They all stop bustling around and stare at me as though I have postpartum psychosis already. Dr. Easey looks irritated. He picks up Milan and unceremoniously plops him on my chest. My hands are still strapped to the table. I struggle to look in my newborn's eyes, but I cannot move my arms. I feel someone tugging angrily at the straps, untying my wrists. I look up into John's brown eyes over his surgical mask, which is streaked with tears. So much emotion in those eyes! With my hands finally free, I begin touching my baby all over his sweet, fat little body. I start rubbing the white, creamy vernix into his skin, massaging him. I smell him, sniffing his neck and behind his ears. I want to lick him, but I already have the sense that Dr. Easey thinks I am a borderline fruitcake.

My bald baby is so beautiful, so perfect, even if he does look a little like Gerald Ford. Milan looks at me and frowns. Then his eyes focus and he squares me with the most intense, penetrating gaze, as if to ask, "Who are *you*?"

This important meeting is cut short by a very rough and painful delivery of the placenta. I look up in time to see Dr. Easey yank the placenta into a bucket waiting on the floor by his feet. When I look in the mirror, I can't believe my eyes. My poor yoni has been transformed into something unrecognizable. It is draped, shaved, stained dark brown, cut, bleeding, and gaping open. It looks like a Thanksgiving turkey ready to be stuffed and trussed. This is when the conflicting emotions begin. I am incredibly high from giving birth, proud that my body is so strong and wise. I am speechlessly in awe of the process. I have just done the most powerful thing I will ever experience in my life, and yet … I am completely pissed.

A growing feeling of anger starts to cloud my euphoria. I feel thwarted that my accomplishment has somehow been belittled, that I have been strapped down like a lunatic, degraded and humiliated in this most sacred of times. It is an increasing uneasiness; at first, it is hard to grasp what is wrong.

Milan weighs in at a whopping nine pounds. Ouch. Must have been all those nauseating Adelle Davis brewers-yeast-and-wheat-germ shakes. My little budgie is taken from my arms to go to the nursery for the high-test newborn exam. Supposedly, he has to wait there until the morning shift, when the pediatrician comes to do his rounds. Milan will be thoroughly checked out during normal business hours. John goes with his son.

Dr. Easey repairs the episiotomy in silence. It seems to me that he is taking an inordinately long time down there. I wonder if he's embroidering his initials. I ask how bad the damage is and how many stitches are needed. I am trying to make shop-talk conversation at three o'clock in the morning with someone who has just cut my vagina to shreds. Surprisingly, Dr. Easey says his first full sentence of the entire night. He proudly states that he is doing his trademark "husband's stitch," which means he is putting in a few extra stitches at the top of my perineum and pulling it tight so I won't be floppy and stretched out from having a baby. How thoughtful. He'll make sure I am good and tight so there will always be enough friction for my husband. I am going to be even better than before! Is this guy serious? I picture my yoni pursed and puckered together with all the flexibility of a vise grip. For the rest of my life I will have a numb spot there.

Dr. Easey finishes up his needlework and comes up to my head. I think, *Now he's going to congratulate me for doing an outstanding job.*

Instead, what he says is, "Some women are meant to be workers and some women are meant to be breeders. You are definitely a breeder."

That does it. The man is a sexist sadist. I need to get out of here. Fast.

I say to him, "I want to go home."

Dr. Easey looks stunned for a moment, then gets an imperious look. "You are aware that hospital policy is that you must stay for at least five days postpartum for observation? You do understand this? *Comprehend?*" he growls. "You absolutely may *not* leave against my orders." He turns abruptly and heads out the door.

"I am outta here!" I yell after him as he disappears down the hall.

The OB night nurse comes back with the orderlies, and they wheel me down some more beige halls to the beige postpartum ward. This is a big, open room with about a dozen beds arranged dormitory style; it is for patients without insurance who are unable to afford a private room. They get me settled in for the night; the nurse squeezes my flaccid belly with a vengeance. She puts a veritable mattress of a sanitary pad on me.

After they leave, I slide out of bed and tentatively try walking. I feel like I have a bowling ball in my butt. I'm sure I am popping stitches with every step, but I am famished—*and* I want my baby. I shuffle with baby steps down the hall, cringing with each movement. I am following the sound of my baby crying to the nursery.

John looks surprised to see me. He is holding Milan.

I say, "Let's go."

The three of us leave in the early morning hours of April 9, 1975. It is written in my medical chart that I left "AMA"—against medical advice.

This is the beginning of my life's work.

RENAISSANCE

LADY'S HANDS, 1975

I have had plenty of time as I lie awake, nursing my baby in the middle of the night, to reflect on my birth experience. Even though my delivery was considered a natural birth because I wasn't drugged, I've come to believe there was nothing "natural" about my experience at all. The rote hospital routines have mechanized the naturalness of birth until it is unrecognizable. There is nothing spontaneous or even sensible about being flat on your back with your hands tied down, like a restrained animal. As a result, I vow to help other women have a more positive birth experience than I had. I just don't know how this is going to manifest, exactly.

When Milan is two months old, I see an ad in the local newspaper for the newly opened New Hampshire Women's Health Services. They are offering abortion services; Roe vs. Wade has passed, and abortions are now legal. The ad is for a PRP, a procedure-room person—a woman to be a hand-holder and comforter for women having an abortion. I think that getting a background in women's health is probably a good place for me to start.

I apply for the PRP position. I go to the interview with my

friend Claudia, who thinks she may be interested as well. I also bring Milan because he is nursing. The director of the Health Center is a classy, no-nonsense, middle-aged woman, who begins focusing more on Claudia than on me. She is interested in Claudia because she has had two abortions herself. The director thinks that Claudia might be more suitable, more compassionate, coming from personal experience. As the director explains the job description to us, however, I can see we are losing Claudia. She looks sick.

The director then levels with me. She expresses her concern that I could be a liability because I have just given birth. I explain that I was fortunate to avoid an unplanned pregnancy in my youth because I was able to tolerate an IUD without mishap, unlike some young women. I state that I certainly respect a woman's right to make the abortion decision for herself. I say I understand the enormity of that decision even more now *because* I have the responsibility of a child.

The director fixes me with an intense, scrutinizing look as I nurse my son.

I plead with her. "Look. You've just got to give me this job. I'll be the best PRP you've ever seen. I want to devote my life to women. I promise you won't regret it."

She sits silently for several minutes. She seems to be considering this eager, postpartum whippersnapper who has the audacity to sit in an abortion clinic breast-feeding her infant.

I get the job.

The director explains that the impossibly handsome Dr. McKinney is the founder of the Health Center. Dr. McKinney is a partner in Fifty Fingers. He is the OB that I like the most; he's so gentle and understanding. Of course, he was not on call the night I went into labor. Apparently Dr. McKinney has recruited his partners to donate time to the clinic to support the cause.

I do not know what possesses me to think I can just cruise right through an abortion procedure without a reaction. I have had a pathological needle phobia and crash-and-burn reaction to the sight of blood since childhood. My idealistic cause of devoting myself to women's health has temporarily taken hold of my common sense. The procedure is described to me in graphic detail. I go into the procedure room with my first woman; I have all the naiveté of a Florence Nightingale wannabe.

The afternoon of my first procedure, as luck would have it, Dr. Easey is on duty. I swear the man looks right at me but doesn't recognize me. Probably just as well, since I went AWOL from the hospital. Maybe if I show him the growing-in stubble on my yoni and that special topknot stitch of his, it might ring a bell.

I am standing next to the woman having the procedure. I am holding her hand. She is a nice woman but very nervous. I am trying to make small talk with her. I see Dr. Easey begin to give her a paracervical block. The needle is a spinal needle, about five inches long. It has to be that long to get up the vagina to the cervix. Even so, it is formidable looking, and I feel my face get inordinately hot. When Dr. Easey begins dilating the woman's cervix, she winces in pain. The remembered pain of my own recent cervical dilation comes flooding back. My uterus starts sympathy contractions that make me gasp. I start to get dizzy. When the cannula is in place and the noisy vacuum aspirator is turned on, I can see the blood flowing through the clear plastic tubing to the machine. I start to see dark spots in front of my eyes. I know I am going down. I give the woman my best sickly smile. I excuse myself.

The bathroom is right across the hall. I fight to make it there before blackness occludes my vision entirely. I close the door and slide to the floor in a heap. Why, oh, why do women have to have so much pain in their lives?

I put my face on the cool tiles of the bathroom floor, and I start to rally.

"OK, girl," I say to myself, "you have got to pull yourself together. Pull yourself up by your bootstraps, or this is going to be a very short-lived career. You march your sorry butt right back in there."

I crawl to the sink and put my head under the cold-water faucet. It revives me. When the nausea passes and I can stand up, I look in the mirror. Not only is my head soaked but the whole front of me as well. My compassion and empathy for the woman has triggered a letdown response. My breasts have gushed milk all over the front of my dress. I know it is now or never. I stuff a bunch of paper towels down my nursing bra to prevent further embarrassment. I slick back my damp hair as presentably as possible. I slip back in to the room, muttering my apologies. Nobody notices my disarray. The woman hugs me and is genuinely grateful for my support.

I stay at the clinic for five years.

At the same time that I start working at the Health Center, I approach Dr. Brown in Henniker, New Hampshire, to see if he will possibly consider taking me on as an assistant. Dr. Francis Brown is a general practitioner. He is the quintessential, old country doctor, still going out to the rural areas, making house calls. He has a shock of white hair and a curly white beard and bright, twinkly eyes behind round, wire-rim glasses. He looks like a skinny Santa Claus. I'm sure little kids expect him to laugh "Ho, ho, ho!" during their checkups.

Dr. Brown, known affectionately as the town's "Doc", is a unique individual; he marched against the war in Vietnam in Washington, DC. In his protest against the unnecessary loss of young people's lives, he signed bogus physicals for young men at the local college to prevent them from being drafted.

New England College bestowed Dr. Brown with an honorary degree, doctor of humane letters, noting that he "pioneered the revival of home births in our state, bringing many of our area's children into this world in an atmosphere of love and security."

He is exactly forty years older than I—we share the same birthday.

Dr. Brown is the only doctor in the state of New Hampshire who still does home births. He generates a lot of criticism from the younger doctors at the hospital for delivering babies at home. They feel it is an archaic practice that is potentially dangerous and that he should stop. Dr. Brown ignores this. His record is good. He has attended thousands of births. He was trained at Rush Medical College in Chicago during the Depression. He explains to me that they would go out "on district," as he calls it. The young medical students got their obstetrical training in the ghetto apartments of Chicago. They sometimes did necessary forceps deliveries on the kitchen table.

He feels strongly that as long as women still want to give birth at home, then he is going to provide them with that option. Besides, he actually prefers a birth at home if the mother is healthy. He thinks all the hospital routine is a bother. He has had a general practice in Henniker in the same house for thirty years and is assisted in his office by his competent nurse and wife, Beulah.

The day I go to meet with Dr. Brown with my proposal, Milan is in a front-pack, snuggled against my chest. I ask Dr. Brown if I can tag along with him to births; that I would like to help in any way possible. I say I would be honored to assist him in his work. He looks genuinely surprised. He says that no one has ever asked to accompany him. I am astounded. He says yes immediately; he thinks this is a great idea. He is getting older and can use a good assistant to help out. He promises to call me with the very next labor case. I am so happy that I cry all the way home.

THE FIRST BIRTH

The first call comes quite soon after our meeting. It is 3:00 AM, and Dr. Brown's cheery voice says, "Carol? Let's go!"

He gives me directions to an apartment in a government-subsidized housing development up on Concord Heights. He says it is the woman's third baby—he attended the first two as well—and that her water has broken, but she isn't contracting yet. He says we should get there soon, though, because the woman is a Christian Scientist, and they tend to have a pretty fast and easy time of it. I am so excited that my teeth chatter all the way on the drive there.

When I arrive at the apartment, Dr. Brown is sitting in an armchair in the corner of the bedroom. He is drinking Dunkin' Donuts coffee and eating a doughnut. I tiptoe into the room and squat down next to his chair.

He grins and hands me the doughnut bag. "Midnight snack?"

The woman is hugely pregnant but hardly breathing at all. She looks to me like a great tigress, looking extremely alert and unafraid. She is lying on her side on a wide platform of a bed; it looks like the entire family could sleep in that bed. Her husband is a handsome African-American man. He is lying next to her, rubbing the small of her back. It makes me momentarily shy to be witnessing such a quiet, intimate moment with two strangers.

Dr. Brown leans toward me and asks quietly, "So how dilated do you think she is?"

I am about to respond "Not much," when I see the woman forcefully push her husband's hand away. So I amend it to "My guess is that she's eight."

He observes her for a little while more. "Hm-m, I think you may be right. Let's check and see."

Dr. Brown gets up, sits on the edge of the platform, and puts on a sterile glove. After he has examined her cervix, he turns to me and says, "You were right on the money, kid."

The woman seems like she is hardly working at all, just light, shallow breathing. Dr. Brown suddenly gets a very alert look and starts listening intently.

He whispers to me, "Hear that catch in her throat? That catch in her breathing? It means she's pushing. A woman like this isn't going to fuss much, so you have to listen to her breathing. When she catches like that, it means she's bearing down."

The woman is half-sitting up, lying against and supported from behind by her husband. She takes one long, strong breath and draws her knees up. Dr. Brown positions himself between her legs and opens up a small sterile kit that contains some hemostats, a cord clamp, a pair of scissors, gauze pads, and a bulb syringe. He sits there, humming a tuneless tune, completely blocking my view.

As if he suddenly remembers that I am there, he leans his body enough to one side so that I can see the progress. I am astounded to see that the head is already on the perineum, and the woman hasn't made a sound! The head is covered by a mass of thick, curly black hair and is descending quickly. Dr. Brown gently receives the baby's head which rotates on its own; then the entire body slides out in one continuous motion. He places the baby up on the mother's chest. It is as simple as that.

Dr. Brown checks out the baby while she is cradled in her mother's arms. He listens to her heart rate and checks her suck reflex with his finger. When the placenta is born, he is the most philosophical that I will ever hear him be. He spreads the placenta out, fetal-side up. He says he loves the placenta because it is the only organ our bodies produce for one specific function; then it dies when its job is done. He says he believes that the arborescent vessels in the placenta create a Tree of Life for the baby and that every tree is different. He feels in some way that it predicts the shape of the baby's life to come. Some trees are very elaborate and complicated, while others are simple and beautifully austere. I have to admit, the branchings and twistings of the vessels are somehow mystically compelling. From this moment on, I become an avid studier of placentas—and futures.

He checks the woman's bleeding. He bids everyone good

night by saying, "Nice job. Nice baby." He never does waste words.

He leaves me to clean up. I am in heaven. I bustle quietly about, tidying up the room, getting the mother and babe snuggled and nursing. I make everyone a snack. I am delirious. I suddenly feel as though I have done this job a thousand times. It is an ageless knowing.

I know exactly what needs to be done and how to do it.

I have finally come home.

I leave the new family at dawn. I see the thinnest crescent of the new moon in the western sky while driving home. I feel that this is symbolic of my life at this very moment, suffused with the dawn of a new beginning. I am filled with joy and gratitude. I am thankful for such a wonderful opportunity and such a sweet introduction.

⚊⚊

As it turns out, the first birth I attend is an interracial baby. The irony of this is that New Hampshire, at the time, is quite possibly one of the most vanilla states in the nation. We've had very little opportunity for racial mixing, or "mongrelization," as my beautiful mixed-race friend, Wini, calls it. Before I leave the birth, the parents check their newborn for Mongolian blue spots, cherry-sized patches of dark coloring in the small of the baby's back. The spots look faintly like bruises. Their firstborn had them as well. They explain that these markings are sometimes found on newborns of African or Asian descent.

Years later, I am training an apprentice midwife who is an experienced obstetrical nurse in the city of Nashua. She has completed her apprenticeship and is waiting to take the state exam to become certified. It is Labor Day, and I want to go hiking in the White Mountains. I don't think anyone is ripe enough to go into labor; besides, who really goes into labor on Labor Day? I ask Val, the apprentice midwife, to cover for me until the evening. Of course, an hour after I leave, a young, single woman—a blue-eyed blonde—goes into labor and has her baby at her mom's house up on Concord Heights. The young woman moved from Florida late in her pregnancy; I saw her for several prenatal visits, and she always seemed to be in good health.

When I get back from hiking, Val says the birth was quite easy for a primip, for a first delivery, but that she is concerned about the baby. She describes the baby as being very dusky, and says that she has used a small tank of oxygen on the baby to try to get it to "pink up." She reports that everything else about the baby is great—good muscle tone and reflexes, strong heartbeat, enthusiastic sucking, etc. It's just his color that worries her. She is worried about a possible congenital heart defect and wants me to go straight there to check him out.

When I walk into the house, the beaming new mother hands me her bundle of joy; his head is capped with thick, black, curly hair. I take one look at this gorgeous "dusky" baby and I laugh.

"Say, Jenny," I ask. "By any chance is the father of this baby black?"

She replies shyly that this is indeed the case, and she apologizes for forgetting to tell me.

I grin and say, "Hey, no problem. Do you mind if I use your phone?"

I excuse myself to the phone in the kitchen and call my apprentice. I am laughing pretty hard by the time she answers.

"Hey, Val," I say. "You know that forty dollars worth of oxygen you gave this baby? Well, this baby is *never* going to pink up enough for you!"

I tease her about this until she politely tells me to shut up.

I personally believe that babies of mixed races are the most beautiful and strongest of all the newborns.

THE SECOND BIRTH

The day after the first birth, I am called to a birth with Dr. Brown that is an entirely different story. This birth is the first for a very high-strung, nervous professional woman, who definitely tests my mettle. This labor takes twenty-four hours, which is not unusually long for a first baby, but Sarah becomes a wild woman. Dr. Brown remains at his office to continue seeing his patients. He leaves me to labor-sit, with instructions to summon him when Sarah gets seriously active.

For months now I have been reading every obstetrical textbook I can get my hands on in the hopes that I can be truly helpful to him. I feel pretty confident in my ability to labor coach and monitor the fetal heart rate and assess progress. In the twenty-hour interim, however, Sarah rips my blouse in several places and bites me on my collarbone, drawing blood. She generally thrashes about and carries on in the most grievous manner. I am trying to be loving and supportive and compassionate, but I am beginning to feel it is a losing battle. I am thankful that I am physically strong enough to hold her.

Her husband, David, cowers after us, looking woebegone and rejected like a beaten dog. She lashes out at him and wants nothing to do with him. When she shouts at me that she can't do it anymore and begs me to knock her out, I decide to call for reinforcements.

When I tell Dr. Brown that Sarah is really fussing a lot and wants to be put out, he asks if she wants to go to the hospital.

"Absolutely not!" she responds in between feral howls.

"That's just as I thought," he chuckles. "This is just her way of doing it. Some women need to have a lot of drama. She'll be fine. But it does sound like she's cooking though, so I'll be right along."

Sarah lives in a huge, drafty old Colonial on a back road in Bradford. It is going to take Dr. Brown a while to get here. In the meantime, Sarah seems to be getting pushy. I walk with her, with her arms around my neck. She stops every few minutes to squat down and complain bitterly about the pain in her back. I suspect the baby is posterior—that the baby is facing up, and the back of the baby's head is pressing on her coccyx. I do counter pressure on the small of her back with the heel of my hand.

When Dr. Brown gets here, he palpates Sarah's belly quickly and confirms that the baby is "sunny-side up," as he calls it. He shows me how to ascertain the position of the baby by noting the place on her belly where the heartbeat is heard the clearest with a Littman stethoscope. If I have to press in deeply along her side with the stethoscope, then the baby is lying in a posterior position and will probably have to rotate to an anterior position in order to be born.

We get Sarah up on her hands and knees to give her some relief and to see if gravity will help facilitate a faster rotation. I am rubbing her back, and I definitely feel her begin expulsive movements. Dr. Brown puts on a sterile glove to check to see if she is fully dilated and ready to push. He says she still has a tiny bit of anterior lip of cervix left, but that she can start bearing down. In a short amount of time, Sarah is pushing and straining mightily. The problem is that every time she begins a contraction and starts to bear down; Dr. Brown inserts his fingers to check the effectiveness and the descent of the head. This causes Sarah to pull back and abort her pushing attempts.

I have been working with this woman for a whole day and night. I feel pretty bonded with her, and I can tell this bothers her. I genuinely like Sarah, despite her unpredictable wildness. I know just how finicky and neurotic she is.

I tap Dr. Brown's hand and whisper, "Francis, get your fingers out of there for a little bit."

He looks surprised and retreats to sit in an armchair, with his arms folded across his chest and with a bemused pout.

Sarah is now semi-reclining, and I sit supporting her knees.

All the while, I am mesmerized by the wrinkled caput of head that is now visible in her vagina. As the head grows larger and bulges her perineum, I look over to Dr. Brown to come catch this baby. He doesn't budge. He hands me the small sterile kit instead. In a semi-panic, I make up some fancy hand maneuvers and massage the thinly stretched perineal tissue around the head to try to prevent it from tearing. The baby's head is born in a nice, controlled way, although it has remained in the face-to-pubes position. I suction the mouth and nose, the shoulders restitute, and the whole body slides out in a gush of amniotic fluid and blood into my hands.

I look down at the beautiful dark-haired girl I am holding. I whisper, "Welcome, little sweet pea."

The baby looks up at me and knits her brows together. She lets out the most god-awful, primal howl I have ever heard.

I laugh. "Yup, Sarah, this is your daughter all right." I hand up the girl, now named Nell, to her dazed mother.

Later, I am wild-eyed and delirious from the experience. Dr. Brown has a funny little smirk on his face. He stitches up the small, second-degree tear at the apex of Sarah's perineum. He seems genuinely cheery as he packs up his bags and bids everyone a good day. But I am worried. I am very concerned that I have overstepped my place and have interfered with his technique. I'm afraid he thinks me too bossy and inappropriate for his practice. I am afraid that I have jeopardized my budding relationship with this wonderful mentor.

The very next morning I drive to Dr. Brown's office, where he is doing clinic hours. I have resolved to be humble and to apologize profusely for meddling in his business. I will promise to never be obtrusive like that again.

He cuts me off in mid-grovel with a wave of his hand. He looks at me with those twinkly brown eyes and says that he learned a great lesson. He says he saw the beauty of a woman attending another woman in childbirth. He realizes that this is the way it should be. He saw that I instinctively knew what to do. It is an ancient thing, and he didn't need to get his male ego into the act. As a matter of fact, he could use some help in the office with the prenatal checkups. These visits would familiarize me with the mothers as well. I am relieved. From this moment on, Dr. Brown and I hunker down to a serious teacher/student relationship.

A Very Long Birth
(or the "Princess Syndrome")

In every birth, the woman teaches me a lesson. This was particularly true in the early days. Betty's birth is runner-up for one of the longest labors I attend, although years later, the all-time winner comes in at eighty-eight hours. Betty's labor, at fifty-two hours, is one of the longest with spontaneous ruptured membranes; it definitely is one of the most exhausting. Betty is a savvy, gregarious journalist who writes a regular column for one of our alternative newspapers. She is considered an elderly primip, in that she is in her late thirties when she conceives her first child. She bristles at the label, and I have to concur. I think it sounds like a guy thing. I'm sure she'll be fine. She is in great shape as she works out regularly at the gym. Her diet is so healthy, it makes me feel guilty.

Dr. Brown and I have been up for a couple of nights with births prior to Betty's. I answer the call and let Francis sleep. I get to her rural farmhouse in Salisbury at dawn, after she calls me about her water breaking, which I confirm with a positive nitrazine test. Because she is not contracting, I suggest she go back to sleep. She says she is much too excited and isn't sleepy at all, so she and her husband, Michael, and I chat quietly in her kitchen throughout the morning. Betty is charming, and she entertains us with stories from her work and scattered local gossip. I keep Dr. Brown posted during the day. He remains in Henniker, doing office hours.

By evening, I am getting a little antsy that Betty still hasn't begun contracting. The risk of a uterine infection is much greater with prolonged ruptured membranes. Dr. Brown isn't as worried as I am, his point being that in her own home Betty has built up a tolerance to microorganisms in her own environment and is already immune to any bacteria to which she would be exposed. Not like the hospital, he says, where one is potentially exposed to some super-resistant mega-bugs, strains of bacteria and viruses that you'd never encounter in your own home. He says the newborn infection rate is four times higher in the hospital than at home. Nevertheless, I say I'd like to try some castor oil to see if she'll get going on her own. He agrees.

I have Betty slug down the "Old Wives'" brew of four ounces of castor oil mixed with orange juice. I explain to her that first she will get wicked runs, but that the full-term uterus is very irritable, so the spasms from her bowels and the resulting prostaglandins will encourage her sleepy uterus to wake up and start contracting. Betty is still very talkative and is chatting nonstop when the first waves of labor hit. She manages to keep talking, although as labor progresses, she falls silent for a moment or two, but then she resumes the conversation. It is a long, hard night and a difficult dilate, but after twenty-four hours, when I check her cervix, she has dilated to eight centimeters. I congratulate her heartily. It is at this time that Betty announces that she doesn't want to do it anymore.

So she stops. Completely. She doesn't have another contraction for twenty-four hours. But Betty keeps on chatting and is the perfect hostess. The morning of the second day, her mom, who is a nurse, arrives from Vermont for the birth. This gives Betty a fresh audience.

Now I'm getting really uneasy with this dysfunctional labor. I call Dr. Brown in the evening. I tell him I need him to help me out with this one. He comes straightaway and checks all the vitals, making sure that Betty isn't getting febrile. He says both mother and baby seem strong enough, but I am beginning to wonder if *I* am going to hold up. Francis and I take turns sleeping in a stuffy attic room, sharing the labor in shifts.

I suddenly remember what day it is. I have lost track.

"Happy Birthday, Francis, you old goat!"

He looks surprised. "Well, that's right, isn't it? Happy birthday to you, too, you spring chicken!"

Dr. Brown is fairly nonchalant about this arrested labor pattern. I assume this comes from so many years of experience. I, on the other hand, begin panicking and pacing around. I have been reading way too many medical obstetrical textbooks. Unfortunately, these textbooks focus primarily on pathological complications. After reading these books for a while, one begins to forget that the majority of births occur naturally and are not a medical emergency.

My anxiety level is rising steadily. I have been extremely careful about sterile technique when doing a rare internal exam. I have been taking Betty's temperature hourly to make sure she isn't developing a uterine infection. The baby's heart rate is absolutely rock steady, not rapid at all. But my fertile imagination is whirling with all kinds of potential disasters. Call it sleep deprivation, perhaps, but this is a classic case of uterine inertia and attendant distress. I just don't feel comfortable waiting it out. And what if she hemorrhages after the birth because her uterus is so exhausted and malfunctioning? I feel like we need to do *something*.

"Francis, I'd like to call Dr. McKinney to see if he has any suggestions for us to get her in good labor again. Is that all right with you?"

Francis allows good-naturedly that we can use all the help we can get at this point. I dial Dr. McKinney's home number. I am surprised how nervous I am in taking this step. Dr. McKinney is a staunch supporter and believer in a woman's right to self-determination. He has stuck his neck out a number of times to ensure that women have as many health options available to them as possible. He is currently Chief of Ob-Gyn Services at Merrimack Valley Hospital. In his own quiet way, he has revolutionized our local medical community's attitude toward women's choices. But I am not at all sure where he stands on the issue of home birth. I am half-expecting a bad tirade. When he answers the phone, I give him a clipped and precise summary of the labor (or lack thereof). I say that I am feeling increasingly uncomfortable with the way it isn't progressing. I ask what he recommends.

There is a long pause. Then he says, without judgment, "Sounds like she needs to be augmented with some Pitocin. If that's what you decide you need, let me know. I'll be happy to meet you at the hospital to get an induction started."

I hang up, thinking, "What a sweetie. What a relief."

"Jesus, Francis, we can't Pit her at home," I say, after repeating my conversation with Dr. McKinney.

"I know," Francis agrees. He tells me some sad stories about inductions in the hospital before the amounts of oxytocin were regulated, and babies died *in utero* from oxygen deprivation. He firmly believes that it is harder on the baby to induce the mother with Pitocin than to be vigilantly patient.

In the meantime, Betty is cheerfully holding court in her bedroom. Even though it is the middle of the night, she is chatting nonstop with everyone in attendance. It finally dawns on me what needs to be done. Now, my assertive nature becomes a true asset.

I walk into the bedroom and am quite firm. Time to clean house.

"OK, that's it! Everybody out! Lights out; party's over," I say. "I'm not kidding. That includes you, too, Michael. Yup, that even includes the cat. Everybody take five. Find a place to sleep, and *nobody* comes back into this room until you're invited."

The room is empty now, except for Betty. She looks forlorn, ensconced in all her pillows.

"Try to get some sleep, Betty," I say quietly. She starts to object, but I say, "Good night, Betty," and softly close her door.

Francis is already snoozing up in the attic. I am amazed at how patient and trusting of the process he is. I find a couch downstairs that has the advantage of being directly under the heating grate to Betty's room. I can hear her upstairs, angrily muttering about being abandoned. I lie down and stare up at the grate in amazement. I am beginning to realize the awesome power women have in labor, whether conscious or not, to shape the path they will take in giving birth to their babies.

"Open up, Betty," I whisper to myself. Soon, I can hear her breathing heavily through the grate about every ten minutes.

I realize that I must have drifted off when I wake with a start. I am incredulous that I actually slept. I now hear Betty moaning quite loudly every few minutes. I decide it is time to check progress. This time when I enter her room, she barely acknowledges me. *Good!* I think. She is in fact fully dilated and ready to push. I wait until a bit of the head is visible on the perineum before I call in the troops. I want to make sure that progress is irreversible this time. Betty is working hard. She has now decided that she wants to meet her baby. It's not all about her anymore.

The entourage files back in, and everyone gets fully comfortable for the big unveiling. With the crowning, Betty's perineum looks mighty blanched to me. I am about to ask Francis to do an episiotomy, when I see the fragile perineal skin shatter like a broken mirror. The baby's pink head pops out. A huge cheer goes up in the room from a bunch of sleepy people. Betty's daughter is wrapped securely in a toasty blanket and put to her mom's breast to nurse.

A while later, I am sitting on the bed, eating an English muffin supplied by the new grandmother. Francis asks me if I want to repair the laceration caused by the rapid delivery of the baby's head. I choke slightly on some crumbs. I remember how shredded Betty's skin looked to me. I have watched Francis stitch some small tears, but I haven't really been paying attention to anatomical detail. But I definitely do want to learn this skill. I ask him if he will talk me through it.

Francis shows me how to inject lidocaine along the edge of the tear, puffing it up slightly, thus exaggerating and defining the layers. He shows me how to identify the apex of the tear, deep inside the vagina, and follow it through to the end. I can clearly visualize the muscle and skin layers. He makes me swab continuously until I can absolutely see what needs to go where, and I can tell him my plan of repair. I can't believe I'm actually going to do this.

He shows me how to confidently bite into the flesh with the curved suture needle, how to bring it out to the other side, matching up the edges perfectly. Francis practices the old style of interrupted stitches, which I find easy to do. It seems to be very strong. A couple of times I sew into my gloved fingers, but slowly, I put the ragged pieces back together. The finished product looks much like the uniform stitching on a football. A football swabbed in Betadine and iced for puffiness.

Betty chats pleasantly with everyone through the whole instructional ordeal. She says she feels great. Again, I feel happier than it is probably legal to feel when Francis compliments my handiwork. He tells me I have done a meticulous job on a very nasty tear.

I am truly grateful for all the gifts that life has given me.

I am grateful and high from the birth, but I am also exhausted. When I return home from Betty's long travail, I bid John good night without even telling him the outcome. I fairly drag myself up the stairs to my bedroom. My body feels like lead, and I am incapable of taking another step. I look in the mirror and am shocked to see that I have bright red rings rimming the irises of my eyes. I have apparently broken the blood vessels in my eyes while pushing with Betty.

Next time, I'll have to fake it, I think grimly.

I scoop up Milan, who is sleeping in his crib. I fall sideways on the bed, intending to nurse him, but within seconds I am in a deep and dreamless sleep. I don't know how much time has passed when I wake to Milan wailing angrily. I feel I am just too tired to cope with a hungry baby. I try to get him on the breast, try to get him to latch on, but he only wails louder. It is pitch-dark in my room. My arms feel like cement and are too heavy to reach up to turn on the light by the bed. What a nightmare. The more I try to get him to nurse, the more hysterical his cries become. I start to cry now from sheer exhaustion and frustration. When I finally get the light switched on, I see that Milan is completely upside down—his head is down by my thighs and his butt is at my breast. I dissolve in irrational, sleep-deprived sobs. In retrospect, it's probably a good thing that he didn't muckle on.

I have convinced the Women's Health Center to train me as a gynecology health-care practitioner. It is the mid-seventies, and legal interpretations of the laws and liability issues have not yet prevented laypeople from being trained to provide well-woman health care. Dr. McKinney, as medical director of the Health Center, has agreed to sign on as my backup doctor for consultation if I have any questions. Originally, I am trained to provide birth-control methods and oral contraception counseling. My enthusiasm for the job persuades the staff to include physical examination in my instruction. Soon, I am trained in the basic skills needed for a well-woman annual exam, such as blood work, breast exams, Pap smears, pelvic exams, and venipuncture.

The Health Center is a collective and has a solid commitment to rotating the skills and knowledge among all health workers who are interested. I am teamed up with some mighty fine instructors. The Center's advanced registered nurse practitioner (ARNP) becomes my friend and mentor. She teaches me the fine art of diagnosing garden-variety vaginal infections, diaphragm fittings, IUD insertions, and uterine sizing. She is a cool, beautiful, professional technician, who is unflappable under pressure.

I am also taught injections, blood drawing, and lab work by the Center's only male staff member. Albert is a full-time phlebotomist and part-time frustrated standup comedian. He is outrageously funny and dear, a patient and smooth teacher. But his jokes are so lame, I tell him to never quit his day job. All in all, I get an incredibly well-rounded education. I feel very secure in my competence and am blissfully happy. By the end of my second year at the Health Center, I am doing all the pre-abortion physical exams and screenings. I am sizing approximately twenty-three first-trimester uteruses on clinic days—I get pretty good at knowing almost to the day how pregnant a woman is by feeling the size and position and weight of her uterus.

My life is full. I am working at the Center during the day, and many nights are spent somewhere out in the boondocks of New Hampshire with Dr. Brown, waiting on a baby. My son is growing steadily into a wise and happy child. John brings Milan to me every lunch hour for nursing. The Center is extremely generous and flexible with my schedule. They cover for me at a moment's notice if I get a labor call. They are very supportive of my work with pregnant women.

The Center begins giving out my name when women call to request information regarding home birth. Women begin calling for a birth assistant in areas of the state that are much too far away for Dr. Brown to travel. He has a catchment radius of only forty miles. I consult him about this dilemma. He states that he emphatically believes that I am ready to spread my wings and attend a few low-risk births completely on my own. The enormity of this responsibility sits like a stone in the pit of my stomach. But I agree that women birthing outside of Francis's catchment area should have access to an attended home birth. Many of these women are determined to deliver out-of-hospital, no matter what.

It is after the call for possible assistance during Betty's labor that Dr. McKinney confronts me about attending the births with Dr. Brown. Dr. McKinney steps into my exam room at the Health Center as I am changing the drape paper on the exam table. He stands there with a boyish grin, but I can see it is forced.

"So, Leonard, tell me about your escapades with Francis Brown."

Unfortunately, I become immediately defensive and blurt, "The births are so different from hospital births, so calm and quiet and loving. I don't know how to tell you, but I know deep in my heart that this is the way birth is meant to be."

His smile becomes frozen. "But they're not *safe!*"

Now I become feisty. "Don't be ridiculous, Ken McKinney! These births are beautiful and reasonable and well-planned. I am surprised at this coming from you! There is absolutely no evidence to support that bogus safety statement, and you know it! Now, if you're going to talk to me, talk to me rationally."

His mouth drops open in surprise. It is an uneasy stand-off, but I do notice he has flecks of amber in his deep green eyes when he is angry. Finally, a clinic worker steps into the hall and gives him the high sign that he is needed in the procedure room.

He looks genuinely sincere when he says, "We need to talk about this."

I nod curtly. My stomach is in a knot and my heart is pounding.

I expel the breath I've unconsciously been holding. I feel I will never get him to understand.

MY FIRST SOLO BIRTH

Inevitably, I agree to attend my first birth on my own, sans Francis. It is a young woman, a primip, who lives in Water Village in the White Mountains. This is much too far away for Francis to commit to do. The woman, Estelle, said she would be delighted if I would attend her, even though I have told her a number of times that I don't consider myself to be very experienced. She and her husband are planning to stay home whether I come or not. She says I still have more experience than anyone else they know. Estelle is in her last month of pregnancy and has had regular prenatal visits with Dr. Faith, a family practice doctor up north. She appears to be completely healthy and low risk. She has an engaging personality. I admire the commitment that she and her husband have to the normalcy and relative safety of birth. I agree to go when called. I enlist the assistance of a beautiful, black-haired coworker named Valerie Gonzales to give me some much needed confidence.

As fate would have it, I am at a birth at dawn in Hillsboro with Francis when my pager goes off. The Hillsboro woman is a frank breech, the first vaginal breech I am to observe, but it isn't meant to be. The woman has just started to push. Francis says he can feel by internal exam that it is definitely a baby girl. He jokes that this is the only time you can do two vaginal exams at the same time. I have to excuse myself to leave to attend Estelle.

Francis walks me to the door. He asks if I have everything that I need in the way of equipment. I say I think I'm all set. I have prepared a small birth bag in an L.L.Bean canvas tote. I have all the essentials, as far as I know. I have gloves, stethoscope, blood pressure cuff, Pitocin (pilfered from the Health Center), and the little sterile kit that Francis gave me. He is beaming at me, proudly. I realize now how very nervous I am and how very much I wish he was coming with me.

I must look panic-stricken because he hugs me and then holds me by the shoulders.

"Look, you'll be fine. You've got a clear head and a calm voice. You know what you're doing. This is going to be great!"

He grins, and his eyes are wicked twinkling. I peck him on the check, run to my car, and head for the mountains.

On the drive to the White Mountains, Valerie is trying to distract me from my nervousness by being funny with juicy tidbits of gossip from work. It isn't working. Waves of anxiety wash over me like a bad drug from the sixties. I think I may hyperventilate or have to pull over because of severe stomach pains. Oh why, oh why, did I get myself into such a situation? What was I thinking? The sheer arrogance of it all! I start wishing I had a job as a counter girl at McDonald's. My belief in the normalcy of birth is on very shaky ground.

Estelle lives in a rustic, funky cabin set way back in the woods. It is accessible only by a long, narrow, winding path. When we get there, Estelle is laboring up in a sleeping loft that is accessible only by a hand-hewn ladder.

I think to myself, *Whew, let's pray we don't have to get her out of here anytime fast.*

Some relatives are gathered downstairs for the big event. Even more family members are crowded up in the loft. It is very close and stuffy up there; at least the baby will be warm enough. The loft is permeated with the musty smell of birth. When I check Estelle's cervix, she is only three centimeters dilated, but she is contracting well. I know by now to clear the decks so Estelle can do her work. I tell everybody that Estelle and her husband need some quiet time together, their last time as only a couple. The rest of the family members take walks outside, as it is a beautiful sunny day. This is good, as it gives Valerie and me time to acclimate and for me to calm down. I make several trips to the outhouse.

Twelve hours later, Estelle is fully dilated and pushing. The labor has been textbook. The baby's heart rate is steady on, and I am feeling pretty secure. All of a sudden, my heart clenches with fear as I look between Estelle's legs and see a glistening sac with floating white flecks. A sac that is growing larger and larger and larger. I know the amniotic sac is still intact, but I have never seen it balloon out like this before. With every push the translucent balloon grows rounder and rounder until it is the size of a fluid-filled basketball between her legs. Oh, my god.

Valerie whispers to me, "What's going on? Is this normal?"

I whisper back, "Beats the hell out of me."

What *does* this mean? I scurry down the ladder to retrieve my bag that contains the obstetrical bible, *Williams Obstetrics,* to find out what is happening. Now, this is a mistake, but I don't know it at the time. This book contains the most horrific, cataclysmic, train-wreck pathology that could possibly occur. I find the section on membranes bulging out like a dirigible. It says that this means there is a malpresentation, that the presenting part is not a well-applied head, thus allowing all the amniotic fluid to gush in front of the ill-fitting descending part. Great. Obviously, I need to find out just *what* is coming down first.

I put on my best poker face, slow my breathing way down, and go back up the ladder. Yup, the membranes are still there, bulging away. I had sworn that I would never interfere with the normal process by artificially breaking the water, but so much for vows. My heart pounds as I take a pair of needle-nosed hemostats and tentatively poke at the sac. It is a lot tougher than I thought. I give it a pretty good jab. This results in an enormous splash that soaks everyone on the mattress. But there it is—dark hair is peeping out. The head! Whew! With sincere gratefulness and relief, I thank the Benevolent Protectress of Childbirth, whoever She is. I get ready to catch this good baby.

The rest of the birth is uneventful. Estelle has a little first-degree tear at the apex of her perineum, a "skid mark" as Francis calls them, not requiring suturing. I make a warm compress of fresh comfrey leaves and apply that to her nick to speed healing. The family members are all delighted with the chubby boy, who is now concentrating fiercely at the breast. I am very thankful to these brave people for trusting in the process of birth. I feel honored that they included me.

On the way home, I laugh and tell Valerie about my momentary freak-out with *Williams Obstetrics*. That was the last time I will consult that harbinger of doom. Valerie is surprised because she thought my demeanor was so composed and reassuring. Huh.

Several days later, we learn that the MD who had done Estelle's prenatal care is furious that they intentionally delivered at home. He is making a big fuss about Estelle's "lacerated vagina." The lesson I learn from all this is that I could be putting myself at unnecessary risk by relying on others to furnish the prenatal care. This could be a setup for disaster.

I realize I could be walking into someone else's mistakes and misdiagnosis. I simply do not want to leave myself that vulnerable. I prefer to assume the responsibility myself for the women I care for.

I start seeing women for their prenatal visits in my home in the backcountry of Warner.

CHAPTER TWO

LADY'S HANDS, 1976

Francis and I continue to go to births together. Sometimes in a freezing country farmhouse with baby chicks incubating by the wood stove, sometimes in a third-floor walkup in the inner city, stifling from the heat. We love our work. Francis is a capable, no-nonsense, wise teacher, melding the art of midwifery and the science of obstetrics. I thank my lucky stars for being at the right place at the right time. Like a sponge, I absorb everything he teaches me.

Francis is a lifelong follower of the old DeLee school of obstetrics, of the "passenger and the passages," the passenger being the baby and the passages being the mother's pelvis and vagina. It is his way of tracking the baby's progress through the birth process, the labyrinthine journey to emerge a new being. He has a habit of sitting in a chair near the laboring woman, his hands mimicking the rotation of the baby's head through the mother's pelvis. He tests me on the cardinal movements by insisting that I constantly tell him exactly which position the baby is in and which station the head is at every step of the way.

This is kind of nerve-wracking, but I get pretty skilled at palpating the baby's position through the mother's belly. I make sure it is vertex or head down by where the baby's heartbeat is heard the loudest. He shows me how to confirm my abdominal findings by internal exam. By feeling the bones of the baby's head, I make sure the sagittal suture, parietal plates, and fontanel of the skull are correctly aligned with the boney structure of the mother's pelvis. The mechanics of birth are a fascinating, unfolding mystery to me.

A QUESTION OF ROOM

It seems that as soon as I learn a skill, it is put to the real test. In this case, Dr. Brown's constant grilling me about the exact positioning of the baby's head proves to be useful. Annie is another young woman having her first baby up in the White Mountains. As luck would have it, she has been seeing the same doctor for prenatal care as Estelle had, the guy who made the big ruckus about Estelle's "skid mark." Annie and her husband, J.W., are quite upset because when they tell Dr. Faith that they are considering a home birth, he tells them that is absolutely out of the question. He is quite sure Annie's pelvis is much too small for a term baby to come through. It is frankly irresponsible and dangerous, he says, to birth out of the hospital in this case; the baby will become stuck in the pelvis, unable to be born, and will die. And Annie could rupture her uterus trying. Dr. Faith orders X-ray pelvimetry—this will measure Annie's pelvic capacity to see if it is adequate—to confirm his suspicion.

I meet with Annie and J.W. at my home in Warner. I listen to their worried story, and I assess Annie myself. She is indeed a small woman, but looks can be deceiving, as most women's pelvises are capable of delivering fifteen-pound babies. I measure her size internally by spreading my fingers and then measuring the space, the way Francis has taught me to do. I feel that her pelvis is normally roomy enough, and her outlet seems more than adequate. But I have her see Francis to double-check, just to make sure. He measures her outside and inside with great old steel calipers, clanking and mumbling and jotting down figures like a mad scientist, until he comes up with an equation that pleases him.

He smiles. "You'll be fine, just fine. Now go home and have a great baby."

Nevertheless, when Dr. Faith calls with the X-ray results, he confirms that Annie has a "marginal" pelvis at best, and she will need to be delivered by cesarean section. She and her husband need to decide on the date they want to deliver their baby and to call him back to schedule the surgery. They call me instead. Great. Now, as cavalier as I may sometimes sound, I truly do not want to be stuck in the middle of the boondocks somewhere with an equally stuck baby. Nor do I want to put anyone at unnecessary risk. Yet I know how important it is to Annie to give this labor her best effort.

It is time to get a medical opinion from the top, from the head banana. I am still very nervous around Dr. McKinney, a fact that aggravates me a lot. It is so out of character for me. He seems to be entertained by my escapades, running around the countryside with Francis. He is always asking about the births in a very amused manner, not derisive, really, just with a little smirk.

I tell him what is going on with Annie's situation, ending by mentioning the mandated automatic cesarean section. He gives it some serious thought. He says that he thinks Annie should at least be given a "trial of labor," an attempt to deliver vaginally on her own. If she fails to progress in a reasonable amount of time, then it probably is cephalopelvic disproportion (or CPD), that the baby's head is too large to fit through the pelvis. In any event, if we don't tarry too long so that everybody is exhausted, we should be able to transfer to the nearest hospital in plenty of time, if we need to. The baby should be none the worse for wear.

Dr. McKinney's real pearl of wisdom comes next. He says, "Besides, the baby's head is the best pelvimeter; nothing is going to test that pelvis for adequacy like the head. Either it'll come out or it won't." He gives me a playful, shy grin.

"Anyway," he continues, "if you're going to be the state's premiere midwife, and if you insist on working in the sticks under barbaric and primitive conditions, you'd better have a lot more tricks in your bag for getting a baby out than most doctors do."

My mouth falls open. I must look like a gasping guppy. *Midwife?* I don't even know what a midwife is, exactly. I envision the unkempt Sarie Gamp, the midwife with the gin bottle in her back pocket, immortalized by Charles Dickens. I have to admit that the gin would have come in handy in any number of births so far, but I didn't even know that midwives were still practicing. Certainly, there are none in New Hampshire. I feel a chill of excitement up my spine. My heart is pounding.

"Why did you call me that? What do you know about midwives?" I whisper.

I feel like I am going to cry, but I don't at all know why. Is this the label for my obsession, for my passion? *Midwife!* I only know I really like the sound of it.

Dr. McKinney tells me about doing his obstetrical residency in Kings County Hospital in New York under the tutelage of some Jamaican midwives. He laughs and says that there he was, a cocky first-year resident who thought he knew everything. He says these midwives were "hard, hard women," who knocked him down to size in no time flat. They made him eat humble pie constantly. They called him "Nurse McKinney." He admired and respected their expertise. He says they were the ones who really knew the undercurrents of what was going on in a birth.

I love consulting with him. He is so gentle and playful and kind. I feel much more confident. I decide to attend Annie's birth.

Annie and J.W. live in an intentional community called "The Swamp," in another quaint hand-built cabin up north. They are intelligent, educated, friendly people who have made a commitment to live on the land as consciously and self-sufficiently as possible. It is the mid-1970s, after all. I have again enlisted the assistance of the lovely Valerie, and we again find ourselves in yet another sleeping loft with a woman in early labor, surrounded by her loving friends. The birth actually occurs some thirty hours later, but only thirteen hours are hard, efficient labor.

I encourage Annie to sleep a lot in the early stages. I have to admit that during the hard labor, I go through a pretty serious bout of self-doubt. By the time Annie gets to seven centimeters dilated, the head is still much higher than I am comfortable with. Much of my concern is that if her water breaks at this point, it can wash the cord down in front of the head, as the head is not firmly engaged in the pelvis yet. What if Dr. Faith has been right all along? What if the head is not able to descend? And then the cord prolapses? I hadn't even thought of this scenario. Again, wishing I worked at McDonald's.

Annie is working hard. She is off in her own world, awash with pain. J.W. is very loving and wonderful, working with her, gently cradling her in his arms, and respectfully remaining quiet as she trances off during contractions. He is kissing her softly on the top of her head. But I can see he is stunned by how forceful and painful the contractions are.

He looks as if he is worried that the pain will engulf his wife completely.

His eyes seem to silently plead with me: "Can't you do something?"

I have learned by this time to keep my theoretical concerns to myself. I go outside and take a short walk to a clearing in the woods. I am getting tired, and I need some guidance.

The night is crisp and clear, and the air in this part of the forest smells pungent with evergreens. The moon, recently full, is now waning, so it has a worn spot on one side, like an old coin. I start conversing with myself. "OK, so I'm beginning to be worried, but it's not yet the kind of worried where my stomach clenches in fear and my intuition says to get her out of here. More like I should give this an arbitrary time frame to see some obvious progress. If we don't budge the head in, say, half an hour more, then we should hightail it out of this swamp." I chat on in this manner for a while longer; but having made a plan of action, I actually feel a lot better.

As I turn to go back, I gaze at the moon, and for a moment I believe I feel true warmth coming from her light. I am immediately suffused with a tremendous sense of well-being and trust. I know everything is going to be all right. This is the first of hundreds and hundreds of serious sessions conferring with the moon.

Back upstairs in the little cabin, Annie is lying in bed, panting mightily. She is glistening with sweat, shining in the kerosene lamplight. I wait for a break, in between contractions, and quietly tell them the truth. I am concerned that the head is remaining so high. I would like to see it move down considerably within the next half hour. If not, we should be gearing up for a trip to the White Mountains hospital.

I also say that I think gravity can help us out tremendously if Annie will get up and squat to bring the baby down. Francis claims that squatting opens the mother's pelvis an additional two centimeters. I believe Annie can use all the room we can possibly find. For some reason, I have found a second wind. I am feeling refreshed and energized, ready to take this on. It seems like this feeling is contagious. Annie looks newly determined and gets up to squat down solidly, her arms wrapped around J.W.'s neck for support. Her husband looks on in awe—and a little afraid of her fierce, tigress-like strength.

Annie is working powerfully for such a little shrimp. I have given her an ultimatum, and she is going to meet it. She is determined that there is no way she is going to that hospital. In half an hour, not only has the head slammed-dunked into the mid-pelvis, but Annie is also fully dilated. She looks like a winning prize fighter, pumped up and raring for the next round. Unbelievable. Where do women find this insane force? Her pushing is just as victorious. She inches the head down with every vessel-straining effort.

I have a small mirror on the floor between Annie's feet. I shine a flashlight on the glass so I can watch the progress of the descending head. The head blossoms her vaginal opening like a moist flower. I am in a very good mood. Now this is fun. I love birth. I love everything about it—the earthy smells, the primal sounds, the mother's blood—it's truly a sacred thing. What a great and crazy profession. One minute you're terror stricken and the next you're on top of the world, thanks to a strong and determined woman. The more I relax into the gentle cadence of this birth and let go of my fear, the more emotion I feel for Annie and her man and this new, emerging little one. I cry tears of wonder and gratitude, but mostly it is joy.

An hour later, Annie's daughter slides into this world, pink and alert and surprised. She really is cute, with a heart-shaped face and a little rosebud mouth. She is the first of many to be born in this swamp community. Annie herself will eventually birth four more girls here. J.W. says he is investing in stock in tampons. This girl weighs seven pounds and has hardly any molding of her head—so much for Dr. Faith's lack of faith in Annie's physique. Years later, I will send Dr. Faith a great bumper sticker that reads:

MIDWIVES DO KNOW SQUAT

This is to tease him. No wonder the guy is gunning for me. I obviously aggravate the snot out of him.

And gun for me he does. Within days of the swamp birth, Dr. Faith is threatening to take legal action against me, to have me arrested for practicing medicine without a license. I personally don't think there is very much medicine involved in what I do. It's mostly good old-fashioned common sense and patience. Dr. Faith says that I am a menace to pregnant women, and there should be an injunction to halt my practice or I should be jailed. Mostly I think he is pissing in the wind, and he is just jealous because many of the women in his area prefer my care. I don't think there is much chance of his making a successful case for litigation, particularly when all of my outcomes have been good.

Just to be on the safe side, however, I consult with a friend who is the attorney for the Health Center to make sure I am not breaking the law. When I tell her of Dr. Faith's threats, she rolls her eyes.

"You really are a nut case, you know that, Carol?" she says. "Some think you're a saint; the doctors think you're a felon. So what are you going to do? Take on the whole medical fraternity in the state?"

She goes on about how I am placing myself in a very unpopular and dangerous position. I say I just want to freely practice my trade, that's all. She agrees to research the New Hampshire state laws pertaining to childbirth and will try to protect me.

What my attorney finds is that New Hampshire is an "alegal" state, or what she calls a "gray state"; there really aren't any specific laws on the books pertaining to midwifery or obstetrics. A majority of states in the nation are gray areas, as midwifery is considered to be so antiquated that it isn't even recognized. It is definitely her legal opinion that I am not breaking any laws. The only statute even remotely addressing childbirth in New Hampshire is an ancient law that states that anyone who cuts the umbilical cord is considered to be doing surgery. So, from this moment on, I have all of the fathers or the siblings of the newborn cut the cord instead. The families find this to be a sweet, symbolic gesture of setting the baby free. How beautiful. I believe it covers my butt.

Meanwhile, Dr. McKinney and I continue to have our weekly arguments about the relative safety of home births. This always occurs after the Wednesday night clinic is over. He starts right in with the "what-ifs...."

This night, however, he says, "So how did that potential WCO in the White Mountains turn out?"

Now my brain flashes through all the obstetrical abbreviations that I know. CPD, SGA, RDS, etc, etc, and the positions LOA through ROP, blah, blah. But WCO?

He flashes a wicked grin. "You know... did it come out?"

Then I get it. What a wisenheimer.

I say casually, "Oh, that WCO converted to an OUT."

He laughs a huge belly laugh that is even funnier than the dumb joke. We laugh ourselves silly—stupid OB humor. For a decade afterward, every time I have to transfer to Merrimack Valley for help with a stuck baby, I will call Dr. McKinney and tell him I am coming in with a WCO. He writes on the woman's chart that it is a WCO, so the nurses all call the problem a WCO. About ten years later, a new nurse finally asks: "What is WCO?"

To which Ken replies, deadpan, "WCO stands for won't come out."

One day Ken asks if I would like to be a medical student for a day. He says that if I'm interested, he will disguise me in hospital scrubs and say I am a visiting Hanover med student. He will sneak me into the OR to observe him doing surgery. *Yes!* He knew I would love that. When we are all masked and gowned and entering the operating room for a tubal ligation, I have a momentary lapse of confidence. This is pretty foreign territory; what if I faint? But my fear is soon overcome by my curiosity. I dig right in there with Ken. He has me look in the laparoscope that has pierced the woman's belly wall. I can see her internal organs. He gives me a guided tour, showing me the gallbladder, the liver, the appendix, and the tiny fallopian tubes that are waiting to be cauterized. I can see the fimbriated ends of the fallopian tubes waving like ethereal sea anemones in a coral reef. Wow! Now this is definitely the nuts.

It is during the next case, a total abdominal hysterectomy, that I completely lose my cool. Ken pulls the woman's entire uterus out and flops it up on her belly for me to see. I can't believe what I am seeing. It looks *exactly* like the drawings in the textbooks.

I am so excited, I yell, "Holy shit! There it is! The mother ship!"

A beautiful, glistening, pear-shaped orb with graceful, embracing fallopian tubes. Awesome! I believe I may be jumping around a little bit. I look up to a roomful of stern, disapproving eyes glaring over their masks. I know what they are thinking— this is one med student who is never going to cut the mustard. But there is one pair of laughing green eyes. I just know he has a shit-eating grin under his mask.

Afterwards, he can't stop laughing. I am chattering away, still so excited about the experience.

He says, "God, Leonard, you are such a nut."

A PAINFUL BIRTH

There comes a time in every midwife's career where she reaches what I call the cocky stage. This is where her arrogance can actually get her into some serious trouble. In my own case of cockiness, I am beginning to feel fairly smug and sure of myself, which is why I think I ignored a pretty obvious ground rule like *Don't work alone.* I learn this fundamental lesson the hard way, fortunately without too much disaster.

Francis and I are at another birth in Hillsboro when Franchesca calls from a neighbor's phone; she's in labor with her first child. Francis is concerned about the woman we are with—she has a history of delivering very quickly and then hemorrhaging in third stage—so he asks if I feel comfortable attending Franchesca on my own.

I say, "No problem."

Franchesca lives in a plywood shack with no electricity in the backwoods of Henniker. She is a single woman and is surviving well below the poverty level. She has been waitressing to support herself until the last month of her pregnancy, when it became physically impossible for her to continue working. She is pale and thin with an enormous belly. She is attractive in a dark, brooding sort of way. She has the air of a woman who is real familiar with very hard times. There is a rough defiance about her, a real scrapper. When I get to her place, she is groaning on her mattress on the floor in the middle of her room. She is in good, active labor.

She is definitely very glad to see me. She gives me a big hug.

"Man, this is wicked," she says.

"I know, tell me about it." I grin.

When I check her cervix, I find she is already dilated to seven centimeters.

Piece of cake! I think.

I tell her that she is doing great and to keep on cooking. A short while later, she starts bearing down vigorously. I think this seems a little too soon for a primip, so I tell her I want to make sure there is no cervix left before she really starts wailing on it. When I check her, I feel a thick wide band of cervix all the way around the baby's head. It is already starting to swell from her pushing efforts. Damn. I know this can be incredibly painful if allowed to become grossly edematous. But I can't get Franchesca to stop pushing with all her might. She simply can't help it. The bearing down is involuntary and violent.

She starts to writhe and thrash around, the pain escalating. She starts to look panicked. I help her get into a knee-chest position, with her butt in the air to try to get the baby's head off her cervix and give her some relief from the pressure. This works for about five minutes. Then she screams and lunges at me.

"Help me!" Her eyes are wild.

She begins pacing around her small space, screaming and pounding the walls with every contraction. She is clawing the air, trying to claw herself away from the pain. She is on fire. Somehow, I manage to get her to let me check her again. This time I find the anterior cervical lip is grotesquely swollen, like a giant blood sausage, hot and tight to the touch. I feel so helpless. I know we are really in for it now. I am wishing I had something for her pain, but we don't carry pain medication. Francis feels it is too risky for the baby. He says the fact that the need for infant resuscitation is so much higher in the hospital is due largely to the use of pain medication. All pain meds cross the placental barrier within forty-five seconds and narcotize the infant. Damn.

I ask her if she wants to go to the hospital for drugs.

She shouts, "Shut up!"

Franchesca is pounding and clawing her mattress. The thin fabric covering soon tears, and she begins digging into the innards of her mattress. She is frantically ripping out the cotton stuffing and throwing it in the air. Everywhere. Soon the entire room is completely covered in white clouds of cotton. A veritable Sealy snowstorm. What a mess. I am trying to calm her and talk her down. I say I know the pain. I also say I know she can do this.

She turns on me like a cornered animal. "Fuck you! Fuck you! You don't know! I *can't* do this!"

I am starting to lose it. My heart is pounding. Then I downshift into another gear. Realistically, the labor will progress, and the baby is doing fine and—I hope—unaware of her mother's terror. What I have here is a woman in tremendous pain, and that's what needs to be resolved first. I remember reading somewhere about putting ice on the cervix to reduce the swelling. But Franchesca doesn't have any running water, never mind ice. And how would I get it in there in the first place? I know I have to do something to bring the swelling down.

Franchesca is crying now. She is exhausted from expending so much energy. I pour sterile oil on my gloved fingers and gently begin to apply counter pressure to the blimp of a cervix, rubbing back and forth, massaging it.

Suddenly, Franchesca becomes quiet. She says, "That feels great."

I press firmer. "Don't stop," she says.

I massage as hard as I dare without lacerating the friable tissue of the engorged cervix. I swear I can feel the swelling disappear and melt away under my fingers. Yes. I keep massaging rhythmically. Franchesca's breathing slows, comforted by the rocking motion. This break lasts only about ten minutes, but it is long enough to get the angry cervix fully dilated and out of the way.

With second stage, Franchesca turns into a snarling, caged animal once again.

She is pacing around in the mountains of white fluff, hollering and yelling at the top of her lungs. My saintly demeanor is getting fried. I want to punch her. This time, instead of bearing down with her contractions, she stretches up on her tiptoes trying to pull away from the pressure. She is literally pulling the baby up out of her mid-pelvis.

She is screaming again. I can't get her to push for the life of me.

"Chess, you really have to focus down," I tell her. "Send that energy down into your butt. You're blowing a lot of precious energy out your mouth. Go like this." I mimic grunting and straining down.

She roars, "Fuck you! Fuck you and the horse you rode in on!"

Oh, great. I am grinding my teeth.

Now Franchesca is leaning over a table, swaying and crying. I have to do something. I am standing behind her. Suddenly, out of the blue, I drop down and slam my knees hard into the back of her knees, causing her legs to buckle. She falls on top of me. She is sitting on my folded legs, but at least she is down. Down and bearing down. She begins pushing mightily.

I think, *Oh, great technique, Carol, drop-kicking your client. Jesus.*

We stay like this, with her perched on top of me, long after my legs have gone completely to sleep. From behind, I can feel her body contort with her expulsive efforts. Her pushing is powerful and effective.

She says the baby is coming.

I say, "Chess, I really need to move around to the front so I can see."

We untangle and rearrange, with me now poised in the catcher's position.

Finally free, I listen carefully to the baby's heartbeat. It hasn't been monitored the whole time I was being the human birthing stool. My heart sinks. Jesus, now what? I definitely hear a marked deceleration in the beat during the contraction. It slows way down, although it picks up after the contraction is over. Head compression. The head is definitely visible and on the perineum, although it is still going to be a while. Another contraction. I listen again. Damn. It sounds worse. Slows way, *way* down; even slower, recovering. This is sounding very funky to me. The scalp color looks dusky. I don't like this one bit. The head is just only starting to stretch the perineum flat. This baby is in distress and still has to crown.

I pick up my scissors to do a pressure cut to get this kid out *now*. I have never done an episiotomy but in this instance, I don't hesitate for a second. I insert the scissors between the head and the perineum and cut straight down. The feel of the scissors crunching through the perineal tissue and muscle shocks me. I am not prepared for how tough and resistant it is. My stomach knots but no time to register this, as the head crowns immediately and is born. The body follows quickly, and Franchesca's daughter, Serena, slips easily into my hands.

Serena's color really is pretty dusky, but everything else is fine. She frowns and looks right at me, like, "Who the hell are *you?*" Ah, her mother's daughter. I can see the resemblance immediately.

I say to the baby, "That was a bit of a rough ride, wasn't it, little shrimpy? Well, you're on the outside now. From now on, it's a piece of cake."

I listen to her heart rate, which is normal and strong. I hand her up to her mother. I check Franchesca's bleeding and find that it is minimal.

"Thank the Holy Mother for small favors," I mutter.

Franchesca is starting to recover. She smiles faintly.

She says, "Wow! I am so sorry, Carol. That was horrendous. So painful! I had no idea." She looks around the room and shakes her head in disbelief at all the white cotton fluff. "I guess I was really bad, wasn't I? I'm really embarrassed that I was so horrible."

I grin. "Hey, no problem. I was an incredible weenie in labor myself. Swore up a storm. You had a pretty unusual situation with your cervix swelling like that. That is genuinely painful. Actually, in retrospect, you did a great job of it, although your mattress may have lost some of its Posturepedic qualities."

By now it is dark outside and not much brighter inside. Franchesca's place is illuminated only by kerosene lamps. Although this is a cozy glow for mother and babe, I soon realize that the room isn't anywhere near bright enough for me to see to do the episiotomy repair. I need direct lighting on her perineum so I can see the extent of the damage. I try with the existing light, but it is way too dim between her legs to positively identify any parts of the puzzle. I need to be sure I haven't inadvertently cut a third degree episiotomy and severed her anal sphincter muscle. That would not be a good thing. Without a second pair of hands to hold a light in exactly the right spot, it would be impossible.

The only alternative I have is to firmly clench my trusty flashlight between my teeth and aim the beam in the correct spot by tilting my head at different angles. This actually works quite well. I am able to clearly see the gleaming white canister of the intact sphincter muscle. The repair is straightforward and goes quickly. For once, I am thankful for having prominent teeth.

I grin, thinking, *Man, oh, man, if Doctors Easey and Faith could only see me now.*

I get Franchesca and Serena all tidied up and cuddling. Serena is nursing vigorously, and Franchesca is resting, sipping a big glass of orange juice. I am sitting on the edge of the now-defunct mattress, going over the aftercare instructions, when we hear a tremendous crash—and then another one. I look up just as the front of my Peugeot sedan comes splintering through the plywood side of Franchesca's shack. Our mouths drop open in speechless surprise. The bumper and grill of my car come right into the kitchen and stop next to the metal dinette table. It is my car, all right; the front license plate reads OS (as in cervical os, the term for the opening of the cervix.) We sit there, frozen, and look at each other.

"*What the ...?*"

I run outside and in the dim light I figure out what has happened. A loaded logging truck had been parked a little way up the hill, done for the night. The brakes must have let go, and the truck rolled down the hill, broad-sided my car, and pushed it through the side of Franchesca's house.

I stand there in disbelief. "All right, that's it! No more calamities! I get it. *I get it!* I'll never practice alone again, I promise. Yeesh! But enough is enough already!"

I am able to back my car out of Franchesca's kitchen and drive it, although the passenger side is smashed in and the window is missing. I tape on a plastic garbage bag as a temporary solution. When it comes time for me to leave a few hours later, I don't want to leave Franchesca alone. Feisty and independent woman that she is, I still feel that someone should be with her in case she needs assistance. She says for me to go find her good friend Jerry Greene. He isn't the father of her baby, but he has offered to help if she needs him. She says I will probably find him at the local bar, where she has been working. I will recognize him because he was in a bad car crash and is severely burned on his face.

I do find Jerry at the bar. When I say that Franchesca has had her baby, a great cheer goes up from all the regular patrons. Jerry looks pleased and eager to look in on her. He is so sweet. When Jerry gets to Franchesca's, he puts all of her bloody linens in a dry tub outside and hauls in water. He scrubs every inch of those sheets until they are bleached clean of any stains. Then he hangs them all out on the line to dry in the middle of the night. He never leaves her. They've been together ever since.

⌐

Always after long births, my breasts are very painful from being so engorged with milk. I can't wait to get home to my own little budgie, mostly because I miss him but also for some relief for my rock-hard breasts. Nursing Milan is one of the greatest joys of my life. Sometimes I wonder if being away at births so much of the time is such a good idea. John is doing most of the child care, ungrudgingly. He is very supportive and proud of my work. But I feel some of Milan's babyhood slipping away from me. Milan is a thoughtful and studious child, who quietly contemplates every new situation. I am hopelessly in love with him and I cherish our precious time together.

One day, as I am leaving for a birth, Milan piles all of his blocks in a pyramid in front of the door, hoping this will prevent me from leaving. I have to dismantle the pile in order to open the door. He is crying as though his heart is breaking. Even though he can't speak, I know he is pleading with me to stay. I look into his deep brown eyes, and I see the anguish there. He truly cannot tolerate my leaving him this much any longer. There is no way I can deny those eyes. I scoop him up in one arm and grab my birth bag with the other, and I take him with me. By the time Milan is six years old, he will have been to over five hundred births.

A BEAUTIFUL BIRTH

A vast majority of the births are sweet, sensual, powerful, and completely uncomplicated. Sondra's birth story is perhaps the most poignant and touching.

Sondra is a wonderful, strong African-American woman with a very large smile, close-cropped hair, and gorgeous dark skin. She calls me late in her pregnancy and asks if I will attend her at home, even though her baby is going to die. She explains that she had an ultrasound done in her first trimester, and her obstetricians told her that her baby is anencephalic. They have found that the baby has a gross congenital malformation; the skull covering and part of the brain has failed to develop. This condition is fatal, and the baby isn't expected to live for more than a short while.

Her OBs are encouraging her to abort the baby, but Sondra finds that she simply cannot. Toward the end of her pregnancy, she becomes concerned; she wants to ensure that her baby's condition at birth be treated with dignity and respect until it dies. She doesn't want any heroics or life support to be administered by the hospital. She doesn't want her baby taken away from her. The more she dwells on this, the more she wants her baby to be born and to die at home, in the peace and love of its own family. So, she calls me.

At this time, home birth is rapidly gaining popularity in New Hampshire and is attracting media attention. My response to Sondra's request is that I don't think we can afford the negative press that I know a newborn death at home will generate. Even though we would all know the cause of death—a congenital anomaly—I believe the media will sensationalize it and treat it as if it were the result of a terrible mistake. I decline Sondra gently, saying I am afraid the adverse publicity could possibly jeopardize other women's freedom to choose their place of birth.

Sondra calls me again on her due date and invites me to lunch. We meet at the Nook in Henniker, where she pleads with me forcefully. She explains with heart-wrenching passion how important it is to her family that their baby is allowed to die gracefully at home, surrounded only by loved ones. She fears that in the hospital, the baby might be treated like a freak. Her fervor is undeniable. I feel that I would be doing her a terrible disservice by refusing her. I commit to attend her birth and to deal with the fallout later on.

Two days later, Sondra calls before dawn to say her water has broken. It is a brutally cold day. Even with the rising sun sparkling on the snow, it is well below zero. I feel my nostrils freeze together as I walk. I fairly drag my birth bag down the half-mile of snow trail to her cabin at Chipmunk Falls on Craney Hill. I have a heavy heart and for the first time, I am really dreading this birth. I realize I am frankly scared.

Their little cabin in the clearing looks so cozy with wood smoke curling from the chimney. For some reason, all of Sondra's ducks are perched on the frozen window boxes, looking in the windows. I have heard that animals are irresistibly drawn to birth. But ducks? When I knock on the door, Sondra's thirteen-year-old daughter, Julie, answers. She is excited. She says her mom feels like she has to push.

I quickly quiet myself. I tell Sondra that I would like to check to make sure there isn't any cervix left before she starts pushing. My heart is pounding. I don't know what to expect. Francis has said there is a good possibility of a face presentation with this condition. He has described to me how this will feel when examining. But, instead, what I do feel makes my mouth drop open and my heart skip a few beats. My fingers search around. I feel hard parietal plates, sagittal suture, the anterior fontanelle—a completely normal skull covering! I don't say anything at the moment because I want to be absolutely sure of my discovery.

I give Sondra the green light. She begins pushing tentatively. She is gazing into her partner, Henry's, eyes. He says softly, "It's time to let go now, Sondra."

Sondra is grimacing now with her pushes. The head is coming down fast. What is visible looks completely normal to me. A fine-looking head covered with thick, black, curly hair. I start to laugh and cry at the same time. When the head is crowning, I am positive the baby is perfect.

I say, "Sondra, give me your hand."

I take her hand and place it on her baby's emerging head. She feels around reluctantly for a moment. Then the realization spreads across her face like the end of an eclipse. Her expression is unbelievable, a look of pure joy. I am flat out bawling now, trying to see to protect the perineum through a rain of tears.

Sondra whispers softly, "My baby."

With tears streaming down her face, she reaches down, and with both hands, Sondra delivers her own baby girl. She gathers her up in her arms and holds her daughter close to her heart.

Henry looks at his baby in disbelief. He has steeled himself for a grossly disfigured child, not this healthy mocha-chocolate cherub who is now studying him intently. He looks at me in questioning shock. I nod with a soggy smile.

Henry crumples in gasping sobs.

"Oh, my god! Oh, my god! The baby is beautiful!"

Big sister, Julie, is nestled at Sondra's side. She is gently stroking her sister's head, looking very confused.

"Does this mean my sister is going to live? That she's going to be OK?"

I insert my finger into baby Aurora's mouth to check for suck reflex. She chomps down voraciously on my poor digit.

I grin at Julie. "Yup, apparently so. This baby looks like a keeper to me."

Sondra is stroking her daughter's face, making a haunting sound that is a remarkable cross between a whimper and a coo. Aurora latches on to the breast as though starving. There are four deliriously happy people in that sunny room, thankful for a wonderful new life beginning.

I drive home from that birth feeling incredibly happy. I am also thankful for Sondra's strength and intuitive sense that bonded her with her child-within's well-being, an unconscious knowing that all was well. I am more than a little awed.

Later, when Sondra and I meet for her postpartum checkup, she is understandably furious at the ordeal she went through. Her attitude was "So much for the wonders of modern technology."

She firmly believes that she was pressured to abort her child simply because she is a black, unmarried woman in rural New Hampshire who already had a child with a congenital defect (Julie had been born with a serious heart anomaly that had been surgically corrected). Sondra subsequently becomes very active in the area of women's reproductive freedom, vigilantly insisting that women be given correct information about their bodies and the right to choose their own destinies.

It is after this birth that Sondra and Henry give me a book called *The Birth Book* by Raven Lang (now out of print), with their grateful thanks for going out on a limb for them. I begin shaking as I look at the black-and-white photographs of women attending other women in childbirth in their homes in Northern California. These are familiar scenes—women squatting down in their rustic cabins, attended by loving midwives. Midwives who are physically supporting heaving mothers. Midwives kneeling, waiting to catch the emerging baby. In the book, author Raven Lang, the midwife, speaks of herself in third person, calling herself Pat, because practicing her art is illegal in California. There is page after page of gentle, beautiful births.

So, there are other women doing what I am doing!

I am not crazy!

I can't believe how euphoric I feel, knowing that I am not alone. I cry tears of joy when I read the 1972 quote from Professor G. J. Kloosterman, professor of obstetrics and gynecology at the University of Amsterdam, Holland:

"Throughout the world there exists a group of women who feel mightily drawn to giving care to women in childbirth. At the same time maternal and fiercely independent, responsive to the mother's needs yet accepting full responsibility as her attendant, such women are natural midwives. Without the presence and acceptance of the midwife, obstetrics becomes aggressive, technological, and inhuman. Today, this 'natural midwife' is emerging from obscurity, making herself well-known to the people she serves and to the system she cannot work within, even where she must practice illegally."

I vow to set out to find these women, these other midwives—my sisters.

A CAR BIRTH

Because all of our clients are carefully risked out prenatally, less than 6 percent of our actively laboring women need to be transferred to the hospital for various reasons. Usually, it's not an emergency; it is failure to progress, or labor has become a long, sluggish affair that need a little goosing. Occasionally, it is simply that the midwife doesn't feel comfortable with a red flag she is being presented with and would rather approach on the side of caution, taking the conservative route. This was the case with Jacqueline, although had I really been listening to all the messages in this fiasco, I never would have set foot in the hospital in the first place.

Jacqueline is a tall, strapping woman with clear gray eyes and a winning grin of perfect white teeth. She and her husband, Ted, live in a beautiful New England farmhouse in the White Mountains, across a little bridge over a crashing crystal creek in their front yard. It is an unusually hot and muggy summer day when Valerie and I drive down their lane. There are many cars parked in their yard. Apparently, this is to be the social event of the season, as the house and lawn are cluttered with well-heeled family and friends.

Jacqueline is pacing upstairs in her bedroom with just her mother, her sister, and Ted. Her bedroom is airy and bright, with wide plank floors and gorgeous, rich, oriental rugs. She is doing great. Valerie and I sit quietly across the room, reading gardening magazines. Jackie progresses to full dilation with no problem and in an average amount of time for a first baby. When she starts to push, however, I am distressed to see a fairly hefty gush of blood. At first I attribute this to "bloody show," or the small amount of bleeding that can happen when the fragile capillaries of the cervix break with dilation.

It is with the second big gush of blood when she pushes again that my senses become hyper-alert. I listen to the baby's heartbeat for what seems to be a long time. It is steady and strong with no apparent distress. Jackie's blood pressure is fine. She doesn't seem to be in abnormal pain, considering she is in second-stage labor. All these findings make me feel a little better, but this is still not normal by any stretch of the imagination.

It is the third gush that I actually *hear*—it sounds like a water faucet. My uneasiness goes into overdrive. My fear is that Jackie may have an abruption or a marginal placenta previa, that the placenta is abnormally attached partially to the lower uterine segment. When this part of the uterus stretches during labor, the placenta, which cannot stretch, separates, and hemorrhage is unavoidable. Time to call for moral support.

When I describe to Francis what is happening, he doesn't panic but says that from listening to my voice, he thinks we should go in. I actually feel relieved. I call the White Mountains hospital and say we are coming in with a laboring woman who is bleeding too much for comfort. Please have the on-call doctor available for us. We will be there within twenty minutes.

I have driven John's car, which is a late-model Volvo station wagon. Ted puts the entire mattress from their bed in the back of the car. Jackie gets comfortable, and Ted and I crawl in the back with her. We set out for the hospital with Valerie driving like hell over potholes. The baby's heart rate is still fine, and Jackie is still pushing and bleeding profusely. The head comes down on the perineum as we approach Laconia during rush-hour traffic. The car stops abruptly from overheating. The fan has catapulted into the radiator.

With all this commotion, the baby is born, and all bleeding stops. The baby is fine, and it really is quite cozy in the back of the car. The windows are all fogged up, and Jackie and Ted are lying on their mattress bonding with their son, Jonathan. As Ted says, their baby was born in their own bed—just not in their own home. I give Jackie a prophylactic shot of Pitocin to prevent any more bleeding and to spit out the placenta. The umbilical cord ceases pulsing, so I cut it, after placing an umbilical clamp on the infant side and hemostats on the maternal side. The placenta is born easily, without excessive bleeding.

By this time, all of Jackie's friends who have been following us in separate cars learn that the babe is born, and all is well. They are ecstatic and begin dancing in the street. Even though we have pulled over to the side of the road, we are causing a traffic jam. People are rubbernecking to see the cause of all this commotion. One of Jonathan's uncles pops open a bottle of Moet & Chandon, right in the middle of rush-hour traffic. He stands on his car bumper and gives a loud toast to the new arrival.

The scene becomes a joyous carnival, with people laughing and hugging, honking and cheering. A man stops and starts to try to sell Electrolux vacuum cleaners. (I am dead serious.) A woman stops and says she is a registered nurse and can she help? At this moment I slide out of the back of the Volvo and turn to face her. I do not realize I am covered from head to toe with Jackie's blood. The nurse looks horrified, rolls up her window, and speeds away.

The dilemma now is that I know we have a doctor waiting for us at the hospital, and I wonder if it would be unspeakably rude to call and cancel, saying, "Thanks for being there for us, but we're all set." I consult with Ted and Jackie. It's OK with them to make an appearance. We'll just pop in and thank everybody for agreeing to help, then we'll go back home. This sounds perfectly reasonable to me. I obviously haven't had much experience transferring to hospitals at this point. I didn't realize that one doesn't just "pop in" and out. Anyway, we all pile into another car and continue down the street to the hospital.

It is when our second car stops dead, drops its transmission right in the parking lot of the hospital, that I know I should have paid attention to my instincts. Instead, some orderlies come rushing out of the emergency room with a stretcher and whisk

Jackie away. I insist the baby stay outside with his grandmother. I don't want a newborn exposed unnecessarily to all the foreign germs of a hospital. As we stand watching, Jackie and Ted enter the ER. I get a sinking feeling in my stomach.

Valerie mutters, "I think all that car trouble was a sign to tell us that we weren't supposed to go to the hospital today."

I look into her dark, suspicious eyes. "Oh, great. Now you tell me."

Soon, Ted comes walking briskly back to the cars, looking quite upset. He says that as soon as they got inside, they were separated. Jackie was wheeled down the hall, and he was made to stay at the front desk to fill out insurance forms. Now, they won't let Ted see Jackie and won't tell him what's going on. Of course, as fate would have it, Dr. Faith is the MD on call.

Mother of God, I think. *How bad can this get?*

Ted is worried that they may be punishing Jackie for electing to have a home birth. He points in the direction that Jackie has been taken, and we see a side door. The three of us look at each other. Valerie, Ted, and I quietly open the door and tiptoe down the hall. We hope we're going in the right direction.

We come around a corner. Ted whispers, "That's him! Dr. Faith!"

The man is getting into an elevator. I run and jump into the elevator with him. I push the close button and hold the door closed. My heart is racing, but I am surprised that he is such a little man. He is at least a head shorter than I, with thick Coke-bottle glasses and squinty eyes. He looks startled by my bloody, disheveled appearance. Actually, he looks like he is going to scream.

I say, "Dr. Faith, perhaps you can tell me the status of Jackie, the woman who just delivered en route in the car?"

The color of his face begins to mottle.

"There were hemostats on the cord! This wasn't an accidental car birth; this was a *planned* car birth! And who the hell are you?"

I am trying to remain calm.

I introduce myself. "I'm Carol. I'm Jackie's midwife."

He is clearly angry now. "Her *what?* Her midwife? What's that? Like a witch doctor? You just drum and chant and burn some sage, and pray the baby comes out all right?"

That does it. I've about had it with this vertically challenged guy. I've had more than enough history with Dr. Faith. I look him squarely in his magnified eyes.

"Tell me, Doctor," I say, "do you have to practice at being such an asshole? Or does it just come naturally?"

He rises up to the full height of his Napoleonic stature, and he spits. He spits right in my face. In my shock, I stumble backwards and release the close button. The door opens, and he rushes out, calling for Security.

I am stunned. Ted and Valerie are waiting for me. We find our way back to the parking lot. Jackie is released a short while later; apparently she has been making life holy hell for her captors. She just wants to go home with her baby and her family. Back at her house, there is much celebrating and ribald ribbing about the need for me to wear foul-weather gear the next time I transfer to a hospital. Very amusing.

I think, *What a job description. Not only do I lose sleep, lose years off of my life, trash my car—no, two cars—and get degraded and belittled and spat upon by a gnome, but now I've also lost a good set of hemostats in the bargain.*

Driving home in a borrowed car, I am speeding because I've been away from Milan for too long, and I just want to get home. It is dark out. Too late, I see the police car hidden on a dirt side road as I roar past him, doing at least eighty. He comes after me, so I pull over, even before he turns on his blue lights.

I say to Valerie, "Oh, shit, what a perfect way to cap this day."

I roll down my window as the officer saunters up to the driver's side. He peers in at us. He says in a thick New Hampshire accent, "You ladies seen a fox around here?"

I look at Val in astonishment.

Her eyes are huge, and she shakes her head. "No-o-o-o."

He says, "Well, there's reports of a rabid fox in these parts. I was just making sure you haven't seen one." He bids us good night and walks away.

I turn to Val. "Did that just happen?"

She lets out her breath loudly in disbelief. Ah, the wonders of country life in New Hampshire—and redneck cops.

As my career blossoms, my marriage is withering. John has become resentful of the amount of time and passion I am expending in my job. And rightfully so. I am seldom home anymore, and when I am, I am sleeping. He is saddled with a great majority of the child care, as his woodworking shop is at home. He is threatened and angered by my intense commitment to my work and my lack of participation in a life that includes him. And I have wrecked two cars with very little compensation. This puts a tremendous strain on our relationship. He has become cynical and reclusive and hurt. The man whose creative and eccentric nature I once loved is beginning to frighten me. We are arguing and fighting constantly. This leaves me feeling desperately sad and drained. I know his heart is breaking as well, but there is nothing I can do to mend it. I am caught in an avalanche of change.

Chapter Three

Lady's Hands, 1977

As my practice skyrockets—from 1973 to 1980, home births in New Hampshire will increase by 300 percent—my friendship and unofficial mentorship with Dr. McKinney deepens. While my apprenticeship with Francis teaches me the art and beauty and patience of natural birth, my dialogues with Ken McKinney instruct me in the cutting edge of current medical technologies of obstetrics. Ken is still challenging me as to the relative safety of out-of-hospital births, but now his attitude is tinged with respect and genuine curiosity. The safety statistics that I know in my heart to be true are still years away from being published.

Ken and I lock horns good-naturedly every time we work together at the Health Center. I think we both secretly love the sparring. We get into an argument about the safety of home births every chance we get. For instance, he is shocked that I do episiotomies only rarely. I would rather repair a jagged tear than a large cut any day. I say I will only do an episiotomy if I think the baby may be in trouble and I want it to be born quickly. He says he was taught that women will suffer from uterine prolapse and incontinence in later years if they aren't routinely cut. I say that doesn't make any sense to me. Episiotomies do far more extensive muscle damage than a possible small laceration.

I show him how I massage the perineal tissue. To demonstrate, I spread my thumb and index finger and use the taut skin of my hand as the hypothetical perineum. I show him how I circle my hands around the crowning head to provide counter pressure. I guide the birth of the head by steady, slow flexion, instead of letting it ram through too quickly. He listens with an amused smile.

I tell him about the fiasco up north with Dr. Faith and his frothing at the mouth. Ken looks upset and embarrassed for me.

"Jim Faith is a nincompoop," he says.

"Yeah, well, that's a lot nicer than what I called him," I say.

Honestly, who says nincompoop anymore? What an endearing, Midwestern-cornpone term. Only Ken McKinney could call someone that and make it sound so devastatingly bad. I certainly never want him to think I am a nincompoop, ever.

He continues, "Really, it's just a turf battle with these guys. They're being territorial. They see you as hijacking their patients. If they had more confidence in themselves and their popularity, they wouldn't feel so threatened. And, if they felt more competent, they'd relax a bit, and this would ultimately be much more attractive to their patients. Then the women wouldn't be tempted to seek you out for more personalized care."

He is in a very expansive mood this night. "It sounds to me like you did all that you could do in that situation. In hindsight, you could have stayed home, but you didn't know that. The bleeding was most probably coming from the cervix as it dilated; the capillaries get so friable in pregnancy. It sounds like it was an abnormal amount of bleeding, so you were right to transfer out of there if you didn't feel comfortable with it. You just didn't know you were going to get beat up about it. I'm sorry that happened to you, Carol."

I have been watching this man work for some time now. I am still left speechless. I am immensely impressed with how gentle and considerate he is with women. I keep waiting for some faux pas, but he only proves himself to be sweeter and more genuine with each passing day. This is a man who truly loves women, who doesn't feel competitive or threatened by women and their needs. He is sincerely respectful and responsive. His touch is as soothing and knowing as any midwife's.

I ask him how is it that he is so different from his colleagues.

"Oh, it goes back to those Jamaican midwives in my residency, I guess. They were set on humbling me, mostly because they could. I want to think it was because they liked me. They used to make me do the nurses' work. One day they said they wanted to teach me what it was like to be a woman patient. They told me to go into the exam room and remove my pants and get up on the exam table with my feet in the stirrups. I lay there for what seemed like an eternity, although it was probably twenty minutes or so. Then a beautiful female medical student came in, nodded to me briefly, snapped on a latex glove, and did a cursory rectal exam. Then she said something unintelligible to me, distractedly patted my knee, and walked out of the room. I lay there staring at the ceiling, my face burning with embarrassment. Then I could hear all the laughing outside in the hall. They were right, those crazy women. It was a lesson I will never forget."

In the winter of 1977, I find an announcement for the First International Conference of Midwives to be held in El Paso, Texas. I can barely contain my excitement. This is where my sisters will be—and all in one place! I dearly want to go, but I know I can't afford the airfare and the conference fee combined. At this point, I am being paid for births with whatever the people can bear. This is usually my gas mileage and the specialty of the house; that is, the best tokens of their livelihoods. I have been paid with tons of cordwood, thirty-six quarts of blueberries, a black angus calf, a freezer full of venison, a house painting, car repair to my radiator, gorgeous handmade down quilts, snowplowing, and Scoobie, the box turtle, for Milan. Even though all these gifts have been given in love, I realize with a sinking heart that none of these is enough to wing my way to the Mexican border.

A month before the conference start date, I walk into my exam room and find an envelope on my desk. In it, I find the airfare and the conference cost, paid by Ken. The attached note says I should have a great time, and he will be curious to know what I learn there.

I sit down hard; I'm shaking and finding it hard to breathe.

THE BIRTH AND DEATH OF OPAL

Franny and Ned are an extremely attractive couple—she, having thick, prematurely salt-and-pepper hair; and he, classically handsome in a John F. Kennedy sense. They live in an ashram a couple of towns away. They come for prenatal care early in the pregnancy because Franny previously has experienced two painless miscarriages, both in her second trimester. Their regular doctor has said not to worry, that miscarriages are relatively common and that they'll be fine. But they are worried.

The part that bothers me about Franny's history is the late second trimester part; this is certainly not common by any stretch of the imagination. After talking with her further, I find that she is a DES daughter—that her mother had been given the steroid diethylstilbestrol (DES) during her pregnancy with Franny. I am afraid that Franny may have a congenital anomaly of the cervix, as many DES daughters do, so I consult with Francis. He suggests that I do a pelvic exam to check her cervix every week in the second trimester for any early changes, so that's what we do.

When Franny gets to the twenty-sixth week of her pregnancy, she calls late in the evening to say she thinks it might be happening again. She isn't experiencing any contractions or any pain, but she has a vague uneasiness and a slight pressure in her lower back. I had just checked her cervix a couple of days prior to this and noted that it felt normal: long and hard and closed. I say I'd be surprised if she has made much change in the interim but tell her I'll meet with her to be sure. What I feel when I do an internal exam takes my breath away. Her cervix is fully dilated and the membranes are bulging into her vagina. Damn! I call Dr. Mc Kinney and ask him to please meet us at the hospital; we are coming in with a very premature baby. He agrees, and we get to the hospital quickly.

Ken sits on the edge of the hospital bed and talks quietly with Ned and Franny about their options in this case. He says he believes the odds at twenty-six weeks are against the baby's survival, even worse for survival without extensive brain damage. After discussing the alternatives, Ned and Franny decide that they don't want heroic measures or life-support systems to be involved. It is very important to them that they hold their baby until it dies.

I know the nurses in attendance are waiting to whisk the baby away, because it is common belief that it is just too painful for parents to see their dead child. Ken states that he has no problem with Ned and Franny's request and actually encourages them to bond with their dying infant. He later tells me that many women who are denied interaction with their stillborns have recurring nightmares that their babies are normal and are still alive somewhere. Ken quietly closes the curtains around the four of us as Franny's water breaks.

Opal is born about ten minutes later. Her tiny, perfectly formed body slides gently into my hands. Her skin has a luminescent, transparent quality, and her miniature mouth begins to gasp for air as her immature lungs struggle unsuccessfully to inflate. I hand her up to her mom and dad, and they gather her up sweetly in their arms. They welcome her softly with tears streaming

down their faces. Ken sits silently observing this. I reach over
and touch his arm. He looks at me saying many things with his
eyes; a softness, a vulnerability there. What a beautiful birth.
Opal lives for about twenty minutes, and then she surrenders.
Her parents hold her for a very long time.

Ken tells Franny that she has a classic incompetent cervix
and that with her next pregnancy, he will do a cervical cerclage.
He can surgically reinforce her weak cervix with a kind of purse-
string suture to get her to term. He gives them an optimistic
outlook for the next time. He hugs them both and offers his
regrets for this little one. His response is comforting. I can tell
he is genuinely fond of this couple.

When it comes time for them to say good-bye to Opal, Ken
does a remarkable thing. The baby weighs a little over one and a
half pounds. He breaks the rules and adjusts the baby's weight on
the death certificate so that it is under the grams necessary to be
considered a stillborn. It will be recorded as only a miscarriage.
He finds a small box and places Opal inside, wrapped in her
warming blanket. He hands her back to her parents to bring
home for burial on their own land. Ned and Franny leave the
hospital with Opal secreted under Franny's poncho. They are
headed home for a bittersweet good-bye ceremony with her
entire extended family.

After they leave, we are silent. I can't find the words to express
to Ken how grateful I am for his compassion. Ken walks me to
my car in the hospital parking lot. He slides into the passenger
side and sits looking straight ahead, without speaking. It is dark,
but a streetlight illuminates the side of his face, which is streaked
with tears. His shoulders heave. I lean over and take him in my
arms. I envelope him, as if to protect him from something too
painful. I lightly stroke his tears away. He crumbles into me and
cries silently for a long time.

As I hold him, I get his scent, and I begin to tremble. I love the
warmth and feel of his body. I want to devour him but instead,

I gently kiss the top of his dark head. I realize he has stopped crying and is remaining very still, as if frozen in place. I suddenly become very embarrassed and straighten up. I pretend to look busily for my keys. We say an awkward good night. I drive home, concentrating fiercely on my driving. I shake uncontrollably.

My mind is racing. What is happening? I can't think clearly. I am overwhelmed. I have emotional overload.

This night has gone from birth to death to desire.

I stop at the clinic on my way to the Boston airport and my flight to El Paso so that I can thank Ken one last time for being so generous. I am extraordinarily excited about this trip and finally meeting the other midwives. I have ransacked all my favorite thrift stores for my conference wardrobe. I am pleased with the results. I have found an elegant, vintage, gray flannel woman's suit, circa 1940s, with a calf-length straight skirt and a jacket with padded shoulders and a nipped waist. It fits me like a glove. I find a black felt beret that I wear cocked to one side. I pin a red silk rose on it. My hair is shoulder length and curly. I fancy I look like Marlene Dietrich. I walk into the recovery room, where Ken is writing in a chart. He looks up and blinks.

His face creases into a huge smile. "Wow, Leonard, you look great!"

I do my best rendition of a blush. I give him a perfunctory peck on the cheek, tell him of my sincere gratitude for his thoughtfulness and head for the Mexican border.

I had hitchhiked across the country several times in the sixties but had never gotten to Texas in my travels. I really feel like a country mouse as I stand in the ornate lobby of the Grand Hotel, clutching my brocade suitcase. What culture shock. There are midwives everywhere, in all different shapes and sizes! There are sleek, cosmopolitan nurse-midwives from urban medical centers; groups of colorfully dressed Mexican parteras, chattering excitedly in Spanish; and many apprentice-trained midwives, like me. My favorites to look at are the tiny, squat, rotund Mayan grand-midwives, with their thick black braids that fall past their waists and their hooked noses and hawk's eyes. I really want to speak with them. I wish I knew more Spanish other than "Hola! Cerveza frio, por favor" and "Dónde está el baño? Gracias. Adios."

In the end, 150 midwives will arrive from all over the country. This meeting will prove to be the historic beginning of the renaissance of the world's oldest helping profession. Many of my heroes are here, the women who are the foundation stones of this new movement. They are charismatic, skilled, feisty, articulate, opinionated, wild, and beautiful midwives. Even with all the diverse backgrounds, what we find most inspirational is our commonality—our steadfast dedication to improving the health and welfare of mothers and babies, and our mutual respect and admiration for each other.

A kismet friend I find here, Fran Ventre, queen of the yentas, best describes the El Paso conference:

"It was an unbelievable conference. It was like we had been hungry for so long, and a banquet was served up. I think for all of us, it was the first time we came together and met all of the people we had read about. And it was unbelievable, the first time this had occurred. It was wonderful, just wonderful. Suzanne Arms was there, Nancy Mills, Ina May, Shari Daniels. That's where I met Carol Leonard; she was just a baby then. I don't mean that in a negative way. We were all babies. It was the most exciting conference I can ever remember, because it was the first one. We all came together and felt like, 'God, there are other nuts just like me. I'm not crazy, we're not crazy.' That's how profound it was. It was a great conference. I don't remember the content, but those of us who came got to meet the people we'd read about for years. Raven Lang was there; to me, big, big names. That's like seeing Elvis. I think the El Paso conference was significant as part of midwifery organization. That's where everybody met. It is our history."

The workshops are informative and educational, but the real event is the storytelling that goes on everywhere until the wee hours of the dawn. It is phenomenal that we have all come to the same conclusions, independently, all across the country. Midwives are listening raptly to each other's stories, laughing, crying, eyes dancing with the joy of it. Absolutely falling in love with each other. It is the beginning of the weaving of the tall birth tales for me. I don't sleep the entire time I am there. We sit hunkered in hallways, squatting in doorways, lying on beds in clusters of enthusiastically gesturing women, exchanging story after story. This is where the real teaching occurs. We are thirsty for all the powerful knowledge we can finally exchange with our peers. It also validates my skills as a relatively experienced practitioner.

The last night of the conference becomes a pajama party. A cluster of us are still awake at 3:00 AM, an occupational habit. We are watching *Night of the Living Dead* on late-night TV. I am scared shitless. I can't watch these movies at all. At the worst possible moment, my midwife roommates mock attack me, mauling and tickling me because I am so freaked out by the stupid movie. Then they throw my stockings out of the hotel window because they say they smell bad. A bunch of grown women behaving like fifth graders.

A midwife from West Virginia does an unbelievably hilarious rendition of a British teaching film, imitating an obstetrician showing medical students how to do a manual removal of the placenta. Her seriously maniacal karate-chopping motions have us in hysterics. Only midwives would think this the funniest thing they had ever seen.

I am so grateful. I have finally found my sisters. I come home, inspired with even more passion, buoyed and supported by the underground network of the wild and brave women who attend births around the country. Our ancient art, which once was associated with the past, the poor, and with witchcraft, is coming out of obscurity to be recognized as a viable new profession.

On my return, armed with heady new information, I am ready to revolutionize the current medical birth practices. Ken reacts by digging in his heels. He becomes more confrontational with me than ever. He is back at me with the safety issue again. How can I ensure the well-being of the mothers and the babies out there in the pucker-brush, when he's seen all hell break loose at the last minute? I calmly state that I haven't seen "all hell," without a few red flags to give me plenty of fair warning that it is about to break-loose. That sounds to me like someone is asleep at the switch.

He rubs his eyes in exasperation. He knows he is losing this one. I am still too hot and full of Juarez grease and salsa to back down now.

I say, "How can you perpetuate a system that depersonalizes and degrades women? How can you continue to do habitual procedures that are totally unnecessary and medically unwarranted, like routine preps of high enemas and full shavings? Or lying flat on our backs like cockroaches on delivery tables, with our legs hanging in stirrups, often drugged and unaware, not even participating in our own birth experiences, for godsake?"

I am mad now; this has been going on for long enough.

He responds by giving it right back. "How can you be so arrogant as to presume to be giving good care when you work without the benefit of continuous electronic fetal monitoring?"

"*What?* What *benefit?* A higher section rate? Ah, jeesh, come on, Ken. Continuous EFM has never been shown to improve outcome and you know it." I lower my voice. "Look, I can do as vigilant a job with my trusty little hand-held Doppler. I know that for certain. And women get to remain upright and active this way. You know, Ken, there's no way you'll ever really know what I'm talking about until you go to a home birth to see for yourself. If you sincerely want to make inroads in maternity care, you'll come with me to one."

Cornered, he nods a feeble assent.

KEN'S FIRST HOME BIRTH

Jessie is a fascinating-looking woman. Her appearance is completely split in half. One side of her head is pale blonde and blue-eyed and fair, and the other side is dark-haired, brown-eyed, and swarthy. It is a little disconcerting at first to focus on her eyes. They have that crazy, witchy look, like those dogs with two different-colored eyes. I soon learn that the color pattern stays true the entire length of her body.

She is a young pharmacist who works at the drug dispensary at Merrimack Valley Hospital. She has gone to Ken's practice, Fifty Fingers, for her prenatal care with her first child. When she says what she really wants is to stay home for the birth, Ken refers her to me.

Jessie lives only a few miles from Ken, on the banks of the Blackwater River. She lives in the crate in which Charles Lindbergh's plane, the *Spirit of St. Louis*, was shipped back to the U.S. from Paris in 1927. The large, rectangular crate is made of English pine and has been made into a summer cottage that has sat on the mossy banks of the Blackwater for almost fifty years. Jessie and her partner have taken up squatting residency in the crate and have made it quite cozy.

Jessie calls in labor in the middle of the night. I ask her if it would be OK if Dr. McKinney came along to observe. She is shocked into silence for a split second, then agrees wholeheartedly. All the women love Ken. He agrees to meet me out on the main road, where the path begins, for the walk in to the cottage.

I am grinning like a hyena in the dark as we crunch along the path down to Jessie's crate on the riverbank. I walk ahead with my birth bags. Ken follows, shining my flashlight at my feet. I am trying to suppress a laugh. It is three o'clock in the morning, and the man arrives looking like an ad for Brooks Brothers, in a button-down shirt and a tie, even though he has a cowlick from sleeping that makes his hair stick straight up in the back. I don't tell him this. Now, he is carefully walking in the mud and the pine needles, wearing his shiny tassel loafers. I giggle. This is going to be fun.

When we get to Jessie's door, he hesitates. He looks panicked.

He says, "Jesus, Leonard, this is trust. I just hope you know what you're doing."

Jessie's labor goes without a hitch. She paces up and down her crate like a caged tigress, stopping only to pick dead leaves off her houseplants. During the hard time of transition, she lies on her side, panting heavily like a great cat. I sit beside her, rubbing her back and giving her sincere words of praise and encouragement. Out of the corner of my eye, I watch Ken as he sits in a chair, nervously flipping through magazines, pretending to be nonchalant about the whole thing.

A slight smile creeps across my face. I really am fond of this man. I know he is worried that all hell is going to break loose, and he will have to bail me out. As Chief of Obstetrical Services at MVH, what would be the consequences of his being caught attending a crate-birth with a maverick, lunatic-fringe midwife? His credibility within the medical community would be shot. This really is a huge risk for him. I admire his courage. I look at him, studiously engrossed in *Woman's Day*, and I feel a rush of tenderness.

At one point, Ken looks up from his reading and sees an

electric cord running from under Jessie's belly and the bed sheets. I know he thinks I have somehow wired her for fetal monitoring. He points to the cord.

"What's that?" he asks.

I answer, "It's a heating pad, Ken. Don't you have these in the hospital?"

He winces and goes back to his reading.

When it comes time for Jessie to push her baby out, she spontaneously gets up into a huge, old, overstuffed armchair and drapes her legs over each arm. She says this feels the best to her. It is great for me; I can see clearly without doing the usual gymnastics. This position seems to bring the head down quickly. Soon, I am oblivious to Ken and anything else in the room. I ask Jessie to slow her efforts down, to blow out through her mouth instead of blocking her breath.

I say, "Beautiful. Gentle. Easy now. Nice!" over and over as the babe's head slowly stretches Jessie's skin taut. As always happens at this point, my focus becomes so complete on the crowning head, that when Jessie's baby girl slides into my hands, there is a stillness behind all motion. I hold my breath until she takes her first, as if my very will can coax the living spirit into her glistening body. Her color changes rapidly, going through a rainbow of hues until it is a healthy rose. I quietly hand her up to her skunk-haired mother.

It is only now that I become aware of Ken's watching intently over my shoulder. I turn to grin at him. He gives me a triumphant thumbs-up.

Jessie names her daughter Amelia Ohram—Amelia after Amelia Earhart, because she has been born in another famous aviator's crate; Ohram because it's Gaelic for "by the shores of the river." It has been a wonderful birth. It is a sunny morning, and Ken and I walk slowly along the edge of the sparkling Blackwater River. Ken is excited and energized by the experience. He talks the entire way back.

He says that this has really been an eye-opener for him. He has been on the verge of quitting obstetrics because it is so impersonal and dehumanizing; the routine of women, drugged and unconscious and unable to push, often requiring forceps. He calls it the "knock 'em out, haul 'em out" school of obstetrics. He's been getting bored and disgusted; he knows there is more to it than that. *This* is the way it is meant to be, with women in their power, in control of their experience.

We sit on a rock, warming ourselves in the spring sunshine. He allows as how he still wouldn't feel comfortable attending births at home. His training makes him feel most secure with an operating room, fully equipped for an emergency cesarean, just down the hall. But why couldn't women have a similar experience, even it they have to be in the hospital? Why couldn't changes be made in standard hospital procedures that would allow women to dictate how they want their births to be? He is all fired up now. He turns to me and asks if I would help him identify the routines that are archaic and unnecessary, changes that will make hospital births more humane. I agree, knowing that I can come up with that list in about two seconds flat.

I look at him as he squints in the bright sun. I think that Ken is absolutely the most handsome man I have ever met. He is a black-haired, green-eyed Scotsman, with the rugged good looks of an outdoorsman. He is tall and muscular and high-cheekboned. Yet his gentle manner makes me profoundly attracted to him. I am content and happy this day, just to have him as my friend.

We reach the cars and turn to say our good-byes.

He says sincerely, "Thanks, Carol, this really means a lot to me."

I draw a heart in the dust on the windshield of his Volvo.

"Great! I'm glad you came." I grin at him. "I thought you'd like it."

A few days later, I bring a friend of mine, who is in her first trimester, to see Ken at his group practice, so we can listen to her baby's heartbeat for the first time with his more sophisticated ultrasound. After she leaves, we are alone in the office, standing next to Dr. Easey's large mahogany desk.

Ken says, "You know, Dr. Easey is getting married tomorrow."

He is scrutinizing me intensely.

"Yeah, so?" I finally say. "What? Why are you looking at me that way?"

He looks puzzled. "The way you tease him at the Health Center, I thought maybe you had a little crush on him."

What? Dr. Easey? Is he serious?

"You have got to be joking!" I explode. "It's *you* I want, Ken McKinney, and it's you I've wanted for a long time. Some days, I can barely stand it. I want to eat you alive!"

He looks at me, completely expressionless, until a violent twitch begins in his left eyebrow. He manages to faintly choke out, "Where? When?"

I say, "Here. Now."

A HANDCUFFED BIRTH

Melissa and her husband, Eric, are of the Bahai faith. They are attractive in a very wholesome, clean-cut way. They are an incredibly sweet and loving couple. Eric is a policeman in Manchester. Melissa is having her first baby, and it is breech. Dr. Brown is seeing Melissa for her prenatal care. He still plans to attend her at home, if all goes well. Francis doesn't hold with the current attitude that all primip breeches are dangerous and should be routinely sectioned. He feels that breeches are simply an error in polarity; that 3 percent of the time, gravity fails to bring down the heaviest part—the head—and instead, the baby simply runs out of turning room with the head still up in the fundus. He is trained in the old DeLee technique of delivering breeches and adamantly feels that vaginal delivery is far safer than cesarean section. He does watch vigilantly for contraindications, however, and he has instructed me on what to look for in labor.

I arrive at their home in Manchester to labor-sit by myself, Francis remains behind to do his clinic hours. He feels it is still early labor and will be a while yet. Melissa is overdue, and I feel her baby is large. She is laboring well. She spends a lot of time in the bathtub, with Eric hypnotically pouring a pitcher of warm water over her hugely mounded belly. The water enables her to handle her contractions surprisingly well. She lies back in the tub, resting, rolling her eyes up to show the whites, as though in a deep trance. She opens up steadily in this manner until she gets to seven centimeters, and then she stops. She abruptly stops everything.

In a normal vertex labor, I wouldn't think twice about having her stop until she is rested and then has enough moxie to continue. But in a breech presentation, an arrest in progress is one of the red flags that Francis has been talking about. His main concern is that with a first baby who is breech, it is an untested pelvis that could possibly be too snug to allow the after-coming head to pass through safely. This is the worst-case scenario of a breech, but one of the possible distress signals is a dysfunctional labor where contractions stop. His theory is that labors like this stall long enough for us to get ourselves transferred to where we need to be.

I call Francis and say that this situation feels funky to me. Melissa's baby feels big, is a frank breech, and is going nowhere. He agrees that we should probably mosey over to Merrimack Valley Hospital. We needn't rush, as she isn't in good established labor anymore. I explain to Melissa and Eric that we are probably looking at a cesarean section, as that is the standard of care in this case. They say they are amenable to this if it is in the best interest of their child. They seem in good spirits, and Eric lovingly helps his wife get dressed for the trip.

Upon arriving at MVH, I learn that Dr. McKinney is out of town, and Dr. Easey is on call. I get that sinking feeling in the pit of my stomach again. I know we are deeply in for it this time. The staff knows we are a transfer of an attempted home birth. My worst fears are confirmed when Dr. Bacon, the anesthesiologist, comes brusquely into the room and tells Eric that he will have to leave, that husbands are not allowed to accompany their wives in the operating room.

Damn! I've forgotten that Merrimack has that stupid, antiquated policy.

I say to the gas man, "Surely you can be flexible and make an exception in this case."

Dr. Bacon clenches his teeth and hisses, "You people are all troublemakers, coming in here with your ridiculous demands. The next thing you know, husbands will want to be with their wives for their gallbladder operations!"

Eric says in a quiet, trembling voice, "Please, Doctor, this isn't a gallbladder; this is my child, my *baby*! I *have to* be with my wife when she has our baby. I promised her I wouldn't leave her alone in this, no matter what—that I wouldn't abandon her. This is our birth together. You must understand; I *have to* be there when Melissa has our baby!"

Eric's eyes are brimming with tears. He is distraught. The anesthesiologist straightens up imperiously and strides out of the room.

I feel helpless and terrible. "I'm sorry, Eric. It looks like you two are going to be separated after all."

Eric stands up suddenly, walking out of the room and across the hall.

"Uh-oh, I know that look," is all Melissa says.

When Eric comes back into the room a few minutes later, he

has something in his hands that I instantly recognize. It is the same leather handcuff that I had been tied down with during Milan's birth. Eric puts the cuff around his wife's wrist, then around his own, and buckles it tight. There is a slight flicker of defiance in his gentle face.

"This may be only symbolic, but I'm not removing this handcuff, no matter what."

The nurse in attendance gasps and scurries out of the room, in search of someone with authority, I assume.

"Mother of God," I mutter. "This is going to be a humdinger."

Next in is my man, Dr. Easey. He is clearly furious. He strides over to the bound couple and fairly shouts, "Stop this, this minute! Stop this ridiculous nonsense! Every minute you waste with your immature stubbornness, *you are killing your baby!* Doesn't it even matter to you that you're jeopardizing your baby's health for your own selfish benefit? This is akin to child abuse!"

Eric's and Melissa's mouths drop open. Dr. Easey whirls back out of the room.

They look at me frantically. I am surprised my voice sounds so calm.

"Look. The reason we came in here is because Melissa wasn't contracting anymore. She still has had only a couple of contractions since we've been here. So that means she isn't much more dilated than seven centimeters. That's not going to endanger your baby by any means."

I take a stethoscope off the blood-pressure apparatus on the wall and listen to Melissa's belly. Her baby sounds fine, a rock-steady heart rate of 144 beats per minute.

"You're doing fine. We have a lot of time to negotiate this, and it's obviously very important to you. As long as Melissa doesn't start cranking again, you can stand firm for what you believe in."

At this point, Dr. Easey asks me to step outside in the hall. He is with Dr. Bacon and some other men in white coats.

"This is all your doing. If you tell them to quit, they will. They listen to you. So make them comply. Tell him to unhandcuff himself from his wife this instant!"

I still sound calm. It's almost as though someone else is speaking.

"I am their midwife. My job is to protect the normalcy of their experience as much as possible, even in an abnormal environment such as this. I can't *make* them do anything, let alone something that I don't believe is detrimental to the baby. I think fathers should be present for the births of their children. If it's a cesarean, then that's all the more reason that he be there for her."

Dr. Bacon is short and to the point. "It is the policy of all Merrimack Valley's anesthesiologists that no family member be present to observe surgery, ever. That's our policy, and it's not going to change today."

I respond, "Yes, Dr. Bacon, I know your position. But I think that policy is founded on the belief that anesthetists are more likely to be sued if a family member is watching when there's an emergency. In actuality, I think the opposite would happen. If there is a problem, and a relative saw all the incredible effort and skill in your response to solving the emergency, instead of sitting in a waiting room imagining the worst, I think that person would be grateful to you for your caring and expertise."

He looks at me blandly. "Save your breath. Save the argument. The man is *not* going in the OR today, and that's that. You'll have to find yourself another hospital."

He turns and marches down the hall.

I turn to Dr. Easey.

"Oh, this is just great. You say home births are dangerous, and I come in here because I need your help—and now you are refusing us?"

He is not enjoying this. "You really are a pain in the ass, you know that, *Ms.* Leonard?"

I nod. "Yes, sir, I do know that, *Dr.* Easey."

I turn and go back into the room.

Several nurses come in to report that Dr. Easey is busy calling hospitals around the state to see if any will allow a father in the OR for a cesarean delivery. They are gawking at Eric's handcuff.

Eric sounds desperately sad and sincere. "Please listen to me. I'm not being belligerent or even trying to make a statement. This is not a whim. I love my wife, and I love my baby. I'm part of this too. I *have to* be there when we become a family."

I can see that the nurses are genuinely touched by his sincerity and are getting a little misty-eyed themselves.

Then I hear Dr. Easey in the hall, swearing in frustration.

"Jesus Christ! This is such bullshit!" Dr. Easey comes storming in. "OK, here's the deal. The only place in all of New England that will take you is Boston Lying-In Hospital. There's an ambulance coming to take us down to Boston. I'll have to go with you in case she gets active and delivers on the way. You're all a bunch of idiots."

Once the four of us are settled in the ambulance, we fly south down Interstate 93. Dr. Easey is glaring at me.

I try, unsuccessfully, to chat him up.

"You know, this is pretty ironic. I transfer to the hospital because I have a big, primip breech and feel I need to be somewhere better equipped, and here we are with the possibility that we could end up doing this baby in the least desirable situation of all."

He is seething. He replies in no uncertain terms. "Don't talk to me. Don't say another word to me."

We spend the rest of the trip in stone-cold silence.

At Boston Lying-In Hospital, it is an entirely different story. The attending ob-gyn is a giant, gregarious Russian in a white coat named Dr. Sergai Borgolinsky. He is amazingly affable and relaxed. It is no skin off his nose if the father—or the whole rest

of the family, for that matter—wants to be there for the section.
The guy must be six foot seven. I am startled at how young he
seems to be, maybe only a couple of years older than I.

He is very friendly and effusive. He keeps saying, "No
'prublem.' No 'prublem.'"

I go up into the medical students observation gallery and sit
in the bleachers, looking down on the scene.

Melissa is prepped and lying flat on her back on the operating
table, with her arms strapped to boards that stretch straight
out from her body. She is alone, except for Eric, who is sitting
at her head, talking to her quietly. Their heads are behind a
screen that is draped over Melissa's belly so they won't see the
first incision. I was raised Unitarian and don't usually get into
Christian symbolism, but the Christ imagery here, with Melissa
splayed as if on a cross, is a little hard to ignore. The vision is
powerful and shocking and makes the hairs on the back of my
neck stand up. Eric looks up and blows me a kiss.

At this moment, all the men in white coats come in and swarm
around Melissa's supine body. They make the first cut, and the
baby is free—a healthy, wonderful nine-pound boy. I feel nauseous.
I look down and give Eric and Melissa the best congratulatory
smile I can muster up. I wobble to the ladies room.

Two weeks later, Merrimack Valley Hospital proudly announces
that it is to be a forerunner and pioneer in the field of family-
centered maternity care by allowing fathers into the operating
room with their wives during cesarean births, thus encouraging
the important bonding process within the family unit.

＊

Ken has become my mentor, my friend, my desire—and my lover.
I have to tell John the truth about my relationship with Ken; it
isn't fair to him to not be honest. I certainly do not expect Ken

to follow suit. When I tell John that I have fallen in love with someone else, he becomes enraged in his grief and his pain. I have anticipated this and have made arrangements to move out of our home and into what is known as the ghetto, on the Heights of Concord. The apartment is in a government-subsidized low-income housing project. This is all I can afford. Even so, I have to borrow the first two months rent from Francis.

But I am happy. Milan's room has a large, sunny window filled with his beloved cactus plants and rock collection. I make the downstairs into a townhouse clinic, where I see pregnant women three days a week. Even though some days I have to raid Milan's piggy bank for gas money, life is good. I become more assertive about my monetary worth and my new fee of $150 per birth. I begin to make enough money to pay the rent with some left over for Milan and me to occasionally go out for a movie and an ice cream.

MY FIRST BREECH BIRTH

It is amazing to me that just when I think I've learned all the lessons I am supposed to get about a particular situation, more come. This definitely keeps me humble. Grace is a willowy blonde with piercing blue eyes and has that old money, WASP-prep-school look about her. She is pregnant with her second baby and has been having her prenatal care with me, in conjunction with Dr. Faith up north, as they live out in the country. I'd like to blame Dr. Faith for misdiagnosing this one, but I can't. I am the last one to see Grace before she goes into labor. I completely miss the fact that her baby is breech.

I arrive at her house in the middle of the night. When I check her, I am appalled to feel a single chubby leg and a huge scrotum hanging down in her vagina. Damn! A single-footling breech. This is not good. Grace's labor is moving incredibly fast. Ultimately, it will be only three hours from start to finish. I know we don't have time to make it anywhere for additional help. I figure it is better to stay where we are and to try to remain calm. One of the real dangers of a single-footling breech is that the cord can wash down and prolapse when the water breaks. Grace has already ruptured her membranes. The baby's heart rate is great, so no cord compression yet. We seem to be doing OK—so far. Time for a consult with Francis. (Time for that bloody job at McDonald's.)

Francis's sleepy voice is reassuring on the phone. He isn't very worried. He says that since this is Grace's second baby, her pelvis has already been proven to be adequate enough to birth an average-size baby. The labor is moving along quite rapidly, so we needn't be overly concerned about disproportion. The place where people get into trouble, he says, is by not minding the store and allowing the smaller presenting part of the body to descend through an incompletely dilated cervix. This will cause the arms and head to extend and get hung up in the cervix, which can result in premature inspiration, possible aspiration of fluid or meconium, and drowning.

As long as I don't have her push until I'm absolutely sure there is no cervix left, the birth should be straightforward—just backwards. And, he says, whatever I do, be gentle, no traction. By pulling on the body, I could cause the head to go into an abnormal rotation, rotating the face up when the back of the head hits the hollow of the sacrum. If this occurs, the chin will get lodged against the pubic bone, and I'll lose the baby. Otherwise, I'll be fine, he says, just fine.

Holy Mother, now I'm *really* nervous.

I take a deep breath, put on my best midwife poker face, and prepare to deal with this ass-backwards child. I wonder what it means for this little guy to be coming into this world scrotum first. Some kind of a statement. Grace does have a rim of cervix left, and she does have uncontrollable bearing-down urges as her son's body starts to slide through the cervix and increase the pressure. It's crucial that she holds off pushing until she becomes fully dilated.

I raise up her butt by piling folded towels under her bottom. I hold the presenting part up out of her vagina, with my gloved fingers in her cervix. This should take some of the pressure off and buy us some time. I sit between her legs, pushing upward against her downward force. I have her blow through contractions to diminish the bearing down. I do a little vaudeville routine to distract her from pushing. We remain this way for what seems like an eternity, until I can no longer feel the cervix.

I give her the green light. "Good to go."

My heart is pounding as the baby's body starts to emerge, mainly because it is so bizarre-looking. First, Aaron's toes are visible in the introitus, looking like a row of tiny pearls. Then his fat left leg is born, and his toes search around as if he is testing the water to see if it is safe to come out. Next comes his hugely engorged scrotum, and then his penis pops out. He pees a fountain of urine into the air the moment it is free. I can't help but laugh.

But his right leg is stretched up to his head, with his foot by his ear. The poor guy is doing a complete yogic split. It makes me sore, watching him stretch in half like that. When his belly and right thigh are visible, I pull a loop of cord down to prevent traction on the umbilicus. I am relieved to feel the cord pulsing steadily—so far, so good. I gently cover his exposed body with a dryer-warmed blanket. No sense getting him upset and taking his first breath too soon. His arms are flexed properly, so the shoulders are born easily with the next contraction.

The next few minutes are critical to this baby's outcome. Now, either the head comes out—or it doesn't. I begin talking out loud. "Come on, little boy baby. You can do this. You've been doing really great up to now. It's not bad out here. Please, little guy, cut me some slack here—just come out. I know you can do it. We have two really nice breasts waiting for you."

He isn't listening. It seems like all movement has stopped—and it remains stopped for what seems like a full minute. I hear a roaring in my head. I am thinking about getting aggressive, but then I hear Francis's voice in my head. I gently raise Aaron's body up just a tiny bit. The head slides down, and I can see his hairline on the nape of his neck at Grace's vulva. I watch as the perineum retracts, and Aaron's little face is exposed. First his mouth, then his nose, up to his brow.

I syringe his mouth and nose. I consider giving him some oxygen while he is hanging out on the perineum, but he is pink and the cord is still pumping loyally.

We are out of the woods.

But this is as far as he gets. He doesn't budge any farther. At this point, it is pretty surreal-looking, because his face is grimacing—and he sneezes. He is looking around between Grace's thighs, her perineum stuck tightly on his head like a stocking cap.

I say to him, "Um, Bud, you're going to look a little ridiculous going to first grade wearing your mother for a hat like that."

After a while, I get antsy. I don't like the thought of the pressure, both to the baby's head *and* the mother's vagina. I prepare to do an ex post facto episiotomy to release his forehead. I pick up my scissors; Grace sees me and looks horrified.

She says, "Oh, no, you don't, damn it!" She pushes Aaron, eight pounds and squalling, into this world.

I am overwhelmed with relief and gratitude. I whisper a prayer of thanks to the Mother of the Universe: *Whew. I owe you one. I promise I will never be sloppy in locating the head ever again. Thank you with all my heart for guiding my hands.*

A few years later, this baby boy will be sitting on the same bed with his older brother, watching as their sister is born. She is a conformist and comes out head first.

Aaron says to me, "She's *naked!*"

"Hm-m-m, so she is. Should we put clothes on her?" I ask him.

He studies his sister very closely. "Nah. She looks pretty cool naked."

"Okay, you guys, what are you going to name her?" I ask the two brothers.

They look at each other and call out in unison, *"Cinderella!"*

⌐⌐

I keep my promise to obsessively verify that a baby's head is down by thirty-four weeks. If I wait too long after thirty-four weeks, the baby is usually too large to turn spontaneously or to be easily turned manually. Because I dearly do not want to be surprised at home with a missed breech again, I get pretty skilled at correctly palpating the baby's exact position. If the baby hasn't flipped around to a vertex position on its own when there is about a month and a half to go, then I attempt to manually turn it by doing an external version. Many obstetrical textbooks state that this is a dangerous maneuver, and I agree—if it is done roughly or forcefully. Francis believes that versions are still safer than cesarean sections. He finds it ironic that no one ever mentions the fact that the maternal mortality rate for cesarean sections is four times higher than that of vaginal deliveries.

Francis says that the most important part of a version is to listen intuitively to your fingertips, to be extremely gentle, yet unwavering at the same time. The trick I find works best is to the get the mother very relaxed by massaging her belly with warm oil before applying any pressure. It also helps to place several folded towels underneath her to elevate her hips. This lifts the breech out of her pelvis as much as possible. I have an assistant listen to the fetal heart rate for any negative response to the pressure throughout the entire turning.

As Francis has shown me, I massage the baby through the mother's belly, slowly pushing the baby's back upward with one hand. With the other hand, I gently "walk" the baby's head downward toward his legs. I check with the mother the whole time to be sure she is feeling no pain. Most often, when the baby's body is transverse, or directly across the mother's belly, the head will dive down into the pelvis, making the mother gasp in surprise. These version babies almost always stay head-down afterward with no trouble. Occasionally, a baby gets to a certain axis and then becomes very hard to budge. In this case, I abandon the effort and revert it back to breech. I never force the manipulation if there is strong resistance. This could indicate an obstruction of some sort and isn't meant to be.

A midwife friend of mine who practices in Vermont used to bring her breech clients down to the New Hampshire border for me to turn. She didn't feel confident or experienced enough at that time to do versions herself. It was a wonderful way for the two of us to spend time together, exchanging trade gossip. We would meet at a rest area outside of Lebanon and sit in the sunshine. The women would lie on the grass, and we'd turn their babies; then they'd go home, and the babies would be born head first. We always made sure to stay intuitively aware. We never ran into any trouble doing these versions, except in one case; I believe my attempted version indirectly saved the baby's life.

My own baby is growing up. Milan is two years old when Valerie and I are at a staff meeting at the Health Center and decide it is definitely time to wean our sons. We are listening to our coworkers struggle with a consensus decision about some piddling thing or other. It is hard to concentrate on the discussion. Our boys are at the breast but are still playing and kicking each other and laughing and generally screwing around instead of nursing quietly. Milan loves to nurse and is usually fairly serious about it, but Ammon, who is a week older than Milan, has always been Destructo Boy. Now, he is rubbernecking at Milan, but he is still at Valerie's breast. He turns around to get

Milan's attention without letting go. He stretches her nipple as far as possible in order to poke Milan.

"God, Valerie, your nipple looks like a quahog neck," I say tactfully.

She groans. "OK, that's it. I've had it with this. I'm tired of being a cow. I want my body back." She rolls her beautiful Latina eyes. "Let's go to the La Leche League meeting tomorrow night to find out the best way to wean these guys."

I admire the work done by the La Leche League in promoting the global resurgence of breastfeeding. I agree to go.

The mothers at the LLL meeting are sitting in a circle, saying their introductions. When it is our turn, we state that we are there for information on how to wean our sons. The women gasp in horror. Uh-oh. I suddenly get that we have come to the wrong place and definitely have said the wrong thing. The LLL women state that they believe children should nurse freely until they wean themselves.

I think, *Yeah, right. At this rate, Milan's going to want a nip of ta-ta before he goes to the junior prom.*

There are more disapproving statements until I begin to feel as if we have accidentally mentioned infanticide.

"Oh, great idea, Chiquita," I mutter. "Let's get out of here."

Chagrined, we head for the kitchen and the little tea sandwiches and cookies. Valerie nods at the back door. We slip silently out the door to the backyard.

"Hey, Val, we're getting pretty good at this," I whisper.

Just then, the resident backyard dog, who is chained to his doghouse, lunges at us, snapping and snarling viciously. Swearing, we duck under some clothes drying on the line. We slink down the side driveway to the car, as every dog in the neighborhood howls at our departure.

Valerie decides to wean gradually, but I know Milan and I have to go cold turkey. It is all or nothing with this child. He is no longer nursing for nutritional value; it is solely for comfort and nurturing. The first night I deny him, I read him a bedtime story, rub his back until he is nodding off, "forget" to nurse him, and tiptoe out of his room. He screams for ten hours as though being murdered. I am a shaking, sweating, hysterical wreck. Several times I almost relent, but I know we will just have to go through this all over again.

At dawn, he stops crying suddenly. I sneak outside and look in his window. He has fallen asleep on his knees, holding on to the railing of his crib, with his face pressed against the oak spindles, as though doing time.

I sit on the lawn and weep silently. Mother guilt is a powerful thing. Had I known then that I would never nurse another baby, I would have gladly nursed him until the prom.

CHAPTER FOUR

LADY'S HAND'S, 1978

The births are booming. Between Dr. Brown's practice, which I will inherit, and my own, I attend 120 home births in 1978 alone. I am madly in love, have a brilliant and creative child, and am enormously busy in my career. What can go wrong?

On a hot, sticky summer day, I am doing prenatal exams in my apartment on the Heights, wearing my bikini. I am sitting on the edge of the wooden cot, pilfered from the New Hampshire State Hospital, which I use as an exam bed. I love this cot. Printed on the side in bold black letters are the words: **Property of the Granite State**.

I have just listened to a woman's belly. The room is very hot and crowded. I hear voices murmuring on the other side of the oriental screen that I use as a room divider. I assume more women have arrived for checkups, as I operate on a first-come, first-served basis. My bikini is sticking to my body, and the ear piece of my stethoscope has just tangled in my dangling beaded earring. I swing around the corner to the living room. I am astonished to see five people dressed in suits standing in my waiting area.

Their mouths drop open, as does mine.

Holy Mother of God! I think. *Now what?*

"May I help you?" I ask, giving them a lame smile.

They introduce themselves as being from the New Hampshire Department of Health and Human Services, Maternal and Child Health Division. They say that their public health nurses have been conducting home visits with new mothers who have had home births, and the women keep giving them my name. This isn't an official visit; they are just curious as to what is going on. I can see that they absolutely mean official business, so I make the split-second decision to play ball. I graciously offer to show them my office.

The largest of the women officiously identifies herself as Miss Betty Erney, RN, director of public health nursing. She immediately asks me if I am a nurse. I reply that no, I am not a nurse. She stiffens and sniffs. I can see straight away that she and I are about to adopt some bad attitudes.

The rest of the group is duly impressed with my setup. I show them the contents of my large, antique, pierced-tin pie safe that doubles as a sterile supply closet. I display my equipment. I even open a sterilized birth kit so they can get the proper picture of how I work. I can see that they have not expected this lunatic-fringe operation to be so efficient and organized. When I show them my autoclave and explain my sterilization technique for them, they are exclaiming happily and are swayed.

All except Nurse Erney. She isn't buying any of it.

She continues to look as if she's sniffing something decomposing. Apparently, she thinks she smells a rat.

She picks up a package of sterile gloves.

"Oh, so you do wear gloves?' she asks, implying that this surprises her greatly.

Officious people like this have always pushed my buttons. I can feel the stirrings of adolescent rebellion start to course through my veins. I politely try to ignore her question.

There is a sign on my front door that reads:

CAROL LEONARD ~ MIDWIFE

Even so, Miss Erney asks the next question. "Well, if you're not a nurse, then what are you?"

"I am an anarchist." I give her my best Pepsodent smile and indicate that the interview is now over. I genially show them the door. As they troop down the sidewalk, I absolutely know that I have just seen the proverbial tip of the iceberg.

A PREMATURE BIRTH

This is a birth that does much to damage my reputation as a competent and credible midwife within the medical community for years to come. It is difficult to decipher what was questionable judgment on my part, as opposed to what was my being pushed up against the wall for the greater part.

Ellen is an enormous farm housewife. She is jolly and incredibly strong, baking pies and rising before dawn to milk their dairy cows. Ellen doesn't believe in "lite" or low-fat anything. She drinks her cream straight. Her husband is a bovine artificial inseminator and has a neck as thick as my thigh. They have a fairly sizeable dairy herd. It is a physically strenuous life, but they are healthy and seem content.

This is Ellen's third baby. She has not had any problems with her other pregnancies. She has seen a family practice doctor sporadically for prenatal care but is very unclear about her dates. (This is before the advent of routine early ultrasounds for dating purposes.) Her doctor has told her that she is much more pregnant than I believe her to be when I first see her. I guess her to be at least a full month behind the due date that he has given her. This confusion is understandable, though, as she has generous amounts of adipose tissue, which is a nice way of saying she is really fat.

It is extremely difficult to size her uterus because she is so obese. She is probably close to three hundred pounds. But she is stocky and solid and strong, everything about her is healthy. Her blood pressure and glucose levels are normal. I agree to attend her at home if all continues to go well.

Not long after I first see her, she calls to tell me that her water has broken, and she's had some contractions but they have stopped. By my calculations, this puts her at thirty-four weeks, way too early for a home birth. My policy is to not attend a birth at home until after the thirty-seventh week, to be on the conservative side. These three weeks make all the difference in the world as far as fetal lung maturity. I tell her I will meet her at the hospital and will coach her through her birth there. She refuses and starts to argue with me.

She says she knows she is at term. She knows her body, and she wasn't anywhere near this big with her other pregnancies. She knows she is due and that all is well. I have an uneasy feeling, but I say that I will come to her house to check to see what I think is going on. Maybe I am wrong. Driving there, I rationalize. *What could be the harm in this? They don't live far from the hospital. If indeed it is a preemie, we'll transfer in plenty of time. Right?*

What I find makes me know I've made a tremendous mistake by not listening to my own hands, by not trusting my original sizing. I can't believe I've been so gullible. This is horrific. Not only do I find Ellen to be five centimeters dilated, with two little feet hanging in her vagina, they are definitely tiny, thirty-four-week feet.

Then, she tells me that her water broke thirty-six hours earlier. *What?* Mother of God! What next? When I listen for the baby's heart rate with my Doppler, I don't hear a thing. Nothing. This is possibly due to the fact that Ellen is so large that I can't hear through her fat—or it can possibly mean that there isn't a heartbeat. This is a mess! We need to get out of here, fast. I am barking orders to Ellen's mother and sister to get things ready for a transfer.

Ellen and her husband watch me benignly as I pack up. When it comes time to motivate, they look at each other calmly but don't move. I am definitely not calm. They ask me to give them some time to discuss their predicament and decide what to do. I think, *There's nothing to discuss!* Instead, I say, "Listen to me. Here's the reality of this situation:

1. We have a premature baby whose lungs are probably not mature enough for him to go it on his own without some assistance, which I don't feel qualified to do.
2. We have a double-footling breech, which in the best-case scenario is a complicated and high-risk delivery that needs to be conducted in the hospital.
3. Your membranes have been ruptured for over thirty-six hours, which significantly increases the possibility of a uterine infection that can result in a septic baby.
4. Your labor has stopped, and I can't even hear your baby's heartbeat to know whether or not he's a happy camper. At this rate, he may not be tolerating any of this. So, let's go!"

They look at each other peacefully. Ellen gives me a warm smile.

"Please give us a minute to pray for guidance," she says softly.

Oh, for godsake. I pace around their big old farmhouse like a caged animal. The house is littered with kids' toys and puppy chew toys. Articles of children's clothing are scattered everywhere. I plead with Ellen's mother and sister. I beg them to go in there and talk some sense to Ellen and her husband.

I explain that this is a very dangerous situation. Ellen's mother goes into the bedroom. She comes out wringing her hands.

She says, "They've decided to put this in God's hands."

God? What's He got to do with this? Is He going to perform a goddamn miracle or what? Damn it, this is just way out of control. This is getting bloody ridiculous!

I storm into their room, almost shouting at this point. "Maybe I've painted too rosy a picture of the probable outcome here. I'm telling you, your God has created a situation where in all likelihood, your baby is going to be in deep trouble when he is born. I don't want to be in the position to have to take over where God leaves off! Do you understand me?

They nod placidly. They say, "We trust in our Lord."

Jesus Christ! That does it.

What more can I say? I never, *ever* thought the day would come when I would abandon a woman in labor—but here it is.

I look at them both. I say quietly, "I'm sorry, but I am going to have to leave. I can't participate in this; it's just too irresponsible. I wish you luck. I pray your God is a compassionate one."

I gather up my equipment and walk out the door. Ellen's mother looks horrified as I leave. Her eyes silently plead with me to stay.

"I'm sorry" is all I can manage.

I get in my car and drive down the country road, along snow-covered stonewalls and stark leaf-bare trees. I am so angry that I pound the steering wheel. Angry at them for being so dangerously naïve and stubborn. Angry at myself for being so stupid as to get sucked in to a situation like this in the first place. *Dumb-ass fool. Now what, girl? You gonna just leave that baby there, knowing it is going to need help, that it will probably die without assistance breathing? Pretend like you can just drive away, wash your hands of it and move on? It's not the baby's fault, for godsake.*

I pull over and sit under an ancient maple tree. The sky is leaden with future snow. God, I hate making mistakes and then having to rationalize every action. I hate being wrong. It's so exhausting. I look up as a giant pileated woodpecker lands on the tree and cocks his head from side to side, listening. I watch him, mesmerized for a long time. When he flies away, I realize I've been listening, too. To myself. I get in the car and turn around.

I walk back into the bedroom.

Ellen's mother says, "Thank God! Our prayers have been answered."

I think, *Yeah, yeah. I'm still pissed, so don't push it.*

In the hour that I've been away, Ellen's husband, the veteran farmer, has given Ellen an enema to get her going again. Ellen is now seriously in the thick of labor and straining hard. Not long after my return, she feels rectal pressure and starts bearing down. I check to make sure there is no cervix left to hang up this little head. I prepare to do all I can possibly do for this little guy, coming out undercooked like this.

The biggest feat is being able to see what is going on at the introitus, as Ellen's thighs are so thick that they bulge in and occlude my field of vision. I finally recruit her mother and sister on each side, pulling her thunderous thighs out of the way so I can have a little elbow room.

The two little legs that are born are completely blue-black.

I think, *Oh shit, he's checked out.*

There is a fair amount of fresh meconium that has mixed with Ellen's enema that is now working to make a fine mess. I change the Chux pads as quickly as possible to try to keep some semblance of cleanliness.

I begin to weep with joy as the tiny little boy slides easily into my hands. He is pink and perfect. I DeLee suction him, and the trap is clear. Ephram opens his eyes and frowns; he looks worried. He gives out a faint cry. I listen to his heart, which is good and strong. He is definitely thirty-four weeks. His legs are discolored from being suffused in the vagina for so long. He is a strong little guy, but I know we are not out of the woods by any means. The placenta is born, and his cord stops pumping. As soon as the maternal oxygen supply stops, he starts gasping. His color gets dusky and his chest begins retracting. He is struggling for every breath.

Sweet Mother! This baby is about to crash and burn. I put an infant oxygen mask on him and start the flow of oxygen.

I say to his parents, "I don't care what you say. I am running interference for God now, and He says we are out of here!"

I bundle up the baby, pick up my O_2 tank, hijack Ellen's mother to drive, and run out the door.

The drive to the hospital is stressful and seems like an eternity, but we make it. Ephram keeps going limp, and his heart rate slows. I continue to give him oxygen. Every time he fades, I gently stimulate him and bring him around by talking to him and rubbing him up. I give him some gentle puffs with my mouth. He responds well. When we get to the nursery, he is alert but he is still retracting.

The woman pediatrician, Dr. Digger, is understandably outraged that this preemie has come in from a home birth. The nursery personnel are getting ready to transfer Ephram to Hanover's intensive care nursery for more comprehensive care.

Dr. Digger and I are standing next to his isolette as she examines his legs.

"Double-footling breech?" she asks.

I nod.

She listens to his lungs, "About thirty-four weeks?"

I agree that would be my guess.

Her mouth is a tight, straight line. She is clearly so angry that she is shaking as she removes her exam glove.

"There's one other thing," I say sheepishly. "The membranes were ruptured for more than thirty-six hours."

She literally flies at me. She draws her hand back and slaps me in the face with the latex glove. She hisses, "How dare you bring such a travesty in here? Now get out!"

My face is burning from the slap, probably more an emotional response than physical. Man, I hate it when this happens. But at least I'm getting used to it.

I say to myself, *Carol, sometimes you're the windshield...sometimes you're the bug.*

I walk down the corridor to the cafeteria for a coffee, but once I get there, I feel as if all eyes are on me. I can hear nasty murmuring. I leave the foreboding concrete walls and go home. I am feeling very dejected and sorry for myself.

Maybe I'm not such a hot-shit midwife after all.

As it turns out, Ephram never does crash. His blood gases and oxygen levels are borderline OK when he is admitted to the hospital. He is a fighter, a determined survivor. They keep him for observation in Hanover for only a few days, and then he goes home. I know we have all been very lucky with this little guy. From now on, it will be my policy to get a guarantee in writing from all parents, stating that they will agree to transfer without argument if I find it necessary.

Eighteen years later, I get a call saying that Ephram is the captain of his high school football team. He is so huge that he is nicknamed the "human refrigerator."

I guess their God had been in a benevolent mood that day after all.

⌐─

I always behave badly around Dr. Digger; I just can't help it, even though years later, she and I will have an uneasy friendship, mostly out of deference to Ken. She is so terminally uptight and straight. I deliberately say things to her to shock her senseless. I think in her secret heart, she loves it. One Valentine's Day, we are skiing, and she and I are riding up a chairlift together, chatting. She is wondering what to do special for her husband for a Valentine's treat, chocolate bon-bons or whatever.

I tell her that I have shaved my pubic hair in the shape of a heart and have henna'd it red as a surprise for Ken for the occasion.

I honestly think she is going to jump off the chair, she is so aghast and scandalized. She skies straight down the mountain without stopping.

I have always wondered if she did it, too.

Ken is busy initiating innovative changes in labor and delivery at MVH that will make the hospital more homelike. I personally think this is an oxymoron, but I don't want to discourage him. I write a list of thirty-three unnecessary practices that are routinely done in the hospital that I find offensive or frankly dangerous. Much of the list comes from a book by my friend, Suzanne Arms. *Immaculate Deception,* is a seminal work exposing unnecessary hospital delivery routines. Suzanne uncovers "an entire system of medical procedures and interferences that have been established to treat normal birth as a risky, dangerous, painful, and abnormal process in which pregnant women have no choice other than to submit graciously." Her book is named the *New York Times* Book of the Year for 1975.

Ken is delighted with my list. He feels it will give women who are on the fence about home birth more options in the hospital for family-centered maternity care. As Chief of Obstetrical Services, he slowly begins to institute the changes. This will put Merrimack Valley Hospital on the map as a pioneer in modern natural-birth practices.

First on the list, obviously, is discarding the wrist restraints. No more being tied down like a deranged animal. Also, deep-six the standard prep of high enema and shaving. No more routine, continuous electronic fetal monitoring for normal, uncomplicated births. No arbitrary, elective Pitocin inductions without some clear medical indication. Fathers are to be allowed access to their families at all times, of course, including cesarean sections and in the nursery.

No more routine drugs, episiotomies, or mandated supine— flat on one's back—positions. No more withholding fluids and nourishment, "just in case anesthesia is needed," and no routine, artificial, early rupture of membranes, which has never been proven advantageous by any evidence-based data. And babies are to be allowed to remain with their mothers at all times.

Through Ken's support and advocacy, virtually all of the thirty-three changes are adopted eventually, the last being siblings' presence at births, which takes until 1982 to be officially approved. He has managed to introduce the novel concept that women can be awake and aware and in control of their birth experiences. That birthing women should be treated with respect.

This is no walk in the park. One of the earliest and most significant changes that Ken proposes is the use of the labor rooms for labor *and* delivery, all in the same bed. This meets with fierce resistance from the other obstetricians. Frankly, they think he has lost his mind. They respond by saying that they weren't trained to do primitive bed deliveries. They say it is barbaric not to use a delivery table.

His colleagues are quite vehement about this, until they get a tidal wave of positive feedback from the women themselves. They slowly come around. I'd like to say the conversion happens in response to women's demands, but it is strictly monetary. They begin attracting patients away from neighboring hospitals. Merrimack gets a good reputation for being progressive. The women seek this out. The delivery numbers increase substantially.

The bottom line is that there is good money in instituting the changes. They turn all the labor wards into individual delivery units with cheesy pictures on the walls, frilly curtains on the windows, a Craftmatic hospital bed, a rocking chair in the corner, and a fetal monitor and emergency equipment hidden in an innocuous-looking oak-veneer cupboard. Yup, just like home.

They leave only one regular, old-fashioned delivery table conveniently down the hall, for last-minute complications. Ironically, as the birthing-room deliveries escalate, the cesarean section rate rises exponentially. Unfortunately, it is the same old practitioners, just in a hip, new disguise. They still don't trust or particularly enjoy birth.

A DASHBOARD BIRTH

The vast majority of the births are not only beautiful and powerful, but they are also a lot of fun. I like Patty a lot. I met her when I attended her first baby, early in the beginning of my career. We have been good friends since then. Patty has long, curly blonde hair and is vivacious and wickedly funny. She is anachronistic—a quintessential hippie "Earth Mother" WASP-reject. She is a back-to-the-lander, farmer wannabe and has lots of animals. She is pregnant again and due any day now.

Ken and I have just co-managed the vaginal delivery of a set of twin boys at MVH. It was a great birth, and I think Ken is a brilliant practitioner. I am standing in the doorway to the emergency room, soaking up some spring sunshine, as a stretcher is rushed in, carrying a woman.

The woman is flat on her back. She calls out, "Carol?"

I look down and see that it is Patty. I can't believe my eyes.

"Patty! What are you doing here?"

She says, "I just had my baby."

I am incredulous. "No, you didn't!"

"Yes! Yes, I did!"

"Well, where was I?" I shake my head in disbelief. "What happened? Where is the baby *now?*"

Patty says, "I had her in the car—it's a girl! Her nickname is Missy, but I started bleeding, so I was looking for you. Couldn't find you, so I came here instead. Now they've taken her away to the nursery."

"They what?" I ask. "She should be nursing to help you stop bleeding. Oh, for godsake."

Patty looks frantic. "I know. I want her back! I didn't mean for them to take her from me."

"This is ridiculous. I'm going to find her. Tell the ER doc to page Dr. McKinney. Have him come down here to give you a shot of Pitocin; that's all you need—that, and your daughter. I'll be right back."

I hurriedly go in search of the traveling gypsy baby. I see my friend Judy, who is the head nurse in the nursery, wheeling a baby cart toward the isolation nursery.

"Hey, Jude! Is that the Dillard baby you got there?"

She nods affirmatively.

"So, listen, Jude," I begin fast-talking, "this baby is already a 'dirty' baby, coming in from the outside. She needs to be back with her mother to help her mom stop bleeding."

Judy looks skeptical.

I rush ahead. "I know it's a stretch, but the baby doesn't have to be admitted; it's the mother who came for help. She's one of my clients."

Judy frowns. "Jesus, Leonard, you really are weird."

But she bundles up the baby and hands her to me. I put Missy under my arm, football style, and run back down the hallway. If it were the nineties, every security alarm in the whole place would have gone off by now, but this is the seventies, and we didn't tag babies back then.

Patty gives me a grateful smile and gathers her daughter to her breast.

Ken is laughing. He says, "You've got to hear this story."

Patty begins to narrate the sequence of events. She had gone to visit her mother but started to get uncomfortable with contractions, so she left and drove home. When she got home, she realized she was locked out of her house. She got back into her Saab to drive back to her mother's house but soon realized the baby was coming nonstop. She tilted the driver's side seat back as far as it would go, put her feet on the dashboard, and angled the rearview mirror so she could see what was happening. She watched the baby's head start to crown, massaged her perineum where it burned the most, and gently guided her baby out into her hands. She sat in the car, happily nursing her baby, listening to her dogs whine and scratch at the door to get in. Her chickens clucked and pecked around in the dirt of her driveway.

Then, she says, she started bleeding much more than what she thought was normal, probably because the placenta wasn't out yet. With the cord still between her legs, holding her daughter in her left arm, she drove her stick-shift Saab into town, looking for a handicapped-accessible drive-up phone so she could call me to give her a shot of Pitocin. Then she realized there was no such phone, so she continued driving to Merrimack Valley's parking lot. By now she was bleeding a lot, so she parked outside the ER and honked her horn until someone came out to investigate. The rest we know.

By now the placenta has been born, the bleeding has stopped, and her daughter is snoozing at the breast. Ken promptly discharges Patty. We wheel her back out to her car, clean up the blood enough to be presentable, and then I drive mother and child back home.

Her husband, Ronald, is standing in their driveway, feeding the chickens. He looks confused as we pull in.

"Congratulations, Dad!" I yell. I laugh at his dumbfounded expression as Patty emerges proudly with baby Missy.

Twenty-five years later, I have the honor to catch a baby for *this* baby! Second-generation midwifery! This has such a profound effect on me. It is such an honor to bear witness to the continuity of life through the generations. It is a fabulous birth, a baby boy named Sam. Missy is fast, like her mom was.

I am waxing poetic when I say to Missy, "If I had known when you were born and I was holding you in my hands that I'd be helping *you* deliver a quarter century later, I'd have said, 'Just shoot me now!'"

After the birth, Missy changes her name to Medusa.

Ken's changes are being adopted rapidly by the night nurses. This is his intended plan—to get the nurses in collusion by making them instrumental in the initial introduction of all things new and different. The night nurses are, surprisingly, the most flexible and cooperative. They tend to be older women who have seen it all and are pretty hard core. They are feisty, uppity, and mouthy. When things get sleepy and boring on the nightshift, they become bossy and loud and argumentative. This keeps them awake and alive. Their skill and knowledge about labor and delivery is legendary, as, collectively, they've been doing this since the birth of Moses.

The younger day nurses are an entirely different story. Fresh out of nursing school, and idealistic, they are still enamored of the paternalistic system that keeps them disempowered. They don't like my act one bit. It is inconceivable to them that I could possibly know what I am doing without being a trained nurse. Their contempt for me is palpable. Their jealousy and confusion about my relationship with their beloved Dr. McKinney only makes matters worse. They are territorial and catty and, some days, are downright nasty. I, for one, try to avoid using Merrimack Valley Hospital during the day, unless it is a dire emergency.

The night nurses, however, are hilarious. The first time I have to transfer at night, they really test my mettle. They want to know what this young upstart is all about. The two loudest nurses are named Dot and Jen. They are a classic dog and pony show if I've ever seen one. They run me ragged, bossing me around. I don't care. I respect their expertise, and I want to know what they know. I am just happy to be running with the "big dogs," so I tuck tail and am submissive. After sniffing me for a while, they decide I have plenty of common sense. They allow me to run in their pack. This is when we start exchanging tricks of the trade, and MVH makes its most radical advances.

We get laboring women upright and active, massaging them in showers and supporting them on birthing stools. I show them how to place a mirror under a squatting woman to watch progress without straining their backs. They appreciate this. They show me how to aggressively press on the rectum to stimulate a gastro-colic reflex to bring the head down. *Ouch,* I think, but it is a good trick to have available. Dot and Jen are the two most outspoken old battle axes, as I call them. They come with me to assist at home births on more than one occasion. They are brave and knowledgeable and kind.

The head "nightmare" nurse, Mrs. Malice, is the head of obstetrical nursing. She is a short, blustery, steamroller of a woman, and even physicians quake in her presence. Mrs. Malice is hell on wheels. Having to interact with her is like going to the principal's office in grade school when you messed up. The first time she calls me into her office for a meeting, I get stomach cramps. She sits across her desk from me. I am totally expecting a brutal reprimand of some sort.

Instead, she affectionately tells me that her mother was a midwife who worked with a country doctor, as I do. She says she remembers helping her mother remove the newspaper-wrapped obstetrics kits from their oven after they had baked long enough to be sterilized. She says she got her lifelong dedication and love of labor and delivery from her mother. I am floored. She likes me! After that, she always defends me publicly, but if she thinks I have overstepped my role, she pulls me up by the short hairs in private.

One day, Ken calls me at the Health Center to ask if I will meet him at White Park for a sandwich lunch. He has something very important to talk to me about. He sounds upset. I am in the middle of a dreadful staff meeting; his call makes me antsy all morning. Ken is sitting on a bench in the park, and he looks terrible. His face is ashen. Milan is oblivious to our tension, he toddles around on his chunky little legs, in his droopy diaper, happily chasing Mallard ducks.

Ken is having a hard time making eye contact with me.

"What's going on?" I ask him, beginning to think I don't want to know the answer.

He sighs and stares out over the pond. "My partners had a meeting to discuss us, although originally, it was supposed to be about lay midwifery. The meeting was a result of that preemie breech that you did. They're all hot under the collar about that and are using that as an example of how dangerous and irresponsible you are. So they had a vote and made a group decision that they can't be involved with or supportive of midwives in general—and you in particular."

"That was thoughtful of them," I say flatly.

"Wait—it gets worse. They requested that I not deal with you or back you up in any way. I said that I didn't think it was morally right to refuse anyone who shows up in the ER needing help. Easey got very angry with that line of thinking. He says midwives don't meet their high standards of training as obstetricians. Then he asked me, point blank, if we were having an affair."

He rubs his eyes hard in frustration. He looks very tired and drawn. "I felt up against the wall. I admitted that we were. To make a long story short, they're ready to can me from the practice.

They've given me twenty-four hours to make a decision—either I stop seeing you, or I have to leave the group. Simple as that." I feel numb, shell-shocked. As different and as innovative as Ken dares to be, he is still one of the "brotherhood." It still matters to him greatly that he measures up and is accepted by his peers. Nothing is ever going to change that. I know this has been a terrible blow to his self-esteem. It is unreasonable to expect him to do anything other than toe the party line. I have the crushing realization that life as I have known it is about to end. I already know what his answer is.

I look at him steadily. I hold my breath. His eyes well up with tears.

"I'm sorry, Carol. It's just too big a risk. I can't be with you anymore."

"I know. I know you can't. I understand." I need to get out of here before I fall apart completely. I peck him on the cheek. "The time I've spent with you has been wonderful, Ken, a true gift. I will cherish this always. Have a happy life. I really mean that."

I feel dizzy. I scoop up Milan and hurry to my car. I need my mother. Driving to her house in Henniker, I am sobbing so uncontrollably that I can hardly see where I am going. I feel as if my heart is breaking. I love this man with all my soul, and now he is gone. I am gulping for air and hyperventilating. By the time I reach my mother's house, I am hysterical and screaming. She runs to the door and grabs Milan. She looks horrified, as if someone has died. Well, someone has, sort of. I crawl under her dining room table and curl up in the fetal position, still sobbing. My mother is a total teetotaler, but she takes one look at me and goes to the cupboard. She pulls out a bottle of scotch and pours me a tumbler full.

"Thanks, Mom, it's not even five o'clock."

"You look like you can use some anesthesia."

She crawls under the table with me and holds my head in

her lap, stroking my hair. "Oh, sweetie, I'm so sorry this has happened to you."

I feel like a little girl with a big-girl heartache. This is the worst day of my life.

I spend the night at her house. She and Milan lie in her bed, watching TV, giggling, and eating cardboard-like Eggo waffles. Milan is nuts about his grandma. I drink more scotch until I am blind, and I go to sleep early. Later that night, my pager goes off. When I call the answering service, they say that Dr. McKinney is looking for me. He's left a message for me to meet him at the Concord Hotel. *Holy Mother of God!* I fly out of the house. When I get to the hotel, Ken is curled up in fetal position on the bed. He looks ill and scared and vulnerable.

"I'm sorry I did that to you, Carol. I honestly thought I could go back to my life the way it had been. But when I thought of never being with you again, I realized how much I love you. I don't want to live my life without you, no matter what the cost." He pauses for a second and has a slight hint of a smile. "I walked into the office meeting this afternoon and gave my partners the international sign of disrespect. I said 'Adios,' then I walked out."

I lie down beside him and curl around his back, spooning. I bury my face in his hair, weeping tears of joy.

He takes a shaky breath. "Oh, man, Leonard, we are in deep shit now."

THE FIRST VBAC

The relative safety of vaginal birth after cesarean section, or VBAC, as this is commonly called, is still very controversial and hotly debated. Most physicians have been trained to believe "once a cesarean, always a cesarean"—that the first cesarean section automatically mandates a cesarean from then on. Their argument being that the cesarean-scarred uterus is weaker at the suture line and is likely to dehisce, or rupture, at a much greater rate than a non-surgically scarred uterus. This may have been true of the old-style uterine incisions, the "classic cesarean," where the incision runs midline vertical from the umbilicus to the pubis through a major mass of uterine muscle.

But the new alternative techniques of the Pfannenstiel incision, or "bikini cut"—which is a low transverse incision through the tissue just above the symphysis pubis but below the thick uterine muscles—seems to reduce later problems significantly. This appears to be because the suture line runs along an area where there is virtually no muscle that can pull apart the old scar tissue with contractions.

Lynn has had a cesarean section with her first pregnancy. She believes it was totally unwarranted and unnecessary. It had been done for "failure to progress" when she was about seven centimeters dilated. She feels that she was thwarted at a reasonable attempt at labor and was denied a vaginal birth. She is extremely angry about her experience. She has become very active and vocal in the new cesarean prevention movement.

As she says, "There is not an angrier woman on this earth than a woman who believes she's had an unnecessary cesarean section."

She becomes very knowledgeable about cesarean practices in the United States, such as the fact that the U.S. has the highest cesarean section rate in the world. This rate has increased 400 percent in the last ten years.

Lynn goes to Ken's ex-practice, "Fifty Fingers," with her second pregnancy, armed with her optimum-birth letter, which is a manifesto listing her demands for her birth, including a trial of labor and, hopefully, a vaginal birth. She has put together a packet of new information and statistics supporting the benefits and safety of VBACs. She feels cesareans are major abdominal surgery, and the recovery time is much more extensive than that of regular birth. She doesn't want to feel condemned to repeat surgery; she wants to be treated like any other low-risk woman in labor.

Her obstetricians' reply? "No way." They say they are not willing to take the risk of venturing into uncharted territory. An intentional vaginal delivery after a section has yet to happen at Merrimack Valley. They not only discourage her plan, but they also later write in her chart that she is a "hysteric" and a "pain in the ass." It is her good fortune that Ken is now a solo practitioner and can make decisions independently. He has been doing a lot of research regarding outcomes from repeat cesareans versus those of spontaneous vaginal deliveries. He agrees to take her on.

After listening to the story of her birth, it becomes clear to me that she has a hospital phobia. This is not uncommon. The pattern is that women will present at the hospital in good established labor, then, after being there for a short while, their labors peter out entirely. This is called the fright-or-flight response in the wild—if a wild-animal mother in labor encounters a frightening situation, her labor stops long enough for her to flee to safety to birth her offspring.

Human mothers are no different. Hospitals have frightened many of us since childhood. Therefore, subconsciously, it feels like a dangerous place in which to birth our babies, so our labors stop long enough for us to flee to protection. Unfortunately, in the current approach to childbirth, this lack of progress is considered pathological, and intervention is begun to remedy an abnormal labor pattern. This protracted labor curve is called "arrested labor" by obstetricians. Ironically, it is called "a rest in labor" by midwives, meaning that Lynn probably just needed to take a nap.

We decide that because of this history, Lynn will feel more comfortable laboring at my apartment until she gets into irreversible labor; then we will hot-foot it to MVH. I live just minutes away, so this sounds reasonable to me. She and her husband, Doug, show up in early labor, laden with luggage, and proceed to take over my bedroom. Lynn zips right along adequately, up to about six centimeters, and then her contractions start to fizzle out.

Ken starts to get antsy. He is pacing around, first looking out the front window, then looking out the back window.

Doug is wringing his hands. Worried, he says, "This is exactly what happened the last time. It's going to happen again; it's the same thing all over again!"

Ken's jaw gets tight. He's really gone out on a limb this time. I look as both men sit tensely watching Lynn, as though they are travelers at an airport luggage carousel, waiting for their Tourister to come out of the chute. Time to clear the decks.

"Dr. McKinney, don't you have some pressing charts to finish at the hospital?" I ask sweetly.

He cocks an eyebrow at me.

I take him aside and whisper, "Look, she's not going to rupture her unit, not with these wimpy contractions. She hasn't even broken a sweat. Relax. We'll get to you as soon as she starts cooking again. I promise."

Ken looks relieved and excuses himself.

Now Doug is sitting next to his wife, fussing and fretting, a bundle of negative nerves. He is getting himself worked up into a state of borderline hysteria.

"It's happening all over again, I know it!" he whines. "You don't understand how psychologically damaging it's going to be if she has another section. She won't be able to handle it. I won't be able to handle *her*. This is an instant replay of the last time!"

I listen to him and realize he is right. This whole pressured scene, setting her up for failure, probably *did* happen the last time, but it doesn't have to end the same way. I see the old dynamics playing out. I decide to intervene.

"Hey, Douglas, I need you to go weed the carrot patch out back." Milan has a small vegetable garden in our backyard.

Doug's mouth drops open. "What? At a time like this?"

I give him an evil grin, "Yes, exactly at a time like this."

He looks at me like I am a mad woman, but he goes out to weed.

Now I can focus on Lynn, and she can focus on the work ahead.

I say to her, "You can take a snooze if you like. I don't care how long you take. Your baby sounds happy, and you've got tons of energy, so do it your way."

She shoots me a look of determination and grinds into gear. Without the inhibitions of external expectations and performance anxiety, she gets down to serious business. Within two hours she is in gale-force labor and eight centimeters dilated. Doug comes in from the carrot patch, and we are ready to go. I drive, with Lynn huffing and puffing in the back seat with Doug.

I think, *So much for Friedman's curve of normal labor progress.*

Once we are ensconced in the labor/delivery bed at the hospital, Lynn becomes an Amazon. She knows she is triumphant; the head is coming down fast. She is clearly enjoying herself now. She stands up on the bed, barking orders to everyone. She squats down on top of the mattress and forcefully pushes out her son. Ken has a demented grin.

We all support her as she reaches down and brings her child up in her arms. She is victorious! It is an incredible sight to see a woman in her power like this. She has been vindicated. Most important of all, what she knew in her heart to be true she has finally proven to herself.

Lynn goes on to become famous in the VBAC and cesarean section prevention movement that spreads across the nation in the late seventies. Ken becomes known in New Hampshire as a pioneer in the VBAC trend. He is sought out by women from long distances specifically for this reason.

A full decade later, Lynn will publish her milestone book,

Very Beautiful and Courageous: The Vaginal Birth after Cesarean Experience. In this book, she writes a touching tribute to Ken:
"He devoted himself and his life to mothers and babies. He never placed himself on a pedestal, but those who knew him would have placed him there. Ken was truly a special being."

⌐

Ken begins setting up his new practice. I think there is more confusion than animosity from the medical community; they just don't know what to think.

"Has McKinney lost his goddamn mind or what?" his colleagues ask.

Ken seems frightened and unsure of himself. What *is* he doing? What if he fails? We find an old ten-room apartment in a brick building downtown that will be perfect for a new clinic, once it is renovated. Ken names his new practice WHCA—Women's Health Care Associates. He starts actively interviewing for a nurse-midwife to assist him with births at MVH. I sit on the floor in the old living room/soon-to-be-waiting room, answering the phone as Ken's receptionist. I am covered in sawdust as workmen busily create a new office around me.

In the first couple of days, there are only a few calls for appointments. Ken is very worried, but I know the women are crazy about him. I try to reassure him. He looks discouraged. By the end of the week, he is booked solid. By the end of the month, the majority of patients from his old practice have switched to him. Women are delighted to have Ken's attention exclusively. He gets so busy that I hardly see him anymore. Occasionally, I spend the night with him in the on-call room at the hospital, just so we can have some uninterrupted time together. He loves every minute of it.

Ken finally decides on a nurse-midwife to hire, a young

woman whose philosophy and approach to birth he feels is similar to his own. Deborah is fresh out of CNM school. I am afraid that I will be jealous of her close working relationship with Ken. The night I meet her, in walks a very tall, exotically beautiful, self-assured young woman with large, dark eyes. Her thick, dark hair is almost to her waist. I think, *Yeah, right, way to go, big guy.* I am pissed.

I am about to have a very unattractive, childish tantrum when I realize that I actually like her. She is smart and funny and warm. Our friendship is sealed that night when I am paged to a birth in Peterborough. She asks if she can tag along, as she has never been to a home birth. I am delighted to have her competent assistance. We have a wonderful time, and we continue to help each other over the years. Ken thinks she hung the moon. Even more women come to his practice to see the new midwife.

It is a tumultuous time. In the middle of this, Dr. Brown has a heart attack. His wife, Beulah, calls to say that Francis is in the hospital. She asks if I will go visit him, as he wants to talk to me. My heart is in my throat as I go to see him. I am afraid that Francis is gravely ill. Instead, he looks fine to me; actually, he seems quite chipper. His white beard is all bushy, and his eyes are still sparkling, but he's had a close call. He needs a triple bypass operation. He says he feels that now is the time for him to retire. I am tremendously sad. I don't want anything about us to change. I still love tramping around the countryside with him. Obviously, this is all over now. This is the end of an era.

Francis asks if I will take over his practice for the women who opt for a home birth. I reassure him that will be fine. I have a couple of women who are interested in midwifery who are assisting me now. I can handle the load. I give him my love and heartfelt appreciation for all he has given me. I tell him to be strong. I leave, feeling dreadful. Now, I am really on my own.

Had I known then how hellacious that spring eventually

would get, that I would attend five births on Easter Sunday alone, I would have panicked.

AN OSTRICH BIRTH

Valerie weans Ammon and promptly gets pregnant again. She says she doesn't know how that happened. I say she is one hell of a midwife if she hasn't figured out how that happens by now. She and her husband, Terry, are happy. Terry is an enigma to me. He is loud and opinionated and dogmatic. Valerie is the opposite—soft-spoken and shy. I never do understand the attraction between them, but sometimes women's choices in men are a mystery to me. Anyway, they make handsome babies, so maybe that's it.

Valerie and I do her prenatal care at the Health Center, and she is fine. Terry calls me when Val goes into labor in Warner. He says he thinks she is getting pretty active. It is the middle of the night, so I make a little nest for Milan in the backseat of my tiny Honda Civic, with pillows and his favorite blanket, Sheetie.

I am excited and rushing to get there.

As we are pulling out of the parking lot of our Royal Ghetto apartment, Milan keeps saying, "Mom … Mom …" as he tries to get my attention.

I shush him, saying it is late, and he needs to sleep and I need to just drive.

He says, "OK, Mom, but you just forgot your birth bag."

Jaysus! Now it takes a three-year-old to keep me organized.

Terry meets us in their driveway and helps carry in the equipment. I can hear Valerie up the stairs, yelping "Aiy! Aiy! Aiy!" in true Latina style. Ammon is awake and waiting to play with Milan, as promised. The two boys head straight for a pile of trucks. They pretty much ignore the other commotion going on, finding a model front-end loader far more interesting.

Valerie is on a fold-out sofa bed. Her head is wedged in the crack between the mattress and the backboard, and she won't come out. At the same time, she is trying to straighten her legs to run away from the pain, so her butt is up in the air. I am trying to chase her lower half around to get a sense of what is happening.

She is still yipping Aiy!" but the baby's head is crowning, so I stand up and run after her kicking legs like a moving target, trying to catch the head. Terry is making an audio tape of the birth.

I say, "Please slow down, Valerie. *Please*, Val."

Valerie finally takes her head out from the crack once Max's body slides free. Max is born with dreadlocks and still has them to this day. Ammon comes over to check out his new brother and lights up with interest, as though looking at a new hamster.

Milan takes a look and says, "Cool." Then they go back to playing with trucks.

On the way home, Milan outlines his approach to births for me.

He says, "When there's kids and it's in the day, I play with them, and I don't watch the baby being born. When there's no kids and it's in the day, I watch the baby. If it's in the middle of the night, and there's toys and the kids are gone or if they're asleep, I play with their toys. If there's no kids and it's the middle of the night, I sleep."

Nice to have it all figured out by the age of three.

Years later, I have the incredible honor of catching *Max's* baby—Valerie's grandchild. On the Winter Solstice of 2004, another dreadlocked kid is born in my birth center, Longmeadow Farm Birthing Home in Hopkinton. True Dowling has the dubious honor of being the *last* baby born at my birth center. I am surprised by the wonderful significance of being older than dirt.

I know I haven't heard the last from Miss Betty Erney, RN, Director of Public Health Nursing. She has apparently adopted home birth as her own personal issue for state investigation. I get a surreptitious phone call from a nurse-midwife practicing in the Seacoast area. She asks me if I am aware of the upcoming meeting at the Health Department concerning the complications from home births.

I ask, "What complications?"

She says, "That's what I thought you'd say. I was wondering the same thing. I don't think it's an open meeting, but it sounds like you might want to make an appearance."

I thank her and hang up. What the hell are they talking about? Complications? Godammit, this is getting to be a pain in the ass.

I stand, uninvited, outside the door to the meeting in the State Building. I take several deep breaths. I am nervous but at this point, I am also angry. I am sick of authoritarians pulling fictional statistics out of their butts. Let's talk *facts* here, folks, not just some empirical knee-jerk bullshit. Okay, now I am ready.

I compose myself, knock on the door, and enter the room. Ten faces look up from the conference table in utter surprise. Betty Erney turns white. I introduce myself. I say that I understand there is some question regarding the births at home. Maybe I can help shed some light on the subject.

The man at the head of the table is wearing the large wooden cross of a missionary. He stands up and warmly shakes my hand. He introduces himself as Dr. William T. Wallace, Director of Public Health. He grins at me, as if to say, "Good show, kid!" He gestures for me to join them. Then he indicates for Betty Erney to continue her spiel.

Miss Erney is tremendously red and unhealthily mottled. I

wonder if maybe she's having a hot flash. She states that her public-health nurses who have conducted home visits and have gathered information from the birth certificates have found that there is a 20 percent higher complication rate at home than at the hospital.

What? My mouth drops open.

Dr. Wallace nods at me. "Can you respond to this?"

I say, "I honestly don't have the slightest idea what she's talking about. Is this percentage broken down in any way?"

After more discussion and looking at the forms, it is discovered that the visiting nurses have recorded the repair of second-degree tears as a complication resulting from home births. Oh, for crissake! That means I have a 20 percent rate for minor tears. Not bad, I think smugly, compared to the almost 100 percent episiotomy rate in the hospital.

Ah, but therein lies the problem, for if one is going to pretend to do a controlled scientific study, one needs to at least keep the pretense of equal values on both sides of the study. Otherwise, it is invalid. I point out this little glitch. I say I consider the results to be skewed and meaningless. Dr. Wallace looks pleased. He asks if I would like to be on his Homebirth Advisory Committee to look further into the controversy. I say I would be delighted.

There is a loud *snap* in the room. We are astounded to see that Miss Erney has broken her pencil completely in half.

As we are leaving, she says to me, "I just want you to know that I genuinely believe that the welfare of mothers and babies is a public-health concern."

I reply, "I know you do. I also know that you are a lot smarter than that bogus study. I just want you to be honest, that's all."

CHAPTER FIVE

LADY'S HANDS, 1979

Now that the lovely Valerie has one little guy at the breast and one in constant turbo-boosted overdrive, I am definitely in the market for a new assistant. Actually, what I really want is a partner in crime—someone to help share the responsibility. I admit I am whipped and chronically exhausted. Poor Milan spends many mornings driving a toy truck through my hair, trying to wake me up as I struggle desperately to crawl into consciousness.

I long for someone who also is possessed enough to lose nights and nights of sleep, occasionally be scared shitless for no money and even less recognition, have no reliable social life, and be scorned and dismissed by the medical community. All this for the sheer love of it.

Susan Bartlett and I had gone to college together and even lived next door to each other for a short stint, but we don't meet until we work together at the Health Center. Susie is of true Yankee stock, industrious and hard working, down to earth, with a dry sense of humor. She and I put together a "dog and pony show," as we call it—a traveling road show to help teach women more about their bodies. This is the late seventies, the height of the self-help movement in women's health care. Susie and I speak to various women's groups to show them how to do their own vaginal exams. We go armed with plastic speculums, a mirror, and a flashlight.

Susie and I take turns demonstrating—one of us drops her drawers while the other exposes the cute, pink, and glistening cervix for all the ladies to look in to see. If one of us is fertile, we show the women the spinnbarkeit, or "dog drool," consistency of fertile mucus. At first, the women are shocked. It is startling how many women have no idea what their reproductive organs look or feel like. Susie and I keep it light and humorous. Eventually, some of the braver women drop their drawers too. They look at themselves for the first time, aided by the flashlight and mirror.

Susie and I are Abbott and Costello with a speculum. We take our pants off in church basements, in universities, at women's clubs, and in consciousness-raising groups. It is educational—and a little bit naughty.

Susie starts coming with me to births when her work schedule allows it. She is wonderful with the women. Francis and I had attended Susie's first birth of her son, Bryant, a couple of years earlier. It was a long, drawn-out, nasty ordeal because Bryant's head was asynclitic and coming down tipped sideways. But he was born successfully at home after thirty-six grueling hours. I think Susie's personal experience makes her empathetic and compassionate with laboring women. We work incredibly well together. While I am flamboyant and extroverted, she is the salt of the earth, gentle, and strong. We are a great match.

We get to the point where we don't even have to speak to each other in an emergency. We already know what the other is thinking. I beg her to come to work with me full time. She is a woman who, I can honestly say, is smarter than I am. I desperately want her to be my equal partner, but she brings up the fact that I don't make any money. Certainly not enough to woo her away from her cushy day job.

Right.

Minor detail.

A HORRENDOUS BIRTH

This is another birth where I blow it by not paying attention to my better judgment. I will later add yet another requirement to my growing list of essential prerequisites, this one being "must have a phone." Cindy and her family are minimally functional street people. This is Cindy's eighth pregnancy and her fifth child.

At her first visit, she states that she can be seen only by a woman. Her husband is so extremely jealous that he will "flip out" if she is seen by a man. Cindy is a large woman with red hair and no teeth to speak of. She looks haggard and a lot older than her years. She says that with her last pregnancy, they weren't able to pay the doctor's bill, so she had to go in "on service," which meant she had to take whichever obstetrician was covering the floor that night. It was a man; obviously, as there were no female obstetricians at MVH at this time. When her husband, Blue, found out that a man had touched his wife's genitals, he beat her black and blue.

In discussing my requirements to attend a birth, I mention that breast-feeding is mandatory. This is not only for the health of the baby but for the mother as well. I feel it is imperative that the newborn at least reap the benefits of colostrum, or the first milk, to ensure survival. This is not possible for her, she says, as Blue has made it clear that her "tits" are his and his alone, and he isn't about to share them with some dumb baby. I can tell I'm going to love this guy.

She says nursing is out of the question. I am relieved, because now I can say I am sorry, but I can't help her. She leaves but is back in a few days. Apparently Blue has had a change of heart about Cindy's "tits" when he realizes that I am the least expensive act in town. He has given her permission to breast-feed the baby. Damn.

As is my weakness, the more I get to know Cindy, the more I actually like her. She is loud and brassy and scrappy. Against my better judgment, I agree to attend her. Blue is another story. He frightens me. The one time he comes with Cindy for a prenatal exam, he reeks of alcohol and looks like Charles Manson. He sits watching us, leering. His mouth is slack and hanging open, like he is turned on by watching us. Yuck! He makes my skin crawl. He is going to be tough to ignore.

When Cindy goes into labor, Blue calls from a pay phone somewhere. He sounds horrendously drunk. I can barely understand a word he is saying. I have had four births in forty-eight hours, and I am not looking forward to this one. I ask Blue if he thinks Cindy is in active labor, if I should come right away.

He says, "How the hell should I know? That's your job, ain't it?"

Great. What a delightful man.

I elaborate. "Does Cindy need to breathe with her contractions?"

There is a long pause. Blue answers in the thickest, drunkest New Hampshire accent I have ever heard. "Yuh, she's suckin' air some."

When I get to Cindy's place, I am repulsed by the scene. They have moved their whole family into a condemned building in a rundown neighborhood. There is electricity but no other utilities. Cindy's children, plus her sister's children, for whom she is caring, are all scattered on mattresses on the floor. The older children are minding the younger ones as Cindy screams loudly. A child with a high fever is moaning on a mattress. There is garbage and empty food containers everywhere. There is an overwhelming smell of dirty diapers and cat pee.

Cindy herself is lying on a filthy mattress on the floor. She has nothing prepared or clean. She is obviously about to deliver, but the bed is so dirty that I want to find something—*anything*—cleaner to put underneath her. I run into the bathroom to yank down the shower curtain but when I turn on the light, hundreds of cockroaches scurry in all directions. I take one look at the grimy curtain and decide against it. I resort to grabbing brown paper bags from the kitchen to cover her bed. Fortunately, Blue isn't here.

Thank the Mother for small favors, I think grimly.

Cindy is wailing loudly. The head is becoming visible. I don't have time to listen to the fetal heart rate, as streams of old meconium, now mixed with fresh, black, oily meconium, gushes out of her, looking like Gravytrain. What I can see of the head looks ominously dark. This is not a good sign. I barely have time to open my birth kit and get out a DeLee suction when the head is born.

The baby's eyes are wide open, glazed, and unseeing. Ken always says that when a baby is born with his eyes open, it means "he's looking for his pediatrician." I DeLee suction the baby immediately on the perineum and get a large amount of meconium in the trap. The umbilical cord disintegrates and shreds like wet toilet paper with the birth of the body. I assume this is due to severe malnutrition.

The baby is in dire straits. I've never had a baby like this before. My guess is that he is Apgar 2 and not doing so well. I can't hear a heartbeat; he is as limp as a rag doll. He doesn't appear to be breathing and has turned from an almost purple-black color to a deathly grayish white with blue lips. This is some bad shit. My mind goes on autopilot. I send the woman who is assisting me at the time to call the Concord Fire Department. She ends up having to run several blocks to a KFC restaurant for the nearest phone.

Cindy is screaming, "Is he alive? Don't let him die!" over and over.

The little kids are crying in fear. I can't hear a thing with all the noise. I clear the air passages by suctioning the mucus from his nostrils and pharynx. I run an oxygen tube into my mouth and begin doing neonatal CPR and resuscitation with my own mouth, with oxygen-enriched breath. His body is lifeless, and his eyes are empty. It seems like I work on him for an eternity, but it is probably only about seven minutes before I hear the welcome wail of the ambulance's siren as it comes down the street.

I frantically shout to the baby, "Hey! Are you in there somewhere, little guy? Talk to me!"

I close my eyes and give him all of my life force with the next breath.

His little body jolts. I think, "Oh, shit, I've blown out his lungs."

Instead, it is as though his soul has decided to enter his body after all. Something shifts subtly in his eyes, and life creeps in. An intelligence looks back at me. I watch as his color changes, miraculously, from ghostly blue to dusky pink. There is slight movement in his limbs. I can't believe what I am seeing. He is like a wind-up kewpie doll that is slowly coming to life. By the time the paramedics walk through the door, Dougie is in borderline-acceptable shape; only his limbs are cyanotic.

But as the paramedics walk in the front door, an extremely inebriated Blue walks in through the back door. I am gathering up Dougie to leave with the paramedics. Blue swings his arm, barring my way.

He slurs, "Where the fuck do you think you're going with my baby? That baby's not going anywhere, you stupid bitch!"

My patience is gone. "Oh, shut up, Blue! Jesus. If you'd been around ten minutes ago, you'd know what was up. So just shut up and sit down, and I'll keep you posted."

We fly out the door.

Things aren't much better at Merrimack Valley Hospital. Dougie is seen by Dr. Winter, who is the pediatrician on call for the ER that night. After checking out the baby, he says, "Why did you come here?"

I say, "Well, I came here because this baby was almost dead when he was born. I want to be sure he hasn't aspirated any

meconium and isn't going to get pneumonia or something. I
know he looks good now, but he *wasn't* good, believe me. I had
to work hard on him to get him started."

He turns to me. "Oh, I believe you. But you shouldn't have
bothered. It is a waste of time. I know this family. They owe me
money. They owe everyone money. People like this are a drain
on society. You should have done this kid a favor and let him die.
They should all be used for dog food. They just lower the gene
pool every time they have another kid."

Holy shit! Is this guy serious? What an utterly arrogant and
privileged asshole. But I am too drained and exhausted to work
myself up to pissed at this point. I simply don't have the energy
for this nightmare.

I have to ask him my worst fear.

"Do you think that in that amount of time, there'd be enough
oxygen deprivation to cause brain damage?"

He responds, "Who cares? This kid is from the shallow end
of the gene pool. He's never going to be a rocket scientist
anyway."

The next day Dougie goes home. Cindy calls me from her
mother's house. She thanks me for "saving" Dougie's life. She
can't begin to tell me how grateful she is.

Then she says something that makes my stomach clench.

"I don't want you to get mad at me," she says, "but right after
you left yesterday, Blue had his way with me."

I start to get nauseous. "I don't understand," I say. "What do
you mean, he had his way?"

She pauses. "Well, he was mad at me that the men from the
ambulance had seen me uncovered, had seen my taint. So he
forced himself on me."

What? I am speechless. He raped her. Postpartum. Reclaiming
his territory. Jesus! What a sick, depraved son of a bitch.

Then she says, "I'm really embarrassed about this. I don't
want to talk about it anymore."

She goes on to say how meaningful the birth has been and that no one has ever paid as much attention to her and made her feel important having her babies. She asks me if I will be Dougie's godmother at his christening in the Episcopal church. This would mean the world to her.

I say, "I will agree to be Dougie's godmother if you promise me that you'll protect him. The first time Blue raises a hand to you or Dougie, you pack your bags and leave. Deal?"

I stand as Dougie's godmother at his christening.

I tell Ken the story of this family and the poverty and the abuse. He gets on the phone and calls some of his colleagues at the hospital.

I hear him say, "If you want to go to heaven, you'll do this one for free."

He arranges for an anesthesiologist and everyone else to donate their time to do a tubal ligation for Cindy for free. Merrimack Valley even donates the OR time. I like to believe this experience empowered Cindy to take control of her life.

She does leave Blue a year later.

I see Dougie all the time. He is a bagger at Shaw's supermarket. He is polite and shy and has flaming red hair.

I, for one, am glad that he's not dog food.

·———·

Dr. William T. Wallace, Director of Health and Welfare for the State of New Hampshire, turns out to be a precious gift from the goddesses Oshun and Yemaya and any other African goddesses of childbirth. Dr. Wallace had been a missionary in Liberia, Africa, for eleven years. It had been his job to work with and train the traditional midwives there. He jokingly said they were proficient in delivering babies under a car's low beams or high beams, as the conditions were that primitive. Despite his bush training, he said the outcomes were surprisingly good.

He believes that midwives are the absolute essential piece of low-risk maternity care; further, trained doctors should be used specifically for complications and high-risk pregnancies only. He feels strongly that midwives should be trained to use vacuum extractors in the event of a prolonged second stage. Plus, he is an all-around dedicated, no-hidden-agenda, quiet, observant, nice guy. How he got to Cow Hampshire, I still don't know, but I thank the powers that made it be. He makes sure our legislative process is sane and tolerable and just. I'm not sure both sides will agree to this, but the fact is, New Hampshire will eventually fashion one of the most reasonable, comprehensive, and workable programs for apprentice-trained midwives in the nation. I respect Bill Wallace immensely.

After compiling all the data from several recent years on New Hampshire's home-birth certificates, the statistics clearly demonstrate that planned, intentional out-of-hospital births are a viable alternative to standard hospital births. Dr. Wallace and the Homebirth Advisory Committee decide it is time to propose legislation that will enable midwifery to become a legally recognized profession in the state. Because I've had no prior experience with the legislative process and have no idea what a circus this is about to become, I participate wholeheartedly.

FRANNY'S CERCLAGE BABY

Franny and Ned have another planned pregnancy about a year after Opal's death. This time they go to see Ken. He does surgery to strengthen her weak cervix right after her first trimester. He puts in a purse-string type stitch called a McDonald cerclage. It goes around the entire circumference of her cervix and is then pulled tight to prevent it from letting go again prematurely. He is fairly confident that this will hold Franny until she is at term, at which time he will snip the suture. Presumably, she then will go on to have a good baby.

Ned and Franny are ecstatic about this as they have suffered enough losses in the past. Furthermore, Ken says, if Franny gets to term, he doesn't see any contraindication to having the baby at home. Prematurity is the only danger in this situation, and we will have already ruled that out.

Ken and I co-manage Franny's prenatal care. We check her cervix weekly for any early change. The stitch holds beautifully. When Franny gets to thirty-eight weeks, she is a full twelve weeks farther than she has ever made it before. We decide it is time for the big snip. They are so sweet and excited about this that it feels like a big celebration.

We aren't sure whether Franny will go into labor immediately. Ken says he'll go along for the ride back to their place. He is more than a little curious about the results. He has a vested interest in the outcome of this, after all. I know he is genuinely fond of this couple.

Ned and Franny live in an ashram that is buzzing with activity and excitement at their return. All the members know that they previously have lost three babies. This coming little one is very special to everyone in their community. But Franny does not go into labor right away. Ken and I sleep in the ashram, undisturbed all night, waiting. I laugh and tease him about being the gorgeous, conservative Arrow Shirt man, all starched and buttoned up, sleeping under a picture of the beatific, white-bearded, flower-encrusted Guru Maharaji. The juxtaposition just cracks me up.

When the hive awakes in the morning, Franny goes into labor. Her labor is fast and furious. Every member of the community is present for the birth. There are twenty-three people silently observing; twenty-three people collectively holding their breath as Harriett makes her debut. Thirteen children ring the bed, leaning on their elbows—and there is not one peep. I've never seen such well-behaved, bright-eyed children.

It's quiet enough to hear a pin drop as Harriet slides easily into this life. There is a collective sigh of relief. Everyone sheds tears of joy as Ned and Franny greet their first living child. And what a kid! I've never seen such wild hair on a baby, ever. Harriet's hair sticks straight up in a punk Mohawk. It looks like she and Don King go to the same hair stylist. Too cute for words. There is a lot of love in this room this day.

Ken is very energized and pleased with this birth. As far as we know, this is the first time a woman with a cerclage has had a home birth. On the drive back home, he begins to develop the philosophy that will unwittingly attract him a lot of attention—positive attention from women patients and a decade of grief from his peers.

He realizes that obstetricians are overtrained and too highly specialized in technology to attend normal births without wanting to interfere and "do" something. He feels that obstetricians need to learn, in most cases, to sit on their hands and do nothing. They can learn this best from midwives. He believes that midwives should attend the majority of normal, uncomplicated births. This will keep the births just that—uncomplicated. This also will allow the obstetricians to conserve their energy and direct their expertise and knowledge to high-risk obstetrical and gynecological cases, where their skills are truly needed and appreciated. This will prevent the obstetricians from burning out and will encourage the midwives to maintain and protect the sanctity and normalcy of birth.

On this day, he commits to becoming a preceptor for the clinical training of student nurse-midwives in his practice.

The time has come for me to move out of the Royal Ghetto for good. A disgruntled neighbor in the apartment adjacent to mine has reported me to the City of Concord for running a business out of my home, which is zoned residential. Apparently, she objects to the steady stream of pregnant women walking up our shared walkway to my front door.

I learn that she has told the City that I throw my used exam gloves out on the front lawn when I am done with them. The truth is that I occasionally give the neighbor kids sealed packets of sterile gloves to use when they play "Midwife." One day when I look outside, I laugh out loud to see these kids "delivering" a baby doll from between the legs of the young girl next door. Obviously, they've been under Milan's tutelage. I suspect this is the real root of the woman's objection to my close proximity.

All this culminates in a love note from the City of Concord Health Department that is respectful but to the point:

July 19, 1979

Ms. Carol Leonard
Royal Gardens
Concord, NH

Dear Ms. Leonard:

A complaint has been received by this Department that the examination gloves used in your clinic at the above address are not being disposed of in a safety manner. Unfortunately, the neighborhood children are retrieving these unsanitary gloves, although this is not your fault.

However, these gloves should be disposed of in a hospital incinerator like those at Merrimack Valley Hospital, the state hospital, or any other veterinary clinic.

I trust I have your interest and cooperation in compliance.

Very truly yours,
Chief Environmental Inspector
City of Concord, NH

Great, now I am being compared to a veterinarian.

As a result of this incident, Ken and I decide to live together. We have kept separate apartments, but the reality is that we are hardly ever apart, so we decide to move in together to save on living expenses. We buy a funky little farmhouse on a country road in west Concord.

I attended a birth in this house, and the new parents tell me they are moving to Boston for better job opportunities. I look around the house at its potential; I believe we will grow to love it. It is a classic clapboard New Englander built in the late 1800s. It needs cosmetic repair—paint and paper—but it has its own earthy charm.

We move in on a spring day, when the giant lilac trees in the backyard are weighed down with enormous, fragrant flower clusters. There are ancient maples ringing the property, a farmer-style front porch, and a large vegetable garden out back. There are several outbuildings where Ken and I will disastrously attempt to raise sheep. Even though we both are insanely busy, we always find time to weed the vegetable garden together. We hunch over silently, side by side, pulling up shoots. This is our therapy and our grounding.

AN ANGELIC BABY

Up to this point, all the babies have been good. It doesn't occur to me that, statistically, I am overdue for a misfire.

Vivian is Ned's older sister. She was at Harriett's birth and was profoundly moved by it. Now, she is eagerly awaiting her own birth at home. Vivian is twenty-seven years old, and this is her second child. She is a special education teacher, specializing in caring for children with Down syndrome. I like Vivian immensely. I am not anticipating any problems whatsoever.

Vivian gives birth to Anna on a blustery, bright spring day

in midmorning. Sunlight is flooding through the bedroom windows as her fair-haired girl slips into the world, all nine pounds of her. She seems robust and healthy. I put her up to Vivian's breast to nurse. After the placenta is born, I occupy myself doing the necessary after-birth chores and tidying up the room a bit. I get Vivian orange juice and a bagel. I am about to fill out the worksheet that the state has given me so they can keep track of me. Vivian says that Anna isn't nursing vigorously. It is fairly unusual for a baby born at home, whose mother hasn't been drugged, to be a lazy nurser. I don't like the sound of Vivian's voice.

I do the regular infant exam. I don't find anything unusual. Her heart sounds good, she seems sturdy enough, but I have a growing unease. Just has I am about to hand the baby back to her mom with a clean bill of health, Anna opens her eyes and looks directly at me. Now I know what has been bothering me. The eyes that peer out from the sweet moon-shaped face are slanted in a perfect almond shape. I quickly check her hands, which are broad and have a single palmar crease. *Oh, sweet baby!* This is a Down's infant.

I place her gently in Vivian's arms, but find I cannot speak. I don't say anything. I am so overwhelmingly sad. Vivian and I look at each other, and then Anna starts rooting at the breast and begins sucking well. I never do say the words "Down Syndrome" out loud. For some reason, the words are lodged in my throat.

As I am packing to leave, Vivian is nursing. She looks up from examining her daughter and says, "Anna looks Down's to me."

I freeze. Then I shrug. "Well, I always ask that parents bring their newborns in to be checked out by their family doctors within forty-eight to seventy-two hours. If she continues to be a sleepy nurser, or if you have any questions, you might want to bring her in sooner than that, just to be sure."

Then I kiss them both and leave. What a coward.

On the way home my little car bumps and splashes through

potholes and muddy ruts from the spring run-off. I cry the entire way. How bizarre that Vivian teaches and cares for Down's children, and now she has given birth to a daughter with the same chromosomal abnormality. What is the probability of that happening?

When I get home, I immediately call up north to Dr. Faith, as he is their choice for their baby's doctor. Jim Faith and I have reached an uneasy alliance, mainly because I refer many of my White Mountain babies to him for their childhood care. He is beginning to find me lucrative.

I tell him that Vivian will be coming in with a Down's baby.

"Are you sure it's not just an FLK?" he asks.

"What's an FLK?"

"Oh, FLK stands for funny-looking kid," he says. "I can't take the credit for that one, though. I didn't make it up. It's a real pediatric term."

"Charming," I reply. "No, this child is not a funny-looking kid. She is definitely Down syndrome; she has all the characteristics. But her heart sounds good. She was a little sluggish, but when I left, she was nursing OK. Oh, Jim, there's one other thing. I feel so guilty—I didn't tell Vivian."

"Poor woman," he says. "OK, when they come in, I'll do the blood work to confirm your suspicions."

Several days pass before Vivian calls me on the phone, crying. She deliberately waited before bringing Anna in for her initial exam. Anna has been diagnosed with Trisomy 21. She has an extra chromosome.

Vivian says softly, "You knew, didn't you?"

I pause. "Yes. I did know, but for some reason I couldn't say it to you. I'm sorry, Vivian, that wasn't very professional of me."

She lets out a shaky breath. "I'm so thankful you *didn't* tell me. I knew, of course; we all knew, but by not naming it, I got to bond with Anna as a normal, healthy kid for the first week of her life.

That was so important to me, so incredibly special. Thank you for giving me that time. That can never be taken away."

Anna grows up to be a great kid. Even though she has her challenges, she really does well for herself, due to all the time and attention that Vivian and her husband devote to her. She loves seeing me. She tells everyone that I am the first person to ever touch her.

The second Down syndrome baby I attend has a sadder ending. The ironic thing about this baby is that his mother's stepbrother was a Down's child as well, so she had experience with this syndrome all during her childhood. This baby, Michael, grows to be a lovable, sweet little boy, but he does have congenital heart defects that require several surgeries during his childhood. He is friendly and affectionate and outgoing. The kids at school love him. He is in special ed, and he is his school's basketball team's mascot. The whole small town of Warner is involved with the raising of Michael.

When Michael is ten years old, while playing with schoolmates at recess, his heart fails him, and he collapses and dies in the schoolyard. The townspeople go into mass mourning, grieving for the brave and affectionate little boy they all loved. But Michael has died doing what makes him happiest—laughing and chasing after his friends at school.

Milan is a great kid to take to births. He is quiet and observant and funny and has become a precocious reader. I attribute his reading ability to all the expectant grandparents who read to him to pass the time while waiting for births. It is a good distraction for the nervous grandparents, and it is truly beneficial for Milan. He begins to read seriously at age four.

One day, I get a phone call from his teacher at Woodside

Preschool. She says that Milan has been explaining the birth process to his preschool cronies. He promises them that he will bring in a placenta for Show and Tell. She is a tad nervous about that last part. She narrates the flowing conversation that Milan has with some young friends, describing birth:

"Here's how babies get born. First there's the crowning," he says. "That means you can see most of the head, like the hair. It's like this …" He holds his hands in a circle over his head. "And there's this pink all around it. Sometimes the opening is a little crack. Sometimes it's a huge circle, a diamond shape, with pink all around it. When it's almost going to come out, the head pops out. Mostly then the head just rotates. Then you hear a 'Wagh!' Then you have to pull the rest of the baby out. It's naked, of course. And it's wet—*real* wet. Sometimes I touch the cord. Once at this birth, the cord was pumping blood. You just squeeze it gently, and you can feel the blood pumping through. But my mom doesn't let me talk to her until the placenta is born."

THE FASTEST BIRTH

Part of the prenatal visits toward the end of pregnancy are spent reviewing emergency childbirth in the event that I don't make it in time. That is a very rare occurrence, as most of the labors end up being a lot longer than the women want them to be. I stress the fact that if a baby comes that fast, there is almost never enough time for the baby to get into trouble. These crash-course childbirth sessions are mainly to give the families confidence while I am en route. I only miss a few.

The fastest birth in my records goes to Melanie from Plymouth. She is in labor for a total of eleven minutes, from soup to nuts. Melanie's first baby takes an average amount of time, about twenty hours, so even dividing this time frame in half for a second baby, which is the general rule of thumb, gives me more than adequate travel time. With her history, I don't anticipate a precipitous labor, but this is what we get. Birth is never boring.

Melanie's husband, Mark, is a professor at our state college. He is a hyperactive, high-strung, nervous guy with an "Oy, why me?" sense of humor. Around Melanie's due date, Mark calls me in the middle of the night, sounding very concerned.

"I don't know what's wrong with Mel," he says. "I think she has the flu. She just woke up, then she threw up, and now she has diarrhea."

I can hear Melanie in the background, groaning and straining loudly. In fact, her efforts have that all too familiar moose-call sound to it.

Holy pushing! This baby is about to be born on the toilet.

"That's not the flu, Mark," I say. "Melanie's having the baby right now. I need for you to get her on the bed, and then you go wash your hands. I'll walk you through this over the phone. OK?"

Mark gasps, "Oh, my god!" and he drops the phone.

A minute later, he is back on the phone. He is panting like he is having the baby.

"OK. I got Melanie back into bed," he says. "Oh, my god, now I can see the head! What do I do?"

His voice sounds really shaky.

"Great! You're doing fine, just fine!" I say, even though I'm worried as hell. "Now, do me a favor. Don't do anything! Just let Melanie push the baby out, and don't you pull or try to turn the head or anything. It will do all that on its own. Just support the baby as it slides out, and when it's out, give your baby a kiss."

I can tell he has the phone tucked between his chin and shoulder. He is breathing heavily.

He keeps saying, "Oy! Oy vey."

Then, "He's out! It's a boy!"

I finally expel my breath. "Good job, guys! Now, Mark, if it looks like he's not breathing, suck out his nose with your mouth."

Just then I hear a lusty cry from the baby.

"No, he's great!" Mark says. "He's all pink and looking around. I can't believe this! He's gorgeous!"

I am poised to fly out the door.

"Nice work, folks, very nice." I am starting to sound like Dr. Brown. "OK, look. I'm on my way. When Melanie feels another contraction, have her push out the placenta. Don't worry about cutting the cord; that can wait until I get there. Just be sure to keep your son wrapped up and warm. Get him nursing as soon as he will. And Mark, you can relax now."

When I walk into their bedroom, Melanie is serenely nursing her son.

She grins at me. "You're going to have to scrape Mark off the ceiling, you know. He's so excited; he's bouncing off the walls. Right now he's on the phone, calling every relative in New York that he can think of to tell them the story."

I check her bleeding and feel the firmness of her fundus.

"Well, he should be proud," I say. "He did a good job, and he didn't panic. When push came to shove, he hung in there and was actually quite together. I'm impressed. You've got a good man there, Melanie."

She smiles at me. "I know I do."

⌐⌐

The day finally comes when the New Hampshire midwives' proposed Midwifery Bill is to be heard in front of committee in Reps Hall. We have gathered all our support people in the New Hampshire House of Representatives. New Hampshire has the largest House of Representatives in the nation. It is the second largest legislative body in the world, the first being in India somewhere. Four hundred twenty-five regular, local people sit listening to proposed legislation all day long. They are paid a measly hundred dollars a year.

We arrange for many home-born babies and toddlers to be present, as well as babies still *in utero*. Our pregnant clients wear banners across their wide bellies that read:

I WANT TO BE BORN AT HOME!

Many parents have come to testify in support of midwives. There are dozens of little kids running around, grinning and flirting with the smitten legislators. The hearing becomes a dog and pony show.

Dogs and trick ponies, that is—until Miss Betty Erney troops in with her people from the state. I have not seen the final draft of our bill since it came out of legislative services, where it has gone to be properly worded in legalese. It is my understanding that the Midwifery Rules and Regulations are to be under the jurisdiction of the Department of Health and Human Services.

To my horror, when I finally see a copy of our bill, it isn't anything like our original draft. Now, midwifery has been placed under the Board of Medicine. And to make matters worse, the proposed Board of Advisors who make the decisions pertaining to midwifery practice consists entirely of *physicians*. There isn't a bloody midwife in the bunch! I am horrified. This bill is a joke. It will simply legislate midwives out of existence.

Godammit, Betty Erney strikes again. She looks smug.

Now I panic. I have spent long hours on the phone with the legislator who is sponsoring the midwifery bill, Representative Eugene Daniell. Eugene Daniell is in his eighties and is a fiery, feisty Yankee to the core. He supports home birth because, as he says, New Hampshire is the "Live Free or Die" state. He'll be damned if anyone is going to tell him where he can or cannot be born or where he can or cannot die.

As Rep. Daniell so sagely says, "People my age got here without all this fancy obstetrical management stuff. And we're all OK—as far as I can tell."

But now the midwifery bill is all wrong! I try to give him a high sign to abort his support, but he doesn't make eye contact with me. He is busy reading the proposed piece. He stands up to speak. I can feel my heart sinking. He looks out over the people, pauses for a moment, and looks puzzled.

He says, "Isn't this Board like throwing the fox into the hen house? Why do these boys always feel the need to tell the girls what to do?"

I laugh right out loud. The man is nobody's fool, which is why he is such a respected member of the House. He has seen this legislation for what it really is—a thinly disguised attempt to prevent midwives from practicing. He proposes that our bill be tabled until it can be reworked into something more satisfactory.

We go back to the drawing board.

THE FALLEN CANOPY

Every fall, I see the Rosal kids at the Sunapee Craftsmen's Fair, tending their father's jewelry booth. Their father is an artisan who makes wonderful, exquisitely wrought, cast-silver jewelry of whimsical wizards and lizards and other fanciful creatures. The children are strikingly beautiful and gregarious, like a small band of dark-haired gypsies hawking their parents' wares.

Joshua, the youngest Rosal, is the only child I haven't seen since he was born in 1979. Now, I finally see him near his family's booth, standing with a group of his sullen, disaffected friends. He is in his mid-teens and is gorgeous, with multiple body piercings, studs in his lower lip and nostril, and small silver rings all the way around his ear. His whole group is dressed in the requisite death-rocker black with short peroxided hair. They are trying to be Goth malcontents, but they are actually quite adorable.

I walk up to Joshua and grin. He has no idea who I am.

I say to him, "The last time I saw you, you were naked, you were bald, and you were crying."

He looks horrified.

His friends say, "Dude?"

Then I introduce myself as his midwife and the first person to ever have touched his hard little head. He looks embarrassed but allows himself a slight smile of relief.

His friends say, "Dude."

His older sister, a stunning, aspiring actress with long, silky black hair, is laughing. She eggs me on to tell the feature event at Josh's birth for him and his friends.

Right before Josh was born, their father, Jack, was in a serious car accident. He broke his back. When Josh's mother goes into labor, Jack is still in a hard-plaster, full-body cast from his neck to his hips. All he can do is bend over straight, perpendicular from his waist. During the birth, Jack stands at the side of the bed and stiffly leans over his wife, horizontal to her body, immobilized. Jack is a big man with a huge, walrus handlebar mustache and wire-rim glasses. Only his head sticks out of the cast; he looks like a beached turtle.

Josh's birth is smooth except for his getting a little bit stuck in transition, when his mother has to work harder than she's used to. Josh's entrance is uneventful, and the other Rosal kids watch wide-eyed and excited. Josh arrives in style, born in his parents' big canopy bed. He is in great shape, his top is as bald as his bottom, and he has a good lusty cry. I hand him up to greet his mother. His father leans in awkwardly to get a better look.

I'm not sure what happens next.

When I get off the bed, somehow I knock the canopy off its frame. The entire canopy falls on top of the nativity scene below. Because Jack is in the body cast, he can't free himself or them. There is a lot of struggling and tangling under the fabric. I am not much help because I am laughing too hard. The other kids are screeching in hysterics. All we can see are lumps roiling around under the covering, trying to get out.

Finally, we get the canopy off of them, and no one is the worse for wearing it.

Now, I tell the teenaged Josh that midwives of old used to believe that when a baby is born in the caul, or born with the membranes intact, this means the child will never drown at sea and is going to always be protected.

I wonder if being born in a whole canopy will be like being in the witness protection program.

Josh is scarlet, but he is smiling.

His friends tease him. They call him the Canopy Dude.

By the end of 1979, I am desperate to work with someone who is reliable. The birth numbers have increased dramatically. I am having a hard time keeping up. I attend twenty-three births in the month of April alone. I am drained of energy. My fatigue escalates until I miss a birth on the Seacoast because I fall asleep after the labor call comes in. I simply cannot make myself crawl out of bed. An obstetrician in the Seacoast area attends the birth in the couple's trailer for me. He is pretty grumpy about it, but it is incredibly sweet of him to cover for me without question. This is the *only* birth I miss due to my being irresponsible, but it makes me wonder about my health.

Most of the time, I feel as though I have lead in my veins. I attribute this to sleep deprivation until I finally have a physical. To my surprise, I find I have become anemic due to my frenetic lifestyle. I essentially have been living in my car, eating shitty food, and consuming unholy, unhealthy amounts of caffeine in order to stay alert. Fortunately, this can be easily remedied with diet and supplements. Not so easy to resolve is the hectic schedule.

I ask Ken if he thinks I should just quit.

He laughs. "That would be impossible. It's in your blood or something. You're possessed. If you stopped, you'd dry up on the vine."

He is right, of course. But I haven't had a day off in five years, not even to go as far out of beeper range as Boston.

I do have several wonderful women who assist me. They are very committed to learning midwifery. But the reality of my schedule is so ridiculous that even the staunchest of them has to beg off. We all have young children, and eventually each woman begins to feel as though she has abandoned her family. The assistants gradually leave to pay more attention to their home fronts. I am at my wit's end and feel I can't continue any longer.

The phone rings one evening right before New Year's.

It is Sue Bartlett. She says, "Howdy, partner!"

I slide down the wall and collapse in a relieved heap on the floor. Tears are streaming down my face. The practice is going to survive after all. *I* will survive.

Susie and I have a lawyer friend who has had a baby at home with us. She draws up the legal paperwork for our business partnership. We name our new partnership the Concord Midwifery Service, and we hang out our shingle.

Little did we know that within two years we will be legal, will be covered by most insurance carriers, and will have a bustling clinic full of women and their babies. Our practice is housed in a funky Victorian office building on the main street of Concord. We still don't make much money, as we are the softest touch in town, but we are happy and successful, and the babies are all healthy.

The Concord Midwifery Service logo is a graceful wild stork flying in front of the moon.

CHAPTER SIX

LADY'S HANDS, 1980

Business at the Concord Midwifery Service is booming in the early eighties. Susie and I try to work together as much as possible, but very often we find we have two women in labor simultaneously. Then we race to see whose baby comes out first. In the office, we see the pregnant women for prenatal visits once a month until the seventh month, then every two weeks until the ninth month. Then we see them weekly until they deliver.

We spend as much time with the women as they need, which averages about forty-five minutes a visit. After the birth, we check the newborns at one week and at two weeks. We see the whole family at one month postpartum. We also do well-woman health care and "interconceptional care," which in plain English means family planning.

The number of home births rises consistently as people become educated about the availability and safety. Our fee still remains at least one-fourth the cost of a physician and a hospital. Eventually, Susie and I receive third-party reimbursements from most carriers, with the exception of Blue Cross/Blue Shield and the new HMOs.

The more intelligent insurance carriers have figured out there are significant savings when couples stay home for their births—there no longer are exorbitant hospital fees. The companies compare the national statistics on the safety of home births versus hospital births, and then they offer parents a two-hundred-dollar rebate to entice them to stay home for birth. Ironically, a couple of our local hospitals have the audacity to refer their low-income women to us for care when the women can't afford their unreasonable fees.

THE WOODCHUCK

There is a picture on my wall in the peanut gallery of which I am especially fond. In the picture I am holding an enormous newborn girl; her big sister is leaning on my knee, and she is checking out the interloper for the first time. In the background, their mother is smiling, and her blonde hair is in a disheveled cloud around her head. She looks angelic. I attended both daughters; this one comes fast and weighs in at eleven pounds. Their mother, Becky, is sweet and soft-spoken. I feel unusually close to her.

When the second daughter is a week old, I drive to their house in the country in Hooksett to do the PKU blood test, which is a heel-prick, on the baby. I am surprised to see Becky sitting on the back stoop, holding a rifle. My mouth drops open. Becky grins at me and nods to her vegetable garden out back.

"See that woodchuck out there?" she asks. "That damn rodent has stripped everything in the garden except the tomatoes. I'm afraid he's eaten his last ratatouille. In a minute, he's going to be stew."

I can barely see a brown, furry bulge munching in the greenery. He looks pretty far away to me. Becky raises the scope to her eyes and fires off a loud *crack*! The brown bulge keels over and stops moving.

I am stunned. I am also very impressed.

She turns back to me and laughs at my stupefied expression. "You didn't know I was a crackerjack shot, did you?" she asks.

I just remember her recently pushing out an eleven-pound baby. "Jesus, Becky," I say. "Is this the new renaissance woman or what?"

Over the years, Becky calls me occasionally with horrific stories of physical abuse from her husband, Frank. Apparently, the abuse escalates; ultimately, I hear through the grapevine that Frank has broken both legs of one of his daughters. He claims some heavy steel fell on her and snapped her little legs. But everyone knows he has beaten the little girl so severely that it will be a long time before she can walk again. Becky moves out with the girls and gets an apartment in town. Frank continues to harass and torment them. He begins stalking Becky. It is an impossible situation. The man is a monster.

Several years later, it is with a pounding heart that I read an article in Becky's town newspaper that tells of a local man, Frank So-and-So, who, as he was welding on a tractor in his backyard, was felled by a deer hunter's stray bullet. One clean shot to the heart from a very long distance, and he was dead. The article goes on to discuss the probability of accidents like this—that it actually is not uncommon to have a couple of deaths per deer season in New Hampshire from misguided shots. The piece then highly recommends the state's hunter-safety program to help prevent random casualties like this in the future.

A year later, I get a postcard from Becky saying that she and the girls are living in Alaska, and that they are doing well. They send their love.

I work with Dr. Wallace and the Home Birth Advisory Committee on designing our midwifery legislation into something that is satisfactory to everyone—well, almost everyone. Many of the state's physicians are still in vehement opposition. They want midwifery to be outlawed outright, even though they have no facts or figures to support their claims that midwifery is dangerous.

We have created enabling legislation that puts the onus of later developing the rules and regulations back on a midwifery advisory committee that works directly with the director of public health services. The proposed six-member advisory committee consists of a pediatrician, an obstetrician, a nurse-midwife, two lay midwives, and a member of the general public who has had a home birth.

This sounds fabulous to me.

The day comes for our midwifery bill to be heard in legislative committee, and we do the whole circus all over again. Little kids are running around with balloons that read, *"I Was Born at Home"*. Many visibly pregnant women have come to defend their right to choose their place of birth. At least this time the proposed statute is a good one.

Some physicians troop in to testify in opposition of midwives in general. I am astounded to see Dr. Faith fill out an in-support card. He turns to wink at me and gives me a thumbs-up. I guess you *can* teach an old dog new tricks after all.

The first physician to speak in opposition to our bill is Dr. Windsor, a British obstetrician practicing in the Seacoast area. He is the chairman of the New Hampshire chapter of the American College of Obstetricians and Gynecologists. Dr. Windsor is an impressive-looking man, very regal and tweedy, with a full shock of white hair. But the minute he opens his mouth, he inserts his foot. He stands grandly and states in his charming English accent that all of the babies who are born at home have suffered varying degrees of brain damage due to incompetence during the birth process.

This is an excellent mistake.

What Dr. Windsor does not realize is that half of New Hampshire's legislators are so old, *they have all been born at home*—this was before the popular exodus to hospitals for deliveries occurred in the forties. The legislators stare at him in disbelief at his rudeness. Dr. Windsor has just inferred that they are all, to some degree, brain damaged.

I am loving this.

Dr. Windsor pauses. He can tell he's not playing to a full House, but he doesn't know why. He has assumed that because he is a medical doctor, the legislators will accept his educated word as truth.

He has miscalculated. Dr. Windsor loses a few degrees of composure but continues his testimony.

"Carol Leonard is a lay meddler," he says. "There is no such thing as a 'normal' pregnancy. All pregnancies are a powder keg waiting to blow. And furthermore, I have it from a reliable source that the reason Ms. Leonard's statistics look so good is because she buries all of her dead babies in the woods."

Now the legislators' mouths are gaping open in earnest shock. What Dr. Windsor also doesn't comprehend is that New Hampshire is such a small state that after my attending a few hundred births or so, I am bound to have assisted a relative or family friend of at least half of the 450 legislators. By my calculations, that's approximately 225 elected officials who know for a fact that these home-birthed babies are alive and well. The longer Dr. Windsor speaks, the further he digs a hole and buries himself.

Rep. Eugene Daniell has a mischievous glint in his eyes. He is clearly going to enjoy the slaughter.

He confronts Dr. Windsor. "Tell me, Doctor, how is it that you are practicing obstetrics here in New Hampshire instead of your home country? Could it possibly be that you are a refugee from socialized medicine? That you have set up practice here to enjoy a significantly greater income? Hm-m? Then is it also possible that you find the growing popularity of these midwives as a threat to this lucrative livelihood?"

I lean over and stage whisper to Susie, "Yeah, and Windsor's cesarean section rate is 75 percent, too!"

Susie shushes me.

Due to the harsh treatment that Dr. Windsor receives, the rest of the physicians remain silent. In the end, our midwifery bill passes and will go to a public hearing before the entire House. This feels good. It is a definite victory. I know the really difficult part is yet to come; still, this experience has restored my faith in the democratic process. I am proud of New Hampshire.

Shortly after this hearing, a friend of mine with a very macabre and twisted sense of humor makes little Popsicle-stick crosses for me to carry in my birth bag. These are for the babies left behind in the woods.

THE BABY IN AN APPLE CRATE

Some of our clients definitely question authority and don't hold anyone else's ideology in greater esteem than their own. This is certainly the case with Mary and her eccentric husband, Harold. Harold has a long, scraggly, grayish-white beard that reaches well below his nipples. He looks like Charleton Heston in the role of Moses. Harold is quite notorious in the state. This couple organizes the migrant apple-pickers in southern New Hampshire and are serious eco-activists. Mary and Harold belong to the Clamshell Alliance of New Hampshire, which is a controversial, radical group committed to blocking the construction of the Seabrook nuclear power plant on our coastline.

The summer that Mary is pregnant, the Clamshellers are fervently doing demonstrations and acts of civil disobedience to prevent the Public Service Company from completing the facility. Mary is protesting the impending threat of the plant becoming operational. She is arrested and jailed for trespassing on Public Service private property. The judge who hears her case is not sympathetic in the least. He sentences Mary to a harsh stint in the Rockingham County Jail. Her sentence incarcerates her well past her due date.

Mary calls me and asks if I will do her prenatal visits in the county jail and probably the birth as well, if permission is granted. I agree to help her out. As I hang up the phone, I have a serious bout of doubt about conducting my business in the clink, as I am quasi-legal myself. But I pack my bags with the equipment I need for a prenatal exam and head to the county jail.

The guards are expecting me. They seem to be amused and curious about my job. I am trying to be as professional as possible, but I realize I am allergic to the environment and want to flee. Initially, I have to converse with Mary behind a glass partition. It is extremely awkward asking her personal gynecological questions, in order to chart her health history, with everyone listening. The lack of privacy, harsh bright lights, and sterile, institutional atmosphere start to remind me of a hospital.

Mary herself is a strapping, powerful woman who seems capable of handling just about anything with unfaltering dignity. She has dark flashing eyes and long, dark hair. She holds her head high and is studiously composed. She is very gracious, even in the slammer.

Mary is very outspoken in prison, demanding adequate vegetarian nutrition and an improved jailhouse menu as required by a pregnant woman. Our visits continue to be behind the partition for most of her pregnancy. Toward the end of her pregnancy, the time comes for me to examine her physically, because she has refused to let the prison doctor touch her.

Mary finagles permission for me to check her in a private room. We are in a small side room that has a cot. We are monitored by a female guard. The guard is large and intimidating and is inordinately interested in what we are doing. It comes time for me to don gloves to do an internal vaginal exam to assess Mary's cervix for "ripeness." The guard, who has been standing off to one side with her arms crossed, comes over and checks my gloved fingers.

I say, "What? Do you think I'm going to slip a file into her vagina so she can break out of here?"

I give her a lame smile, but it doesn't work.

The guardette has absolutely no sense of boundaries. Her presence is hard to ignore. I try to focus solely on Mary and her baby and the information my hands are telling me. As I do the pelvic exam to feel Mary's cervix for softening and opening, the guard's head is blocking my field of vision. She is leaning against me to observe more closely. I try to body-check her subtly by turning my shoulder at an angle to edge her out of the way. She is immovable. Perhaps this woman is a budding student of midwifery, but I am getting claustrophobic.

I say, impatiently, "Say, ma'am, do you think you can back off just a hair so I can have some elbow room to maneuver here?"

The guard shoots me a poisonous look, but she does back off. She straightens and resumes her crossed-arm sentry position.

My examination tells me that Mary is getting very near to delivery. She needs to make arrangements with the prison for her impending birth. Ultimately, she petitions the governor of New Hampshire about her plight. He pardons her so that her baby will not be born behind bars. I am tremendously relieved. I was not especially looking forward to catching a baby surrounded by unsmiling, implacable matrons. Mary is released from jail and goes into labor four days later.

Mary and Harold live in a dark-wood yurt they have built themselves in a clearing in an apple orchard. They generate their own electricity from a small stream nearby. The yurt's curved interior walls that spiral in on themselves remind me of a nautilus shell. The innermost room, the inner sanctum, has a round skylight that filters in soft sunlight.

Silas is born in this womb-like room. The birth goes fine. I put my hands on Harold's hands and help guide him as he receives his own son. It is very touching, except for some inexplicable reason, Mary's perineal tissue lacks flexibility, and she tears through her anal sphincter muscle. I can clearly identify the two round canisters of the severed sphincter. A third-degree tear. The birth of Silas's head had been nice and controlled. The only explanation I can think of is that this is due to her languishing inactive in prison for months, without much walking or exercise.

I call Ken to ask if he will see us in his office to assist me with the repair. He is surprised at my sudden conservatism and is insistent that I can handle this repair at home. He asks me if I can positively identify the two ends of the muscle, which I can. He says to just put in a butterfly stitch through both sides and pull it together in a figure eight, and then continue the repair as usual. I say I'll give it a shot.

When I go back and look at the tear again, however, it doesn't look as straightforward as Ken made it sound. Maybe it's because I've never done this repair before, but my confidence is waning. Now I find that I am even having difficulty locating the apex of the tear. It isn't that it looks particularly nasty, but I have learned long ago that if I have nagging doubts, I should listen to myself. I apply a sterile gauze pack to her perineum, then call Ken and say we are coming in. He laughs and calls me a weenie, but he fits us in.

Harold and Mary line a wooden apple crate with a soft, handmade baby quilt. They bring newborn Silas to Ken's office and are sitting in the waiting room, with Silas asleep peacefully in his apple crate. The women in the office are astounded that this baby is out and about at only two hours old. Mary is very proud of her son and enjoys showing him off to all the cooing women.

Ken takes a look at her perineum and shows me how clean the tear really is. He coaches me easily through the repair. I think he truly loves teaching obstetrics. He is a gentle and articulate instructor. The repair is fun and educational. He shows me how to do a new, continuous stitch and a swift and sturdy instrument tie to lock it all together.

I love this man with all my being.

When we get back to the yurt, Mary says she wants to eat her placenta, like animals do in the wild. Most folks who have their babies at home are satisfied to bury the placenta on their land and then plant a fruit tree or rose bush over it. This is a nice symbolic act that nourishes the tree as it had the child. The child knows this is his own personal tree as he grows up. But not Mary, the quintessential Earth Mother. She wants to devour this tough organ as a replacement for blood loss.

Studies show that the placenta is exceptionally high in iron and protein. This helps to rapidly elevate a postpartum woman's red blood cell count. Mary states that she knows it will help her recover faster. It's fine with me; after all, it is her placenta—she definitely grew it herself. Mary's first thought is to blend it in a Cuisinart with orange juice. I think this sounds like some kind of gruesome cannibal cocktail. She resorts to drying the placenta in a slow oven for a couple of days until it can be pulverized. She mixes this dry powder by the tablespoon in tomato juice like desiccated liver. Over the course of a month, she ingests the entire thing. I tease her about drinking Bloody Marys.

———

The great thing about schlepping Milan to births in the middle of the night is that this causes him to develop a very flexible and adaptable personality. One night he might wake to find himself in the midst of a Harley-Davidson motorcycle gang's birth with bearded, bandanna'd, beer-guzzling bikers sobbing unabashedly at the beauty of it all, and the next night he might wake to Fundamentalist Christians solemnly reading scriptures through the entire affair. It certainly is educational.

The first time Milan hears some deeply religious folks talking in tongues at the moment of birth, he leans into me and whispers, "Mom, are they Lithuanian?"

I have no idea where this comes from.

Milan always gives me a high-five when we are done with a birth and ready to drive home. One night during an ice storm up north, he is awake and unusually chatty for four o'clock in the morning. Typically, Milan sleeps pretty soundly while I am driving, but this morning he is asking many questions about the mechanics of birth.

I can tell he is struggling with a particularly perplexing problem.

I ask, "What's on your mind, sweetie?"

He says, "I know that a baby is made when the father's sperm joins the mother's egg, but what I don't understand is, how does the father's sperm get in there in the first place?"

I think, *Whoo, boy, here it comes—the facts of life, and he's only four and a half.*

To his credit, he's seen enough births to rival most beginning obstetricians that I know of, so I decide to give it to him straight. I begin to tell him the drill in the most kid-friendly, scientific, nonchalant manner I can muster. I can see he ponders this for only a few seconds.

He throws up his hand to signal "Stop!" He says to me, very seriously, "I'm too young to know this."

I say, "Yes, perhaps you are. Let's check back in on this one in about ten years, OK?"

I don't recall that we ever did continue this conversation when

he became old enough. I think by then he had it completely
figured out.

SHOULDER DYSTOCIA

Ken and I have gone skiing out West for our winter vacation,
when a friend and colleague of mine runs into a midwife's worst
nightmare. Roberta is a midwife practicing in the southwest part
of the state; she has attended home births almost as long as I. We
are close friends. I respect her expertise, and we have covered
for each other on many occasions.

Ken and I have just gotten home when the phone rings. It is
Roberta, asking Ken to meet her at the hospital to do a repair
of a deliberate fourth-degree episiotomy that she has just cut. I
can tell by the sound of her voice that she is shaky and upset.
Roberta tries to remain calm as she unfolds the story:

Makela engaged Roberta to be her midwife. She wanted her
second baby to be born at home. Her first birth of a good-sized
baby had no problems. This prenatal course had been normal,
so Roberta was not anticipating anything out of the ordinary. I
met with Makela several times as I agreed to be backup for this
birth if Roberta needs me.

Makela is a bright, savvy, hip woman with a thick dark braid
down her back and a big laugh. She is fun to be with. We like
hanging out with her longer than usual during her visits—she
is that engaging.

Unfortunately, Makela's baby ends up being an eleven-and-
a-half-pound girl, causing a severe shoulder dystocia. Shoulder
dystocia is a serious complication of delivery, one that everyone
working in obstetrics dreads. The problem is that the head
is born, and before the midwife or doctor realizes that the
shoulders cannot be delivered, and the baby is stuck—the cord
becomes compressed, and the baby can become fatally oxygen
deprived.

The reality is that a true shoulder dystocia is incredibly rare. Although everyone in the business dreads it, the probability of its occurring is, statistically, less than 0.15 percent of all births. The size of the baby does figure into the equation; obviously, larger babies run a greater risk. We are practicing at a time when it is in vogue for home-birth pregnant women to follow a diet extremely high in protein to ensure maximum brain development of the child within.

The average size of babies born with Concord Midwifery Service is well over eight and a half pounds. It is interesting to note that in approximately one thousand babies that CMS attended in the years between 1975 and 1987, there are no fatalities, but there are two birth injuries, both due to shoulder dystocia. United States National Vital Statistics show that physicians in hospitals have 4.54 perinatal *mortalities* per thousand births, not to mention their morbidities.

This is not to say that all big babies are a greater risk; on the contrary, the biggest baby on Susie's and my record is born in our office because the parents live too far away for us to attend them safely. They drive through the night and birth on our exam bed, and their baby weighs 12.3 pounds. The mother is not a diabetic; they are just large country folk. Both parents look like they work for the World Wrestling Federation. The baby is in great shape; she looks like a junior Sumo wrestler when diapered, with no neck and thunderous thighs. This baby girl is healthy in every way, but her bulk and baldness make her look disturbingly like a diminutive Kojak. Her mother doesn't even sustain a skid mark.

Shoulder dystocia can happen in any birth setting, in the hospital as well as home; where it is equally unpredictable. As *Williams Obstetrics* notes: "There will always be the unexpected case, despite a carefully obtained history that may identify the likelihood of a shoulder dystocia developing and the resulting sequelae of a traumatic delivery."

I believe a couple of dystocias that I observe in the hospital happened when inexperienced physicians panicked at the size of a head and caused an impaction of the shoulders by rushing and not waiting to see what happened with the next contraction. Instead of waiting to see if the shoulders restitute properly, the immediate use of fundal pressure and aggressive traction on the head forces the shoulders down in an abnormal position, all but guaranteeing failure. They end up deliberately breaking both of the baby's clavicles in a last-ditch attempt to free the shoulders.

Obstetrical textbooks refer to sweeping an arm across the chest to deliver it. My experience with true shoulder dystocia is that after the head is born, the head is abnormally sucked back in with the next contraction—this is literally called the "turtle sign"— and the midwife can't get her fingers in anywhere. She can't get a purchase on anything—forget "sweeping." There is not a more desperate feeling in the world.

I have found that stuck shoulders can be dislodged by using a technique that midwives call the "maternal screw maneuver." This requires the mother to immediately flip over onto her hands and knees. It is amazing how agile a woman can be, even with a head between her legs, if she knows her baby is in danger. What this maneuver does is rotate the shoulders into one of the oblique diameters of the pelvis. The previously posterior shoulder passes beneath the symphysis and can now be delivered as the anterior shoulder.

Roberta did all this—but nothing budged. This is the true nightmare of all who work with birth. Roberta is finally forced, as a last resort, to do the unthinkable. She cuts a large episiotomy through the vaginal floor to make enough room to deliver the posterior shoulder via the rectum. This proves life-saving for the infant, but there are devastating consequences from the length of time of the dystocia. The baby girl, Carlotta, begins seizing soon after birth and is transferred directly to the intensive care nursery in Hanover.

Ken meets Roberta and Makela at Merrimack Valley Hospital, and he repairs Makela's perineum under general anesthesia. Roberta is beside herself with grief but is strong in her conviction that she has done everything in her power to get the baby out as quickly as possible. Yet Carlotta suffered significant neurological damage from oxygen deprivation; she is permanently handicapped.

Roberta and Makela and I spend a lot of time afterward, grieving and being comforted just by being together.

—

A few months after Carlotta's birth, our midwifery bill is heard at a public hearing in the House of Representatives. This time the place is packed to standing-room–only capacity. Throngs of other people wait out in the hall. Halfway into the testimonies, a contingent of several physicians from the perinatal high-risk medical center in Hanover approaches the podium and addresses the chair. Their delegated speaker is a neonatologist, who states the following:

"RSA 326-D is an act for the regulation, development, and improvement of lay midwifery. It is our professional opinion that the entire concept of a lay person providing medical services at the time of delivery and providing newborn care immediately after delivery runs counter to the philosophy and recent trend in American medicine of providing the best care possible to all people. We are not willing to participate in any way in state certification of a non-medically trained person. We feel that such certification lends a degree of legitimacy and, in a sense, is a state seal of approval to an activity that we feel is unwise and unsafe."

I lean over to Susie and whisper, "Ah, very clever how he

worded that little spiel. You will notice he neglected to document any of this 'unwise' activity with hard-core facts or figures."

The doctor continues: "For example, recently in Hanover we've seen firsthand the tragic results of out-of-hospital birth in the form of a newborn that has been rendered a complete vegetable from being delivered at home."

Roberta is sitting with us, and I hear her gasp. I look over and see a single fat tear roll down her cheek. She is silently weeping with sorrow.

I think, *Oh god, this is terrible. Those sons of bitches know damn well that the baby isn't damaged just because of where she was born. It could have happened to them in the hospital in a heartbeat.*

The man drones on about the horrors and hardships for this child and her family in the future.

Suddenly, there is a commotion in the back of the room.

A woman says loudly, "Excuse me! Excuse me! I'd like to speak now!" She jostles and elbows her way through the crowd to the front of the room.

All I can see is the woman's back and her long dark braid.

My mouth drops open.

I nudge Roberta. "Look, it's Makela!"

When the disturbance settles down, Makela turns defiantly to face the room. She holds Carlotta aloft for all to see. Carlotta looks chubby and beautiful, with her chocolate-cream skin and new, sparkling, diamond pierced earrings.

Makela says, "This is the 'vegetable' that they are referring to." There is a murmur through the room. Her voice is clear. "This is also my baby, my daughter, Carlotta. It is true that she is brain damaged. And it is true that she was born at home. And I do know that life ahead for us is going to be very hard. But what I also know is true is that this complication of my birth would have happened in the hospital with the same results. These people cannot tell you any differently. This is not an accident specific to place of birth, and hospitals cannot guarantee a perfect outcome. It makes me angry that these doctors are even suggesting that. I know my midwife is skilled and experienced and compassionate."

Makela takes a deep breath. "These women, my midwives, are like sisters to me. They took care of me in my grieving. They have loved and supported me and have given me strength in my pain. No one has asked *me* if I would do it the same way over again, knowing the outcome would be the same in either place. Would I still have my baby at home with my midwives?" She pauses. "My answer is yes—yes, I would!"

There is a lot of snuffling and blowing of noses. I look around and see there isn't a dry eye in the House. The Hanover delegation packs up their briefcases and files out, not to be heard from again.

How incredibly brave of Makela.

Our midwifery bill passes the House by a wide margin.

AN INTERTWINED BIRTH AND DEATH AND DEATH AND BIRTH AND BIRTH

In ancient times, midwives traditionally worked with families from "womb to tomb," bringing in new life and laying out the dead. They saw living and dying as opposing aspects of the same cycle. The two were of equal importance, as two passages through the same door: one coming in, the other going out. Midwives were as intimately involved in every manifestation of death as they were in those of life. They recognized that positive power cannot exist without negative power. Midwives traditionally supported and taught the dying, and cradled the corpse as well as the infant, each to its own particular new life.

Susie and I begin training apprentice midwives. We have some incredible women come through Concord Midwifery Service's doors, apprentices who go on to become very competent midwives with busy practices of their own.

One woman I love to work with is named Raven. She has jet black hair and a hooked nose—on her, the nose looks beautiful. She is fun and wild and has been trained as a licensed massage therapist in Colorado. Raven and I first meet in the late seventies, when she arrives early in her pregnancy with her first child. She has a tattoo of a morning-glory vine on her belly. The vine grows bigger and longer and more fecund as her pregnancy progresses.

Her baby girl, Willow, is born upstairs from the pub where Raven works. The birth is wonderful, as Raven is adept at focusing and directing her energy. The labor is very smooth, and she delivers, squatting. After Willow's birth, I go downstairs to the pub and announce the good news. A hearty cheer goes up from all the regulars, and there are pints of Guinness all around. The pub dwellers tease and question me as to how it is that Raven's blood is covering my elbows and my knees. There are some wild speculations. I don't tell them the truth—that a midwife spends a lot of time doing contortions on the floor.

Raven's daughter is beautiful, and her mother cherishes her deeply. When Willow is nine months old, Raven goes back to work downstairs in the pub, leaving her partner to watch the baby. When he turns away for a split second, the baby scoots over to the stairwell and tumbles head first down the long flight of wooden stairs. Willow dies later that evening from head injuries. Raven is devastated. She goes into a long period of mourning. Her relationship with that partner does not survive the accident.

The very same month that Willow dies, March 1980, another woman, Charlotte, loses her son, Trenton, as well.

Charlotte has been coming regularly for prenatal visits. This is her third baby and she is in complete good health. Charlotte is a bit older than her husband, Tommy, whom I adore. Charlotte is a fiddle player. I love seeing the two of them, and I feel unusually close to both of them. Charlotte calls about a week before her due date, very concerned that her baby has stopped moving and kicking.

I must admit that I am somewhat pat in my response to such a concern, because pregnant women worry about this a lot, and their babies are generally fine.

Even though it is a very busy night at the office, I tell Charlotte to come right in, that we will listen to her belly to assure her all is well.

All is not well. Charlotte says that the day before, when she was taking a walk, she felt turbulent, violent movements, and then her baby was still. I listen to her belly for what seems like a very long time, moving the Doppler back and forth. I hear only emptiness in return. It is a terrible, vacant sound, not even a maternal souffle. I hope my Doppler's batteries are dead. I use Susie's Doppler and listen even longer. Still nothing. I finally have to deal with the realization that Charlotte's baby is an intrauterine demise.

Oh, Mother of God, this is going to hurt.

I whisper softly, "I'm so sorry, Charlotte. I'm pretty sure your baby is gone."

Charlotte looks at me in horror.

She begins a haunting, primal, keening sound that builds steadily in decibels. Soon, her wail fills the entire office building. I never want to hear that sound again as long as I live. I go quickly to the waiting room to dismiss all the women who are waiting to be seen. They all look pale and stricken. They know what that sound means without my saying a word. They all quietly leave.

I call Ken to tell him what has happened. He says that if Charlotte doesn't go into labor soon, she can be given a prostaglandin suppository to get her laboring to expel the fetus. I have seen a few women induced with prostaglandin before. I think this is a very rough way to go. The women I have been with have experienced severe side effects from the drug and have become incredibly ill during labor. I am hoping Charlotte won't have to go that route.

Charlotte gets her first contraction fifteen minutes after I tell her that her baby has died. She is in hard labor by the time we get to the hospital. She births her son, Trenton, two hours later. Ken is surprised at what we find to be the cause of death. There is a true knot in the cord that has tightened to cause a total stricture of circulation. The maternal side of the cord is so engorged with blood that it resembles a large blood sausage. The fetal side is blanched white and is as thin as cooked spaghetti from the knot to the baby's umbilicus.

The story is painfully clear. The knot was created from active movements of the baby and somehow, it was pulled tight. This is the part that perplexes Ken. He believes this is extremely rare. He says that the incidence of true knots of the umbilical cord is less than 1 percent, and even then, they are usually just a novelty. A gelatinous substance within the umbilical cord known as Wharton's jelly usually protects the cord and keeps it pumping and rolling around like a slippery eel. The fact that this knot actually serves as a true knot and stops circulation is a tragic fluke.

Fluke or not, Charlotte and her husband now hold their stillborn son. Their grief is soul-numbing. I hug them briefly, but I feel like they need to be alone. I feel like this time period has had enough grief in it to last me a decade. I need to be by myself to assimilate all this.

I wander down the hall and end up in the unused delivery room where Milan was born. I stand next to the old delivery table that still has the wrist straps in place. I remember with joy and sorrow all the stories as they come flooding in. I lie over the delivery table, sideways, with my head hanging down over the side. My body is racked with exhausted sobs.

I don't know how long I cry or sleep there, but when I open

my eyes, there is a shaft of sunlight on the floor. I see two white-stockinged legs and two feet in sensible white shoes.

I look up to see a pert, pretty, young day nurse, newly on her shift. She is looking at me with disdain.

She says caustically, "Get a grip," and walks out.

About a year after the death of these two children, Raven calls me and asks if I will take her on as an apprentice. We talk for a long time. I know she has the calling, but I also feel her mourning and grief are still too raw. I suggest that she study areas of women's health that she finds compelling and call me when she knows the time is right. About a year after the first call, she calls back, and we both know she is ready. Raven moves to Concord and begins a formal apprenticeship with Concord Midwifery Service.

At the same time, Charlotte becomes pregnant again. She and her husband are understandably worried about a repeated bad outcome. Ken reassures them that the probability of this type of cord accident happening again is probably one in a million. He is so adamant that they don't dwell on it. A previous dead born is a contraindication for a home birth. But when Charlotte gets to term with a vibrantly active baby, we all know the past is a moot point, and we prepare for this baby's arrival at home.

The night Charlotte goes into labor proves one of the worst snowstorms I can remember in New Hampshire—and that's pretty bad. Roads are closed and snow drifts are impassable. I am thankful that Ken had the foresight to get us a beater four-wheel–drive, green Jeep Pioneer for exactly this type of emergency.

Raven and I inch through unplowed roads to get to Poor Farm Road in Weare. There is one steep ice-covered valley, where I don't know if we will make it. We keep sliding and spinning and are not able to make the crest of the hill. Four-wheel drive doesn't work on ice. We are in the middle of the woods. If we don't make it, it is going to be one hell of a long walk back to civilization. Finally, I tell Raven to hold on to her wig hat, as I am just going to gun it. We see snow spraying and trees flying by and somehow we are on the other side of the valley on our way to Charlotte's house.

Charlotte births Freya in a cozy room upstairs in their log cabin, surrounded by all her various relatives, grandparents, kids, and dogs. As Freya emerges, I hear Raven sob. Her face is streaked with tears, and her eyes are shining with joy. I'm embarrassed to say that sometimes I get so caught up in the mechanics of birth that I almost miss the sacred events that occur simultaneously. It dawns on me what a healing the birth of this baby girl is for Raven, as well as for her parents. Charlotte has figured this out long before I do.

After cuddling and nursing her daughter for a short while, Charlotte hands her infant to Raven. It is a blessed moment. Three people who have experienced the worst nightmare—a pain that only parents who have lost a child can know—now share in the joy of life returning. Freya becomes the princess of the family.

A short while later, Raven calls to tell me she has fallen in love with a man who is significantly younger than herself. They have conceived unintentionally, but they are delighted. The young man is a sweet, sensitive, artsy type and perfect for Raven's earthy temperament. I think it is a good union, and he proves to be in it for the long haul. Raven's morning-glory vine starts growing again.

Raven attends the majority of the births with me. As her pregnancy progresses, she becomes cumbersome and finds it hard and awkward to assist with some of the floor catches. Late in her pregnancy, when her belly is quite melonesque, we drive together to a birth up north. I am speeding to get there in time, when a large red fox runs directly in front of the car. I swerve to miss it, but the Jeep Pioneer is very top-heavy, and we start fishtailing badly. As we swerve from one side of the road to the other, we barely miss the guardrails. The Jeep goes up on two wheels, and it feels as though we are about to flip, but it finally smacks down upright, gets under control, and stabilizes. I pull over to the side of the road, badly shaken. Raven is curled over her belly, protecting it. As she uncurls, she gives me a scathing look of silent reproach.

I say, "Oh god, Raven, I am so sorry! I guess it's pretty stupid to get everybody killed on the way to help a baby to be born. That doesn't make any sense. I'll slow down now; I promise."

I mean this sincerely. I look at Raven and feel such affection for her and her baby. I have developed a deep attachment to the two of them. It frightens me that I could have been responsible for doing them harm. I drive under the speed limit the rest of the way. We still end up taking naps waiting for the baby's debut.

Raven calls early one morning and says she has been contracting since she woke up. It is time for me to come. I am thrilled. I am just going out the door when the phone rings. It is Charlotte. I have not heard from her in a while. I say I'm glad to hear her voice, but I'm on the fly because Raven is in labor.

Charlotte says, "Ha! I knew it! I knew something was happening. Tell Raven to be strong; we're all sending her our love." What an amazing connection.

When I walk up the stairs to Raven's apartment, I can hear her loudly chanting, "Om-m-m." I laugh as I walk in, saying it sounds like the Ganges River in here. Raven is in the bathroom, standing on her toes on one leg. The other leg is on the counter with her knee in the sink. And that's where Alaya is born—sort of in the sink.

Raven says this is the only position that feels good; she doesn't want to move. It doesn't look at all comfortable to me, but I'm not the one having the baby, and probably nothing is going to feel so great at this point anyway. It looks more like an advanced yoga position. I kneel behind Raven as Alaya is Om-m-m'd gently into my hands. Alaya looks like an elf, with jet black hair and a tiny hooked nose.

I give Alaya a kiss. "Welcome, little elfie. You're finally here."

The great thing about being in the bathroom is that it makes cleaning up afterward a cinch. We get Raven and Alaya comfy on the daybed in the living room and prop them up with pillows and blankets. Alaya's father is singing a beautiful song he has written for his daughter's birth.

There is a knock on the door. It is the retired obstetrician, Dr. Tom Ritzman, whose office is downstairs. He is standing there with a bottle of Champagne and a dozen long-stemmed roses. He is grinning like the Cheshire cat. He says that at first, when he heard Raven's noise, he thought there was a yoga class up here, but then the sounds became all too familiar to the old obstetrician. He rushed out and bought the new family a gift to celebrate. What a dear man! He greets Alaya warmly and heartily congratulates everyone, then goes back downstairs to work.

Now everything has come full circle for Raven.

A LESSON IN LISTENING

Hilda is a blonde, buxom, Germanic woman with an endearing gapped-tooth smile. She sits on our exam bed at her first visit and tells me, in great detail, the story of her previous births. She wants a home birth with her third baby because she has so many complaints about the care she received with her prior two hospital deliveries. The main complaint being that they almost drop her babies.

Hilda says that with the first two births, she knew she had to push, and she was positive the baby was coming. But in both instances, after the doctor checked her, he said she wasn't anywhere near dilated enough to deliver, and it was impossible that the birth was imminent. Both times, just as the doctor turned to walk away, the baby shot out, narrowly avoiding a disastrous fall.

I respond, "That's such a typical, arrogant, guy thing—to tell a woman she doesn't know what she's talking about, that there's no way it can be happening—when she can feel the baby between her legs! Right? God, the audacity of these men."

Hilda goes into labor and I drive to her house in the country. When I arrive, she appears to be working relatively hard. She is antsy and is pacing around her living room. She stops every few minutes to grasp some furniture and breathe deeply. I start following her around, rubbing her back when she leans over to help her better cope with her contractions.

Her husband, who considers himself a professional philosopher, is poised in a rocking chair next to the woodstove. He is smoking a pipe and thoughtfully stroking his beard. He is expounding on his version of existentialism.

He pauses long enough to say, "Hilda. Hilda! Please bring me my tea."

My mouth drops open. He has got to be kidding. How can he be so unaware? I am about to get nasty, but I realize my opinion of his behavior isn't going to mean diddly-squat at the moment, and getting confrontational with him will be even less beneficial for Hilda.

For her sake, I only say, "I think she may be a tad busy right now."

He looks put out and disgruntled.

Shortly after this tableau of domestic servitude, Hilda goes upstairs and lies down on their futon bed. She has only been there for a couple of minutes when she says she can feel the baby coming down. I put on a glove and quickly check. I feel thick, rigid cervix at only five centimeters dilated. It is unyielding and unstretchable—absolutely, positively not ready. I tell her this and turn to walk away.

I hear her sound.

It has only been mere seconds from the exam, and she has not even had another contraction. But the sound is undeniable.

I think, *Oh, my god! That's right! I'm being just as bad as the boys!*

I whirl around and drop to my knees, just in time to guide Hilda's baby out. I am chagrined that I have been as callous as the guys. I give Hilda a sheepish smile.

She is very gracious and never does mention it.

We get mother and child comfy and nursing in the third stage. I ask the father to get his wife some orange juice.

He says, "I can't."

I want to ask him if his arms are painted on, but instead, I say, "Oh? Why is that?"

He answers, "Because it's not made, and it's frozen."

Great. Now Hilda has three small children and a mate who doesn't know how to make juice from frozen concentrate. Make that four children.

I call Hilda's mother, who is delighted to come to spend a few days with her grandchildren and to see that her daughter gets some much-needed rest. Obviously, we aren't going to change the dynamics of this couple's relationship in a matter of hours. But we always make sure that the mothers have adequate help and support in the immediate postpartum period. This ensures quality alone-time with the new baby and a speedy recovery.

The ease of this birth astounds me. It brings to mind Jeanne M's birth in Warner. Jeanne is a hard-core mountain woman who lives in a remote log cabin and bow hunts her own venison. At the end of her pregnancy, she wakes up from a sound sleep because she hears a baby crying. She thinks she is dreaming—until she reaches down to find her baby, pink and squalling, between her legs. She wakes her husband, who calls me. I get there in time to assist with the delivery of the placenta. Jeanne tells me the only pain she feels is the after pains as her uterus clamps down strongly from such a precipitous labor.

I am in awe and wonderment about the disparity of women's birth experiences. It is never predictable. It is never the same.

But hard or easy, I love every minute of it.

I wouldn't trade my life for all the tea in China.

CHAPTER SEVEN

LADY'S HANDS, 1981

I am attending a birth in Manchester when our midwifery bill passes the Senate. We had been told its passage was a fait accompli, so I am mostly just relieved when Susie calls me from the Senate.

She shouts, "Crack open the Champagne!"

We have worked hard, and by the time the bill reaches the Senate, it is unopposed. I am proud. New Hampshire is the ninth state in the nation to legalize midwifery. Susie and I and a couple of our apprentices get all dressed up and go to the signing of the new Midwifery Law at the governor's office. Two nurse-midwives who have worked diligently on our behalf also show up for the ceremony. I believe one of the reasons we are successful in our legislative efforts is because the nurse-midwives and the apprentice-trained midwives have all worked together as a sisterhood.

Governor Hugh Gallen is beaming at us. He seems like a friendly, accessible man. He says that he is honored to be the one signing in this law and that we should be very proud of ourselves. As far as he knows, New Hampshire is the only state in the nation with a *voluntary* midwifery certification program. We have our picture taken with him as he signs it, and we all have huge smiles. Governor Gallen looks very healthy in this picture, but he will die from a mysterious illness a year later.

In 1981, the hostages are freed from captivity in Iran. The day their liberation is announced, I am attending a birth for a former coworker and her husband, whose name is Richard Freed. When his son is born, he says jokingly that he is going to name him Hostages R. Freed.

This is also the time period when I was still performing circumcisions. Francis has taught me how, and when he retired, he gave me his circ set, which I feel comfortable using. The problem for me is that I feel strongly that circumcising infant boys is totally unnecessary and extremely painful for the poor little guys. Although I know there is no medical basis for removing the foreskin, I justify doing it for several years.

I rationalize that those who choose circumcision for religious reasons will have it done in the most gentle and humane way possible. Instead of going to the hospital for the procedure, where in all likelihood a medical student will do it for practice, with the baby strapped down on a circ board, I have the parents hold their child and have the mother nurse her son until the pain gets too great. This way, the parents participate in the procedure and can comfort their child as much as possible.

Circumcisions, however, give me a stomachache, mostly because I find them so barbaric and grisly painful. Finally, my conscience makes me stop doing them. But prior to this decision, the Freed's bring "Hostages R." in for a circumcision when he is a week old. When I take down his diaper, H. R. Freed has a yellow ribbon tied around his penis.

In early 1981, Susie and I move Concord Midwifery Service to a larger office space. As we are renovating the rooms, we have one of our very rare arguments—on the correct and most efficient way to hang wallpaper. I've lost, so I am grumpy. Susie waits until I am underneath an exam bed, stapling a fabric cover over it, to tell me that she is pregnant.

I freeze in mid-staple, trying to absorb the enormity of what she has just said. We are working at maximum birth capacity. I think that she thinks I'm upset, because she hurriedly assures me that her pregnancy will not hinder her ability to take calls in any way.

And she is right; she is a machine. I hardly even notice that she is pregnant.

THEA'S THREE BOYS

Thea is one of the tiniest women to come through our doors. All four foot eleven of pure feistiness. She is blonde and spunky with a contagious grin. She cruises through her pregnancy without a hitch until around her thirty-fourth week. I see her in the office, and as I am palpating her belly, I get the clear message through my hands that something is desperately wrong.

When I check abdominally to make sure the head is down, I feel a broad, firm globular mass high above the symphysis. I have the immediate, sinking feeling that the baby's head is abnormally large—it feels to be almost as big as Thea's. I wish I was wrong. I am honest with her, to a point. I say that I'm not absolutely sure what's going on and that I would like for her to have an ultrasound to better define what I am feeling. We rarely do ultrasounds, but it is a handy diagnostic tool when it's needed. This is a good example of definitely needing a clearer picture.

As I leave with Thea to go to her appointment, I whisper to Susie, "I'm pretty certain that Thea's baby is hydrocephalic."

The ultrasound confirms my worst suspicion. Hydrocephaly—excessive accumulation of cerebrospinal fluid that distends the brain—occurs in about one in two thousand fetuses. It is almost always fatal. Even though this congenital malformation is very rare, it is a stark reality for us at the moment. Thea is understandably devastated. I think she handles the diagnosis courageously, although it will take some time for her to assimilate the gravity of this kind of news. Her care is transferred to Mary Hitchcock Medical Center in Hanover, a facility that is better equipped to monitor a high-risk pregnancy like this one. When Thea is a few weeks before term, her doctors decide to induce labor before the baby's head becomes too large to be born vaginally.

The Hanover obstetrician who cares for Thea during her birth is a very gentle and hospitable man. He isn't at all threatened by my presence; his ego is intact, and he doesn't need to strut his stuff to garner admiration or praise. I feel comfortable on his turf; I like his style. He graciously treats me like a colleague and involves me in the decision-making process. What a refreshing approach! Based on radiographic findings, he feels that Thea probably can birth her baby vaginally, but he will closely assess her progress. He is prepared to do an emergency cesarean, if it becomes necessary. And, he adds, if Thea delivers normally, he has no problem with my receiving her baby.

As it turns out, Thea and her baby get a bit stuck during pushing. The good doctor completes the delivery with the use of high forceps. This is one of the very few times I am grateful for the invention of this usually misused tool.

On September 4, 1981, Thea's son, Peter, is born alive but with severe hydrocephaly, as well as an associated condition, spina bifida—an open neural-tube defect. Thea loves and protects her son fiercely. The professionals attending Thea at Mary Hitchcock are wonderful. They are skillful, supportive, and compassionate. They show Thea how to care for her son by covering his exposed spinal cord with sterile saline packs. Peter's head is shunted and the cerebral spinal fluid is diverted from his brain. Even so, he is not expected to live for more than a short while.

Thea brings her boy home. Against all odds, he lives for six months. I believe it is her sheer love and determination that keeps him alive. By the time Peter finally succumbs, Thea is pregnant again. She wants to have her baby at home, but her husband is understandably traumatized by their previous experience. He feels more comfortable birthing in the hospital with Ken.

On September 4, 1982, exactly one year after Peter was born, Thea gives birth to Paul, a perfectly healthy boy, in a birthing room at the hospital. It is a lovely birth, with all of the family present, but Thea still wants a home birth. Exactly one year later, on the same date, she gets her wish.

On September 4, 1983, Thea gives birth to her third son, John, in her laundry room. While in labor, she had walked there—with difficulty—to get some clean diapers to fold for the impending birth. I trailed after her to the laundry room, and that's where we end up. Birth is never predictable.

Because Thea is so short, she braces herself, straight armed, in the space between the washer and dryer. This leaves her feet dangling about six inches off the floor. This is how she wants to do it—suspended in midair.

I, on the other hand, am lying on my side, wedged in between both appliances. I am trying my best in these cramped quarters to guide the baby out. The amniotic fluid is dripping on my head. Dryer lint is sticking in my wet hair. I am covered, head to toe, with fuzz balls. When I finally stand up, I look like a gray Yeti.

It truly amazes me that Thea's devotion caused her to birth two other sons on the birthday of her deceased child—the power women have over their bodies. And she got her wish and had a home birth.

At last count, Thea had six boys, four born at home.

I am asked to participate in a round-table discussion in Hanover about the state of midwifery in New Hampshire. It will be filmed for Dartmouth Medical School's closed-circuit TV. The panel consists of several obstetricians, a few nurse-midwives, and me, representing apprentice-trained midwives. I am slated to speak first about the new midwifery legislation that has just become law in New Hampshire.

To this day I can remember what I wore for that discussion because of the conversation that ensues with the MD, a perinatologist from Vermont, who was seated next to me. I am wearing a conservative Harris-tweed suit in a beautiful mauve heather. He is the joker whose car in the parking lot has a bumper sticker that reads:

HOME DELIVERIES ARE FOR PIZZAS

The doctor leans over to me and whispers, "There's going to be a lay midwife here today, you know."

I feign surprise. "Really?"

He says, "Yes, and I have it on good authority that she bites umbilical cords with her teeth to sever them, instead of cutting then with scissors. Some kind of primal, animal thing I guess."

Now I really am surprised. "Oh, my god!"

Obviously, the man assumes that I must be a nurse-midwife, probably because I look more professional than he has anticipated.

I can't resist. "So what does she look like?"

He looks around. "I don't think she's here yet. You know those lay midwives all look alike. They all have greasy, stringy hair and wear ill-fitting dresses and big work boots. And they all have a violent hatred of the medical establishment."

It is my turn to present my talk. As I am introduced and get up to speak, my neighbor looks stricken.

I flash my teeth at him. Biting cords, indeed.

Bite my pizza.

The Most Dangerous Birth

Of all the births, there is only one where I am concerned for my own personal safety. The goddess in charge of protecting her midwives certainly worked overtime on this one.

In 1981, there was a lot of media coverage about a militia man, Bo Haggett, who has stormed into my former place of employment, now renamed the Feminist Health Center, and has threatened the health workers at gun point. He claimed he was there to "liberate" his teenage daughter. He was going to prevent her from having an abortion, which was scheduled for that afternoon. He was there to save her from the "slaughterhouse." Apparently, he shot a phone off the wall when a health worker tried to call for help. He generally created a lot of mayhem and confusion. My friends were terribly frightened as he physically removed his daughter from the premises. The anti-choice people claimed it as a victory for their side.

Several months later, I get a call from the Penacook High School guidance counselor, asking if I will consider taking on the care of a sixteen-year-old in her charge who is progressing in her pregnancy but has not had any prenatal care. I agree, if the young woman appears to be in good health and if she and I click.

The teenager, Crystal Haggett, comes by herself. I like her immediately. She is very committed to having a home birth. She has been eating well and is taking good care of herself. She seems to be a responsible young woman. We have a long discussion about the trials and tribulations of single motherhood. She says she has the support of her parents.

I drive alone to her parents' trailer deep in the woods on the night that Crystal goes into labor. It never occurs to me to be leery of some of the living situations I confront. I guess I believe that my work is so sacred, so holy, that I am blessed, and therefore, impervious to danger. I am much more concerned with the safety and well-being of the mother.

When I arrive at the trailer, it is crammed full of sleeping children, as Crystal has ten siblings. Crystal is laboring on a narrow bed in a small room, with just her mother and father present. Clinically, everything seems to be OK, but I get the distinct feeling something is wrong. My intuition nags at me as Crystal labors into the night. She is making some progress, but it is slight. With every contraction, her father leans on top of her and breaths through it with her.

At some point, Crystal's parents ask me, in a conversational way, where I got my training. Usually, I say I was trained by Francis and also mention the Health Center. Maybe it is the crucifixes on the walls, or possibly the gun rack with the many rifles and shotguns and ammo, or maybe it's my own innate sense of self-preservation, but on this night I say only "Dr. Brown of Henniker." They seem to like that answer.

The night wears on and I get a little sleepy. I watch Crystal working with her pain and her father holding her down and rocking her with every contraction. Then I see it. I see her ever so slightly pull away from him, repulsed. This is when I identify the problem with lightning clarity. Now I know what has been eating at me all night.

Crystal's father is the father of her baby.

My skin crawls. I feel nauseous.

Holy Mother of God! I've got to get her out of here!

Then, in a flash of recognition, I realize who the father is. Finally, I understand the perilous position that *I* am in as well. I know in one swift second that this guy won't hesitate to hurt me very badly if he learns that I am an original board member of the "slaughterhouse."

I try to still my pounding heart as I check Crystal's cervix. I explain to her parents that she isn't progressing properly; that she is hung up in labor, and this can have dire consequences to the baby. (This is perhaps the only time that Friedman's curve has come in handy.) We need to transfer to Merrimack Valley Hospital immediately.

Then I call Ken, waking him up, to say I'm coming in with an arrested labor.

He says sleepily, "What? You *never* come in like this. It doesn't make any sense. Sweetie, what's going on?"

Because I am being overheard in the tiny trailer, all I can do is repeat myself with my trumped-up facts. I say, verging on panic, "Ken, you've got to hear me! We are coming in *now!*"

He says, "OK, OK, whatever you say. Jeesh—pushy, pushy. I'll meet you there in twenty minutes."

I have never been so relieved to see MVH in my entire career. Ken strolls down the hall in his scrubs and his white clogs. The back of his hair is still sticking up.

"What's going on?" he asks, rubbing the sleep out of his eyes.

I tell him the scene and that the father is Bo Haggett. Ken's eyes grow wide, and he gets very pale.

"Jesus, Carol, you could have been hurt!"

I wrap my arms around him and take a deep breath, finally feeling safe.

"Tell me about it. But I wasn't, and now we have to get Crystal away from her incestuous father, or she'll never have that baby."

Somehow, Ken weaves an obstetrical bullshit story that frees Crystal to labor on her own. There is much loud protestation from her father, which gets him banished to the waiting room. Crystal proceeds to do a fine job. She gives birth to a healthy baby boy, Alexander.

The next week, the media is all over the story—a diligent father has "saved" his daughter from the "terrible mistake" of terminating her pregnancy. Now, they are all just one big, happy family. The *Boston Globe*'s weekend magazine carries a full-page glossy cover story on how wonderful it is that a grandfather has been so protective of his grandson's life. These well-meaning journalists obviously don't know some of our darker country ways. The anti-choice movement makes this baby their poster child. It makes my blood boil, knowing "the rest of the story," but ethically, as Crystal's midwife, there is nothing I can say or do. I feel tremendous sadness for Crystal and her son and what the future holds for them.

Crystal comes to the office for her postpartum checkup when Alexander is a month old. She is terribly upset. She says her mother and father forced her to go back to work as a waitress at the local diner soon after her baby was born. But the distressful part is that her parents make her pump her breast milk every morning, and then they stay home, parenting the baby, feeding him with her milk, while she goes to work to support them. They have taken over the raising of the child as their own.

She states to me that this is an intolerable situation; she feels as if she will go insane if she doesn't leave. I look in her eyes and ask if she will promise to call me if she ever needs help, no questions asked. She nods, and I give her three hundred dollars. I never see her again.

A few days later, Crystal calls me from New Jersey to say that she bundled up her son and fled her parents' trailer at five o'clock in the morning, hitchhiking down the highway. She says she and Alexander are with some good people in New Jersey who are taking care of them. She feels safe and that I should not worry.

A day after that, the local police come to ask me if I know the whereabouts of the runaway with the baby. They say her father wants her arrested for kidnapping.

I say, "Let me remind you that this is Crystal's baby, not her father's. And no, I don't know where she is. I did hear from her, and I know that for now she's OK and that she feels safe, but that's all I know."

Crystal never, ever, goes back.

⌐

Of course, Crystal's story brings up the issue of abortion, which most midwives try to avoid like the plague. No professional midwifery organization to date has adopted an official position on the abortion debate, preferring to ignore it in the hope that it will go away. Although our ancient craft is to preserve the sanctity and holiness of birth—and therefore, life—the title "midwife" still means "with woman."

To me, this means that midwives are beholden to honor and respect a woman's decision, no matter what side of the abortion question she ends up on. We are charged to support and aid her in all phases of her reproductive journey, not just childbirth. This needs to be done with a clear heart, without judgment.

Midwives of antiquity often helped women procure abortions, either induced with abortifacient herbs or otherwise. The midwives of old used "quickening," or the first perceptible fetal movements felt by the mother, as the indicator that it was too late to abort. They believed that the soul entered the body at quickening. The first felt movement signaled that the baby had individuated from the mother by making its presence known. Prior to the soul's entrance, the pregnancy was simply a part of the mother's body, a growth of a cluster of cells. Quickening happens at roughly sixteen weeks gestation. It makes sense that midwives would assist women up to the point where they believed the baby became a distinct entity of its own.

Quickening is also the first real bonding event, a clear communication between mother and child. As a midwife, I use quickening as my personal milestone to help women in their decision-making process. If their ambivalence has been so great as to render them undecided until they detect movement, perhaps it is wiser for them to continue the pregnancy. Some veteran abortion proponents will object to this theory, saying sixteen weeks is too restrictive or limiting. Again, this is my own comfort level with the issue; every situation should be considered on an individual basis. Personally, I don't think that church or state should be involved in any manner in this most intimate decision a woman must face.

In keeping with midwives' ancient traditions, Ken taught me how to safely perform the technique commonly known as ME, or menstrual extraction, for early termination of unwanted pregnancies. Now, with the availability of very accurate pregnancy tests only ten days postconception, the more appropriate term for the procedure is EUE, or early uterine evacuation. This is a relatively simple suction technique that can be done safely up to the seventh week of pregnancy. It is nontraumatic, relatively painless, and, because of the flexibility of the cannula, or extraction tube, it carries little risk. The best book on the subject is Chalker and Downer's *A Woman's Book of Choices.*

Ken is firmly committed to women's freedom of choice and authority over their own bodies. He feels the purported pro-life faction has not so much to do with honoring life as it is obsessed with controlling women and limiting their autonomy by suppressing their power of self-determination. He wants to be sure I am skilled in the technique, in case Roe v. Wade is ever overturned and we are denied legal recourse.

He is worried that women will once again resort to seeking unsafe procedures, with disastrous or fatal results. He instructs me and has me perform many EUEs in his office under his supervision. I have since taught the technique to some of my sister midwives, who are prepared to go underground to safely help women, if this ever becomes necessary. In the meantime, I keep current with this skill by helping my close friends whenever necessary.

I thank Ken for this gift and the simplicity of it every time a sister is empowered by it.

———

Susie and I are training two very capable apprentices, both of whom are obstetrical nurses. They are technically skilled, but the hardest part about teaching nurses is getting them to trust in the validity of their own judgment. They need to have confidence and to develop trust in their intuitive knowledge. It just happens that Susie has ended up covering the southern part of the state more often, while I get to drive bloody Route 4 to the Seacoast area more times than I want to.

The midwife that we are training on the coast, Mari, is fun and loving, although at times curmudgeonly. She becomes a dear friend, so I don't really mind the trips I make over there. Besides, the Seacoast is beautiful and has a large home-birth population that crucially needs a local midwife.

As Mari becomes more confident in her skills, she starts to challenge me—a lot. Not exactly arguing, really, more like a congenial power struggle. Often, we bicker like two old ladies. Like the night I am trying to teach her how to suture a classic second-degree tear. For some reason, she puts the stitch in sideways, almost parallel to the wound, instead of straight across. It has been a lovely birth, but now it is three o'clock in the morning, and I can't understand why she keeps doing this. I've been up for days, so I am getting cranky.

I say, "Mari, that stitch needs to go straight across the tear."

She says, "I know. It *is* straight across."

"What? You call that straight across? That's the most cockamamie straight across I've ever seen!"

"Well, it looks straight across to me."

"I can't believe this. You're hallucinating. Take it out."

"What do you mean, 'take it out'?"

"Take it out and start over again. That's going to pucker her whole perineum. She'll have a crooked smile."

"Well, it's going to be just as bad to have so damn many puncture wounds."

And so it goes, the two of us growling and squabbling between the woman's legs. Fortunately, the woman is happily bonding with her newborn and is oblivious to the cat fight going on below the Mason/Dixon line. And thank the heavens for long-acting lidocaine.

When Mari takes her second try, it is still cockeyed.

I say, "Mari, what the hell is going on? You're doing it again!"

She pauses, and then begins to laugh. "Oh, now I bet I know." She backs the suture off and then goes in, straight across, a perfect stitch.

She turns and looks at me with one eye closed.

"I forgot. I'm blind in one eye."

"Oh, great! That's just great, Mari—a one-eyed midwife. Jesus, you're a piece of work."

One night, when Mari has her own practice, I am covering for her while she is out of town. One of her clients calls me, in labor. I have never met this woman, which is actually unusual, but the woman sounds pleased that I will be assisting her. When I get to her home, she is very active. She thinks she might be beginning to push. I put on a glove to check her progress.

What I find upon examination takes my breath away. In front of the baby's head, I feel the baby's finger.

I think, *Damn! A compound presentation! This is not a good thing.*

I feel around a little more. All of a sudden, the baby's finger breaks off into my fingers.

Holy mother of pearl! How horrible!

I am trying not to shake or let on how shocked I am. I keep

my midwifely composure. I hold my breath as I slowly withdraw my fingers.

When I look down at my hand, there in between my fingers is *a clove of garlic.*

Then I understand. I laugh out loud.

"Ah, by any chance did you have a vaginal infection?"

The woman nods affirmative. "Oh, I'm sorry," she says. "I forgot to tell you. Mari told me to use garlic to treat it."

Garlic is commonly used for vaginal infections because of its antibacterial properties. My heart rate finally regulates. I can breathe again. I never do tell them that I thought, somehow, I had amputated their child's finger.

In August of 1981, Dr. Wallace appoints the six members of the Midwifery Advisory Committee to the Director of Public Health Services. We are charged with drafting rules and regulations relative to the "qualifications for the practice and teaching of midwifery, and procedures for the practice and certification of midwifery."

The committee members include a pediatrician and a nurse-midwife, both of whom commute from the Seacoast religiously for our meetings. I always appreciate their dedication and commitment to the process. They are knowledgeable and considerate. The two apprentice-trained midwife members are an experienced midwife, whom I care about deeply, and me. We balance each other perfectly.

The obstetrician member is Dr. Gerald Hamilton, Ob-gyn, who is a midwife down to his very soul. Dr. Hamilton comes to the meetings encrusted in exquisite Native American jewelry—gorgeous silver and turquoise adornments—with longish hair and cowboy boots. He is a caring and meticulous practitioner and surgeon. The member of the general public is a crackerjack attorney, who has had a baby born at home with us.

The meetings are chaired by a very savvy nurse-midwife with a master's degree in public health, who works for the department. All in all, it is a phenomenal working group. Ultimately, we will spend 150 hours in meeting time, plus hundreds of individual work hours over a four-year period. We develop a program of which we all are proud—I believe we evolve a program for apprentice-trained midwives that is one of the best and most comprehensive in the nation.

A HOSPITAL BIRTH

On rare occasions, a woman comes for a home birth and then is risked out because of a contraindicated, preexisting medical condition. In these cases, the women are referred for a hospital birth, but that doesn't necessarily guarantee that they receive adequate care.

In Sylvie's case, she had four normal births but had developed a bleeding disorder (disseminated intravascular coagulation, or DIC) with her last pregnancy. She'd had an undiagnosed, severe placental abruption, which was not picked up by her doctor, and that caused her baby to die. The result was an uncontrollable hemorrhage, and Sylvie almost bled to death. The likelihood of this happening again is slight, especially with a live baby. But even a possibility of a repeat occurrence is not a risk that we are willing to take at home.

I agree to accompany Sylvie in the hospital as an advocate and labor-support person. Her husband refuses to go because he was so traumatized by the last experience. Sylvie and I are sitting in the sunny hospital labor room, chatting quietly for about an hour. Her labor picks up noticeably. We are attended by a sweet, ancient nurse, who either has been silently observing us or sleeping—I can't tell which.

A doctor comes in, cursorily checks Sylvie, says that she is only five centimeters dilated, and walks out. Immediately after this, Sylvie definitely switches gears and begins to breathe deep into her bowels. She catches her breath and then releases it with a quiet groan, her energy focusing down.

Just then, an efficient middle-aged nurse walks into the room, takes the ancient one aside, taps her wristwatch, and whispers, "It's time for your coffee break."

The ancient one now is suddenly wide awake. She nods gratefully and hobbles out of the room. I am astounded that she would leave at this moment.

I think, *So much for the magic and mystery of birth. When the java calls, you just gotta go.* Such a flagrant disruption of the continuity of care.

The new nurse is professionally cool and distant to me. Now she stands with her back to us, reading Sylvie's chart. She hasn't introduced herself to Sylvie, not that Sylvie is aware of the transition that has occurred. Not that Sylvie even cares at this particular moment, as she is oblivious to anything other than the work her body is doing.

I am about to tell the new nurse that Sylvie is in second stage, but I don't. I figure she's been working here for years. She is an experienced labor-and-delivery nurse. I assume she can make that assessment on her own. I sit next to Sylvie on the side of the bed, rubbing her back. I watch her bear down silently through a few more contractions.

Suddenly, Sylvie groans loudly and raises up her legs, and we can see the head starting to crown.

The nurse quickly leaps over and squeezes Sylvie's knees together. She yells, "Don't push! Don't push! I've got to get a doctor in here!"

She runs out of the room.

Sylvie looks shocked and confused. She is trying to comply by struggling against her body.

I engage her eyes and smile. I say calmly, "You're doing great Sylvie. You're absolutely fine. Now just do what your body tells you to do."

With the next breath her son slides easily into my waiting hands.

I say, "Hi, little man! Nice job!"

I wipe off his face with a towel, visually check him out, and then place him up on Sylvie's chest. Then I cover them both with the bed blankets. I can hear the nurse paging for a doctor STAT. I am getting Sylvie a glass of water when the nurse and a male medical student rush back in.

The medical student says loudly, "It's OK, hon, you can push now!"

Sylvie and I look at them in disbelief.

I point to the bundle at Sylvie's breast.

The nurse writes up yet another incident report, and I am summoned to speak to the head of obstetrical nursing, which always makes me feel like I'm being called to the principal's office. Unfortunately, by this time old Mrs. Malice has retired and her replacement is a hip, young, professional nurse with a plethora of degrees. This woman had home births herself in another state, so it is always mind-boggling to me that she has forgotten her roots. In spite of her steely veneer, however, she and I somehow establish an uneasy respect for one another.

This time, the umpteenth visit to her office, I am cited for misconduct.

She says, "There's been a complaint that you have delivered another baby in this hospital. You know you're not allowed to do that. You are not on staff at this hospital."

I say, "Oh, so that explains the lack of a paycheck from you folks in my mailbox every week."

She says, "Cut it out, Carol. I'm serious. You're really pissing people off when you do that, and then I have to deal with them."

"Well, look at it from my perspective. I come into the hospital because I have a problem, something that's out of my league. I think my client may need more specialized care than I can provide. So I come here, assuming she's going to be adequately cared for, and then she's not. It's not my fault an experienced OB-nurse doesn't recognize when a grandmultip is pushing."

I place both hands flat on her desk. "I do admit that if she and I had communicated a bit, the snafu may have been avoided. But she chose not to acknowledge me or ask my opinion or involve me in the care in any way. What am I, chopped liver? I'm a midwife, for godsake. I'm not going to sit by and let a woman blow out her perineum because she's left unattended. If she was getting proper care in the first place, I wouldn't have to do a damn thing!"

She responds blandly, "And the report states that you were not wearing gloves."

These were the pre-AIDS days, when we didn't have to be as concerned about contracting a blood-borne disease *from* someone as much as we were careful to not introduce contamination *to* the mother or the baby during delivery. Most out-of-hospital midwives I knew preferred to scrub well and to assist the birth of the baby gloveless.

I answer, "I don't think a baby's first touch in this world should be through latex."

She sighs. "Look, you know the drill. You can't touch the mother or the baby, no matter what. Let's see if maybe you and I can *not* see each other like this for a couple of months, OK?"

⸺

Ken and I are married on a beautiful Indian summer day, when the air is crisp and clear but the fading summer sun is still warm enough to have the celebration outside. We are married at Pumpkin Hill Farm in Warner at the height of the fall foliage season. The sky is a brilliant blue, and the trees are spectacular colors of rust, orange, yellow, and swamp-maple red. Susie's farm is just down the road, so I get dressed there. I have found a fine, antique-linen, off-white gown with a pleated front. I am so nervous and shaking that I can't button my own dress, so Susie has to dress me and put on my mascara. She is very pregnant at the time.

She says, "It's not often that women get to marry the man of their dreams, you know."

I say, "I know. I'm so in love with this man. Maybe you should pinch me."

The ceremony itself is attended only by immediate family. Milan's father, John, and I have remained good friends for our son's sake, so we joke by having him give me away. ("Take my ex-wife—*please.*") Ken's best friend, Bill, is a justice of the peace and is the officiant. Milan is the ring bearer. Ken and I have written our own vows.

Afterwards, our friends join us to celebrate. Many of Ken's colleagues from the hospital combine with my less conservative friends to make a very eclectic, fun mix. Dr. Easey is noticeably absent. Friends wander the grounds of the farm; the gardens are still lush with late-blooming flowers and perennials. There is a jazz quartet and free-flowing Champagne, and the laughter gets progressively louder as the day goes on.

In the early evening, just as the sun is setting, Ken puts his arm around my waist and leads me up a hillside behind the farm to a grove of trees. We stand beneath a blazing maple. He surprises me by taking out a little box that contains another ring made by the same friend who crafted our wedding bands. This ring is a plain gold band, set with a perfect oval New Hampshire garnet. Ken says the garnet came from Mount Monadnock in Peterborough. It is stunning in its simplicity.

He says, "I cherish our rings, Carol, as I cherish you. In them I see that our lives are now in an unbroken circle, a circle that wherever we go, we will always return to the other."

I kiss him softly. We hold each other for a very long time. I love this man, my soul mate, with all my being.

Back at the farm, the revelers are getting raucous. People straggle away as the night wears on, leaving us with wishes of eternal love and happiness. Late in the evening, Dot, the notorious night nurse, comes marching back into the building, madder than hell. She is covered in mud from head to toe.

I say, "Good grief! What happened to *you*?"

She says that when she and Jen started to drive away, Jen got stuck in a ditch on the side of the road. Dot got out and tried to push the car from behind, but Jen's spinning tires sent mud flying all over Dot. And if that wasn't bad enough, when the car finally got free, Jen lurched ahead, causing Dot to fall face first in the mud.

Ah, the dog and pony show strikes again. Dot is grumbling, but I am giggling hysterically. We are in the bathroom, and I'm trying to wipe the worst of the mud off Dot's fancy party dress with wet paper towels.

"Jesus, Dot, I never thought I'd be cleaning *you* up!"

She just growls, "Damn Jen. She's trying to kill me."

SUSIE'S WINDOW SHADE

Susie gives birth to Kirstyn one month after my wedding. If I've had any fears about Susie's ability to keep working through her pregnancy, they prove completely unfounded. Susie is in the office, conducting prenatal exams, on the night she goes into labor. I refuse to believe it; her pregnancy has just flown by. But now the reality is here.

In between clients, Susie stops occasionally to breathe deeply, until I can't stand it.

"Yeesh, you're making me nervous! Why don't you go home and get some rest before this thing really kicks in?"

Her sister, who is an obstetrical nurse in Boston, calls me the next morning to say that Susie is five centimeters dilated. It is time to come.

She scolds me, "You can't deny that Susie is pregnant any longer. This is the real deal, and it's happening *now*. You have to cope."

Driving to Susie's farm, I realize her sister is right. I am a wreck. I need to get a grip. I try to figure out why I have so much anxiety about this birth. Certainly it's not that I will be without a partner for a while. Surely I'm not that shallow? I dig around a little deeper.

Susie is like a sister to me. My fear is that this birth might be long and painful like her last one. I really dread seeing that happen. It dawns on me that this is the first birth I've attended for someone I am so close to, like a family member. I am afraid my emotional attachment to this birth might affect my judgment and skew the professional perspective. For the first time, I feel the enormity of the responsibility.

I am worried that somehow I might fail her.

As it turns out, I needn't have been so stressed. Not by a long shot.

The birth is wonderful and actually fun—well, for me, anyway. Susie still has to work pretty hard, but at least the labor is relatively short. This time, Kirstyn's head is properly flexed and comes down quickly.

The birth is being photographed for an article about home births for a local publication. It is a crisp, sunny fall afternoon. Susie is ensconced on their large bed in the airy upstairs bedroom of their big old Colonial farmhouse. She is wearing one of our "bowling" shirts that reads "*Concord Midwifery Service*" on the front. Being ever the entrepreneur, I keep pulling the shirt down over her belly so we can get some valuable PR from the photos. Susie keeps pulling it up because it is too tight and irritating as she contracts.

This goes on until finally Susie snaps at me. "Godammit, will you stop already? This is like a window shade—up, down, up, down. You're driving me crazy!"

Kirstyn's arrival is greeted with tremendous joy and celebration. She looks much as she does today—blonde and very fair, petite, and pretty. I am greatly relieved and wildly happy that things have gone so smoothly. At one point postpartum, I ask Susie if she thinks she might be bleeding a tad more than normal. Does she think she needs some Pit? She replies that she has just had a baby and that I am the midwife, for chrissake, and she goes back to nursing. Right. I know that. Her sister rolls her eyes and says she'll take care of it. I thank the stars that someone objective and level-headed is attending this birth.

Later, Susie's sister and I are sitting on the stairs drinking a beer. I get a little misty-eyed as the full realization that Susie is a new mother dawns on me. She is scheduled to take a three-month maternity leave, so I am mentally gearing up to cover the practice solo for a while. I should have known better.

Susie is such a dedicated midwife and in love with her profession that she is back at work in the office—with Kirstyn in a front pack—when her daughter is two weeks old.

Milan is in first grade in the Millville School. His school is across the street from the prestigious Ivy League prep school, Saint Paul's in West Concord. Millville is an interesting red-brick building that served as a schoolhouse for the children of workers in a local mill that is now nonexistent. Milan greatly admires his teacher, Phil, and is an avid reader and an enthusiastic student.

One day in late winter, my pager goes off, and I am instructed to call Milan's school. My heart is always in my throat when this happens; being a mother, I always fear the worst. His teacher, Phil, says that the children have been incubating baby chicks and all have hatched without a hitch except for one. Apparently, the last little guy still has part of his shell stuck to his head and he is running blindly, frantically, into all his siblings. This upsets the children greatly; they are crying for the helpless baby chick. Phil says he can't remove the remaining shell without ripping the chick's eyelid off. He says that Milan said that his mother is a midwife, and she deals with stuff like this all the time. She will come and save the baby chick.

I say, "Um, Phil, my specialty is perineums. Don't you have a student in your class whose parent is an ophthalmologist?"

Phil is serious. "I'm not kidding, Carol. This is urgent. You gotta come do this. The kids are majorly starting to freak out. *Please.*"

When I get to Milan's classroom, I find the baby chick really is in dire straits. The poor thing somehow has the last remnant of eggshell glued to its eyelid with thick dried yolk. No amount of pulling is going to loosen it. The chick's eyelid is as fragile and as transparent as rice paper. The children are standing around sniffling, tears coursing down their sad little faces.

They are watching me expectantly.

I think, *Oh, great. How do I get myself into these situations?*

I am starting to sweat.

Milan is looking at me. His eyes are brimming with trust and confidence.

The pressure is on.

I flush the dried yolk with a syringe barrel of warm water until it is softened enough to remove with a mosquito-clamp hemostat. Pretty delicate surgery. The chick can finally see, and he runs and huddles in the corner of the box with the rest of his fuzzy yellow clutch mates.

The first graders let out a collective sigh of relief.

A few days later, Phil's first grade sends me a giant yellow paper chick, with thanks and the scrawled signatures of all his students.

Milan tells me he is proud of me.
Life is good. Life is very, very good.

CHAPTER EIGHT

LION'S HEART, 1982

Our preferred method of birth control is the diaphragm. Rarely, we insert a contraband IUD or illegally prescribe oral contraceptives for a non-nursing mother if requested. We are still skeptical of the overall safety of these methods, so we mostly stay with the tried-and-true barrier methods; the "Frisbee" or condoms with spermicidal jelly. We fit women for diaphragms at four weeks postpartum, as many of our clients describe themselves as "ultra-fertile." They claim they get pregnant if they get a drop of semen on their big toe.

One such woman arrives with yet another unplanned pregnancy, her eighth. She is upset because she has been using her diaphragm religiously. She is confused as to how this could possibly happen. I ask her if she is sure she used it every single time.

She replies, seriously, "I'm positive I used it every time, because I had it tacked to my headboard so I wouldn't forget."

Not long after this story, one of our clients comes for her yearly well-woman exam and Pap smear. She brings her two daughters, who are in their early teens, with her to her annual checkup. They are grinning at me like hyenas; they have an air of expectation about them. I find it a little odd that the girls are so psyched for their mom's Pap smear. They are great kids, but they didn't have this much anticipation, even when their baby brother was born a couple of years ago.

I am chatting with their mom. The two young women are standing next to me, giggling, as I insert the speculum. I open it to view the cervix.

I scream *"Ah-h-h!"* and jump straight up in the air.

The girls are hysterical and laughing helplessly, rolling on the floor.

For looking back at me from inside their mom's vagina is *a giant eyeball!*

Their mom wipes tears of mirth from her eyes. She stops gasping enough to tell me that the three of them conspired together. They painted a big, bloodshot eyeball on her diaphragm.

Funny, really, very funny.

I say, "Here's looking at you, kids."

A COW NAMED CAROL

Of all the babies born with us, only one is named in my honor, and I am extremely flattered. It is a baby cow.

Joyce is a physical therapist working at Merrimack Valley Hospital. Her husband is a cow farmer. Joyce calls and makes an appointment for an interview about a home birth, but I never do meet her prenatally—she goes into labor before we can meet. She has had care with a physician but feels that he really doesn't care about her, personally, at all. She has developed such an aversion to seeing him that she gets stomach pains when she has to have a prenatal visit. She calls, in labor, and says that she's not going anywhere. She is staying home. Will I come anyway? I have a solid policy not to attend births like this; this is a recipe for disaster.

But of course, I go.

It is late at night when I get to their farm. A March wind is howling ferociously around their hilltop. It sounds as if the wind will violently rip the clapboards off the house. Shutters are banging and curtains are blowing on the inside of the house where drafts sneak through ill-fitting storm windows.

Joyce and her man are very pleasant. She is cooking right along. She seems cordial and relaxed for a first baby; even more so, when I check her and find she is ready to push.

Her husband beams. "Just like a heifer!"

He keeps comparing her to his cows and the ease of their births until I get a little testy. I remind him that this is his *wife*, after all.

Joyce gets up on her bed and squats to deliver. I am astonished to see that she has completely shaved off all of her pubic hair. I have never seen a bald vulva before. I am shocked at how it looks like a prepubescent girl is having a baby. The dichotomy is a little disorienting.

Joyce does a splendid job of birthing her baby, with incredible ease for a first-timer. When I remark on this, her husband says again that he knows she is just as rugged as his "girls" are, God bless 'em. He never had a doubt that she'd be fine. Never once thought she might need a Come-along.

I remind him that this isn't always the case, that human females sometimes have a difficult time of it. He claims that humans create much of these problems with their minds by being overly analytical, and they think too much. The discussion goes on in this vein for a while until he says that they have a heifer that is due to calf any day now. When that happens, he'll call me so that I can see for myself.

True to his word, several days later the farmer calls early in the morning to summon me to a calving. Milan and I arrive as a hugely pregnant cow begins lowing. Milan sits up on a bale of hay, where he can have a good view but be out of the way. I am rubbing the heifer's back and telling her she is doing a great job, which makes the farmer snort and roll his eyes. Eventually, the farmer tells me he is going in for breakfast and that he'll be back out after eating.

As soon as he leaves the barn, the cow turns to look at me, groans, and lies down.

A couple of pushes later, I see a dark, glistening amniotic sac bulging between the behemoth's legs. On closer inspection, I see two hooves and a little snout with a very large purple tongue hanging out.

Holy baby cow!

If one were to see a human baby with a tongue lolling like this at birth, one would be in very deep manure, indeed.

I wonder if it is normal for a calf to be born in the caul—in the membranes—like this, or if I should try to make an airway. I try to scratch the sac with my nails but to no avail; it is as tough as Naugahyde.

I am considering poking the sac with a pitchfork, when the whole calf slides out in a tremendous gush. I am astounded— this baby is *huge!* My heart is pounding at the sheer magnitude of everything. Do I try to suck out its nose? Or listen for a heartbeat? How can I resuscitate this baby when I can't even pick it up? My heart is crashing as I worry about all this.

The baby calf snorts, shakes her head as if to ask "Where am I?" and attempts to stand up on wet, spindly legs in the straw.

As the calf begins to wobble and stand, I feel my legs wobble and my knees get weak. This is all so *enormous!* This new calf will weigh in at seventy-five pounds. Give me a portable little human baby any day! The baby behemoth is adorable, with large dark brown eyes and very long eyelashes.

Milan is tenderly stroking her soft butterscotch-colored fur, saying, "Awesome. This is so awesome."

I must look a wreck, because the farmer is laughing as he

comes around the corner from the stall, where he has been watching the whole birth.

"Jesus, you look turrible, deah!" he guffaws.

Joyce is grinning as she comes out of the house with her infant to greet the new arrival. By now, the mother cow is licking her baby clean. The new heifer is starting to root around for the teat, seeking out the colostrum that will ensure her survival. I have to admit to the farmer that I think the mother cow did a powerful job. He seems tremendously proud of his "girl."

He nods. "Yuh. She's a corker."

As Milan and I are leaving, they name the new heifer Carol.

In the winter of 1982, Ken and I take a much needed ski vacation in Park City, Utah. Ken is pushing himself to extremes to meet the demands of his patient load. He is exhausted from constantly making himself available to all the women who need him. When Ken is exhausted, he goes through long silent periods where he becomes uncommunicative, almost sullen. These times are painful and confusing to me. This is almost always followed by an extremely playful and gregarious period, where he is talkative and affectionate. It is becoming Jekyll and Hyde-ish. I never know which man I'll be married to when I come home from work.

Will it be husband number one? He is the reserved, dignified doctor from the Midwest, who sits quietly in our living room, reading the paper, wearing his reading glasses and a button-down, lightly starched oxford shirt and tie. He simply nods at me in greeting, having given his all at the office. He is drained of any animation; he is almost … unfriendly.

Or will it be husband number two? He is the gorgeous, raven-haired guy running around in the backyard, with nothing on except a ratty pair of Patagonia shorts, tanned and muscular, mowing the lawn with a boyish grin and a tumbler full of straight gin. This is the same guy who gets a tattoo of a rose on his big toe at the Bradford Fourth of July fireworks, where the young mothers with their children stop at the tattooist's booth and whisper to each other in shock, "Oh, my god! Isn't that Dr. McKinney?" as Ken grimaces in pain.

My husband has two sides that are polar opposites. I love them both.

The ski vacations out West are a busman's holiday of sorts, as they are actually a tax write-off. The American College of Obstetricians and Gynecologists (ACOG) sponsors a conference in Park City so ob-gyns can get mandatory continuing medical education (CME) credits. They combine this with great skiing and deduct it as a professional expense. The guys have an educational seminar in the morning for half an hour before the lifts open, then another cocktail meeting in the early evening, after the slopes close. Then they tell the IRS that they are working hard.

Most of the conference attendees ski either Park City or the new, ridiculously posh Deer Valley ski area, with its waiters and helicopters, uniformed chefs, and brass pineapples. Ken and I duck out as soon as possible and head for the more rugged and challenging terrain and snow bowls of Alta or Snowbird. Being used to skiing in the East on our infamous "boiler plate," we laugh when Western skiers complain about icy conditions. Our thigh muscles burn from skiing in unfamiliar deep powder. We pack a picnic lunch of sandwiches and beer into a back snow-bowl and doze in the sun, sated. These times recharge Ken tremendously.

The wives of the ob-gyns always have an afternoon tea or genteel cocktails, which I learn to avoid like the plague after attending only one—especially after mentioning my line of work to these refined ladies. Their response, "Midwife? Dear

God! Wasn't that made illegal at the turn of the century, along with prostitution?", lets me know, positively, that I don't want to attend another soiree. It just takes too much effort to appear properly bred and polite with the doctors' wives; I can't sustain the uptightness. I politely excuse myself after about half an hour, saying I forgot my hankie.

I'd much rather argue with the Mormon cab driver about the pros and cons of polygamy or the origins of the temple gown and its significance to women's self-esteem, as I do on the way back to our condo.

One night, after the requisite cocktail seminar, Ken comes back to report that an incredibly impressive and articulate nurse-midwife has presented the evening's talk. Not only is she brilliant, but she also is very supportive of apprentice-trained midwives. He talks to her afterward and tells her that he is married to a midwife. She says she would like to meet me, because she has some important news that might interest me. Ken's enthusiasm for my connection with this woman is undeniable. I think that a midwife instructing the obstetrical "brotherhood" on anything is phenomenal. My curiosity is piqued.

The nurse-midwife is a petite woman with curly, jet-black hair and enormous, shining dark eyes. Even though she has been in California for over a decade—she teaches midwifery at Stanford University and is the head of the midwifery program at San Francisco General Hospital—she still has a very thick New York accent. You just can't take Brooklyn out of the girl. She has the kind of razor-sharp mind that leaves me a little dizzy and feeling sluggish. I hesitate to tell her about my background in midwifery; I am afraid of being rebuffed.

I must have passed her scrutiny. She says, "Have you heard about the meeting in Lexington, Kentucky, to encourage a dialogue between nurse-midwives and apprentice-trained midwives? It was called by the president of the American College of Nurse Midwives [also known as the ACNM] and is set for

next month. I think it is an extremely important meeting. Fran
Ventre is going, I know; I think you should go, too. I think your
voice will be invaluable."

I am flattered that I am being recruited on such short notice.
Sister Angela Murdaugh, president of the ACNM, has arranged
for this meeting to further communication between the two
different modes of entry into the profession of midwifery. Some
of her colleagues think she should be impeached for involving
the outsiders—the "non-nurse" midwives.

Sister Angela's response to that threat is, "Good. Impeach
me. I want to go back to my little clinic in sleepy, rural Texas
anyway. I can't stand Washington!"

I believe it is imperative that both types of midwives work
together. I know that we owe a lot of our legislative success in
New Hampshire to the fact that we have the active support of
the state's CNMs, and both groups have worked in concert. It is
a clear case of "divided we fall, united we stand," if we are to gain
more legal recognition for our work and common goals.

This is ultimately how I become involved in the founding of
our national professional organization for midwives in North
America. The irony is not lost on me, that this chance meeting
occurred in the seat of the American College of Obstetricians
and Gynecologists, while the boys were out to play.

A month later, Fran Ventre and I meet at the Boston airport
and fly to Kentucky together. I am excited, but I have never
in my life met anyone who talks more nonstop than Fran. She
talks the entire flight. *Holy yenta!* This woman can go on. She
pauses to take a breath, I start to interject, and she's already a
full sentence ahead of me.

But what Fran is telling me is informative and full of insider
gossip, dark secrets, and revelations. Feeling like a rube, I drink
vinegary airplane wine and listen carefully to her stories. I
learn who all the important players are. I know without a doubt

that what is about to happen will have far-reaching historical significance.

Our meeting is scheduled during the ACNM's annual convention, so the hotel in Lexington is teeming with midwives. It has an electrically charged atmosphere similar to the El Paso conference—except these women are more well-heeled. Standing out in the crowd is Ina May Gaskin, one of my folk heroines. She is pulling a cart loaded with her groundbreaking 1975 book, *Spiritual Midwifery*. She looks exactly how I imagined—a long, graying braid, colorful Guatemalan clothes, and intelligent blue eyes. I am a bit star-struck and tongue-tied, but she is just normally friendly and seems genuinely interested in me as well. I relax and feel comfortable and accepted. I am surprised at how many women I already know from the trade. The political networking begins immediately.

I make signs that announce the meeting in our hotel room to assess how much interest there might be for an umbrella organization to unite all midwives. We really have no idea how this idea is going to be received, especially here. Using some of the guerilla tactics I learned from anti-war demonstrating in the sixties, I post signs in elevators, in hallways, and in the lobby, introducing the concept of the "new AMA," which is what we call ourselves originally—Ina May's twisted idea of a joke: the American Midwives Alliance. We hope a few women will be curious and will attend our formative meeting.

As it happens, our room is packed, and midwives are crammed in the doorway and down the hall, straining to hear what we have to say. I am deliriously happy. There are probably close to a hundred midwives thronging in enthusiastic support. It seems to me that most are younger midwives, a lot still students. Perhaps because of this, they have a certain idealism, a naiveté. But they all are craving more freedom and autonomy in their work.

Many of these nurse-midwives tell stories of working with or having friends who are apprentice-trained midwives and how much they admire and respect their less-accepted counterparts for being radical enough to buck the system. They say this, even though they know these same sister midwives face legal harassment and confrontation from the medical establishment in every facet of their practices.

The "new AMA" has made enough of a startling impact that the issue is addressed in the open forum of the convention. Not surprisingly, many of the older and more seasoned certified nurse midwives express grave misgivings and resistance to allying with the "fringe midwives," citing their own long history of arduous years, working to garner respect and inclusion from the male-dominated medical profession. Their fears are entirely understandable. They are concerned that the strides they've made over the years in an effort to gain acceptance from ACOG could be undermined and their reputation jeopardized. This could result in opposition to practice and possible loss of hospital privileges. We are anathema to them.

And yet, the younger nurse-midwives stubbornly stand their ground. They are butting heads with authority. They express their belief that nursing should not necessarily be a mandatory prerequisite for midwifery study. Midwifery is a separate profession in its own right, of which nursing is only one component.

Out of all this debate, the Midwives Alliance of North America is born. The women have expressed a hunger for an umbrella organization that will unify the two types of midwives and bridge the chasm between the "two sisters separated at birth." They want a comprehensive, holistic approach to the midwifery model of care, using the best of both routes of entry.

The Midwives Alliance of North America (hereafter MANA) was founded in April 1982 to build cooperation among midwives and to promote midwifery as a means of improving health care for women and their families, and to establish midwifery as an accepted part of the maternal/child health-care system in North America. The impetus for

*the formation of this organization came from a group of midwives with
diverse educational backgrounds who believed that the time was ripe for
unity.*

I return home from this meeting with my briefcase stuffed with
checks and many slips of paper with the names and addresses of
new members. I have been recruited to be the acting treasurer
and membership person of this fledgling organization. I don't
have the heart to tell anybody that I never balance my checkbook.
I see this as a challenge and a serious learning experience in
financial responsibility.

Little do we know from this heady experience that a powerful
new organization has just been born, one that will become an
international mover and shaker—and that will withstand the
test of time.

A WATER BIRTH

In the early eighties, the use of water for birth becomes all the
rage. Much of this is due to Frederick Leboyer's published work
on the Leboyer bath, which is the use of a warm-water bath for
the newborn immediately after birth. The theory behind this
technique is that water simulates the intrauterine environment
and returns the baby to weightlessness. This relaxes the baby
and releases any tension the baby may have sustained in the
birth process.

Unfortunately, now the focus is on the obstetrician who does
the honor of floating the baby in his simulated sea, as if only now,
the baby will recover and relax after the grueling experience of
being pummeled by the relentless contractions of the mother's
abusive body. Leboyer believes that the baby's experience of
labor is a terrifying struggle with a mother that is hurtful. I find
this concept disturbing and bordering on misogynistic; grown
men imagining the womb and vagina as a potentially harmful
and scary place. In actuality, studies have shown that hard labor

and the resulting elevated catacholamine levels are beneficial to the newborn and its survival-coping mechanisms.

The main positive impact of Leboyer's work is to awaken awareness in many hospital settings that the newborn is a new *person* who needs to be greeted with gentleness and respect, not bombarded with sensory overload of bright lights, loud sounds, rough handling, and the emotional insecurity of separation. They find that babies who are loved and held and touched by their parents fare much better than babies who are not.

Obviously, babies born at home stay right where they are supposed to be—on the breast. Paradoxically, we find that it is a good idea to *not* bathe the newborns until the greasy vernix that coats the baby's skin, with its beneficial antibacterial properties, is completely absorbed.

Next comes the vogue of literally giving birth under water. This one makes Francis particularly nuts.

When this practice begins to become popular, Francis grumbles, "We are no longer whales you know; we have evolved. We are now land mammals."

He feels that the baby should be challenged to adapt to the extra-uterine environment as soon as possible, to get the circulatory/respiratory processes switched over smoothly, without confusion. He believes that water birth is a gimmick. Francis is vociferous about the fact that human beings no longer sport gills, and we are "air-breathers" these days. But soon, hospitals are jumping on the bandwagon and installing Jacuzzis in their birthing suites, even though the tubs are rarely used.

Francis and I do, however, almost always use water for pain relief. My personal observation of women's behavior while laboring in water is that while the relief of the water is profound and the mothers are grateful for it, at the precise moment of crowning, a vast majority of women lift their bodies out of the water and sit on the edge of the tub for the actual birth. This occurs with no coaching from me; I am ambivalent as to whether they should be in or out. This has happened enough times that I conclude that delivering under water is probably not a natural process.

Many midwives are enamored of water birth, and I get a lot of criticism for expressing my opinion. I think what is truly important is how loving the midwife's hands are when first greeting the babe, whether in a bed or in an ocean. In this respect, I think the water-birth trend has done much to humanize births in institutions. It has increased awareness of the sensitivity and needs of the newborn, as did the Leboyer baths. This is certainly true of the water births in Russia, where the introduction of gentleness and respect is truly a novel concept.

A water birth that later always makes me smile is with a client who is a registered nurse, living in an apartment complex toward the Seacoast. Gloria is tall and outspoken and very funny, so it comes as no surprise that she is directive and bossy in labor. What works best for her, during the throes of transition, is standing up in her shower with the massage showerhead set on "pulse," directing the stream of water on her clitoris. This gives her tremendous pain relief, and it looks like it might be a familiar habit. This is fine and dandy with me, until she is in there for so long that she runs out of hot water and the water becomes icy cold. She continues to spray as if in a trance and doesn't seem to notice that the water is now freezing. She is clearly pushing now.

I say, "Ah, Gloria, sorry to bother you at a time like this, but is this water temperature still OK with you?"

She growls, "Be quiet! I'm not moving!"

Okey dokey, whatever you say. As the baby's head begins to crown, I have to crawl into the shower with Gloria, kneeling on my knees in front of her, looking up as the icy jet pummels my eyes, trying to see what is going on through the spray. With the glacial torrent streaming down my face, we remain frozen in this tableau until the baby slides free. Gloria finally turns the damn thing off, and we sit down in the tub together to greet her daughter. My teeth are chattering; I am soaked to the bone.

I feel like a drowned rat, but I am grinning. "OK, Gloria, next time you have a baby, remind me to bring my swim goggles, snorkel, and foul weather gear, will you?"

Ken and I travel to his family's fishing camp in beautiful Ontario, Canada, every summer, like spawning salmon. The camp is on a remote glacial lake, Lake Lauzon, north of Lake Huron. The nearest town is a dusty mining town, Blind River, which still has a saloon with two entrances; one door marked "Ladies" and one door marked "Escorts." The camp is accessed by miles of bumpy dirt roads. It is rustic; there is no electricity, and it is illuminated only by gas lamps. Behind the camp rises Mount Baldy; this is the highest point of land on the lake and commands a spectacular view of Lauzon. The lake itself is primordial. Many nights, the moon shining through the mist that rises from the water imbues the lake with an ancient mystery.

Ken, an only child, built the camp with his parents in the mid-1950s, when he was in his teens. His mother is now deceased, but we meet up with his father, Mac, at the camp every summer. Mac is a wild one. He's a hard-drinking Scotsman with plenty of opinions, a mischievous wit, and a shock of snow-white hair. He is loud and skillful and hard-working, but he also is very competitive with Ken and occasionally has a mean streak. Mac is proud of Ken's accomplishments, but he is also often excessively critical of Ken, even though I know he loves him deeply.

[Postscript: My own mother will marry Mac in less than five years making my father-in-law also my step-father and my mother also my mother-in-law. PPS—this is true.]

The ritual at Lauzon is to drink Labatt's Blue all day and fish for small-mouth bass. In the evening, we make an open campfire on the rocks of the shore and cook the fish that we caught that day. Then we eat them and drink Mac's whiskey all night. The menu is *always* the same—bass coated in cornmeal and cooked in a huge, black cast-iron frying pan; cabbage coleslaw, chopped into minuscule pieces by hand; homemade tartar sauce; home-fried potatoes with onions; and blueberry cobbler made from the prolific blueberries picked from the slopes of Mount Baldy.

Ken and I always wake up stiff and cold, lying on the smooth rocks next to the lapping shore, huddled together in an insufficient blanket, spooning each other for additional warmth. We have buried our noses in each other's armpit to escape the chill. It is the middle of the night, the campfire is cold, and our boisterous Canadian friends have all gone home. But the stars are wheeling brightly overhead and sometimes, if we are lucky, we see the lights of the aurora borealis on the northern horizon. We always hear the insane night cry of a loon.

Ken at Lauzon is, undoubtedly, the most peaceful and content that I will ever know him to be.

The Only Mortality

My dreams about impending births are always disturbingly prophetic. I grant them a lot of credence because I know they are based on intuitive and unconscious factual information. My dreams are an invaluable tool in my practice. Many times I am forewarned by a dream that is a prediction of a future emergency, so I am prepared in advance. The following story illustrates my dreams' role to the extreme.

Barbara is an eighteen-year-old woman living in the North Country, who calls late in her pregnancy to ask if I will help her out and attend her birth at home. She has had no prenatal care because she belongs to a strict fundamentalist Christian sect that does not believe in medical care in any form, as they think that all outcomes are the will of God. (This church is not connected in any way to Christian Scientists, whom I respect.) Her church members have planned to do the delivery themselves, unassisted, but Barbara gets nervous at the last hour; hence, the call to me.

The New Hampshire Midwifery Rules and Regulations, however, have quite an explicit section that prevents us from assuming the care of a woman with no prior care after thirty-six weeks. This rule is more to protect us, the midwives, from getting into a rocky situation. I explain this to her and encourage her to contact her local hospital to make satisfactory arrangements.

A week later, this young woman shows up at the office. She pleads with me to assist her, as her church is refusing to let her go to a hospital. After speaking with her further, I discover that she is the daughter of an old acquaintance of mine, so I agree to help her—against my better judgment. During this initial visit, Barbara mentions that her husband, Ron, is forty years old and had two daughters by a first wife many years ago. I don't question her further about this. Barbara seems to be in good health and reasonably informed about her body and birth, so my reluctance is diminished somewhat.

Soon after this first and only visit, Barbara calls in the middle of the night to say her water has broken. I tell her to go back to sleep and to call me when she begins contracting regularly. I fall back asleep and have a terrible anxiety dream that wakes me in a cold sweat.

In the dream, *I have her husband, Ron, arrested for child abuse, but he is released on his own recognizance, and he comes and slaughters a sow on my bed, leaving a large pool of blood.*

I am so frightened by this dream, and I haven't even met this man!

I wake Ken and tell him about it.

He says, "Huh, that really is bizarre. I wonder what that's all about."

Soon after the dream, Barbara calls back to tell me it is time to come.

As I am leaving, I give Ken a kiss good-bye. He oinks at me.

I say, "That's not funny, Ken. I find this whole thing disturbing. It's making me feel kind of sick."

He yawns and scrunches down deeper in the covers, preparing to go back to sleep. "OK, sorry, sweetie. Be careful. I love you."

When Susie and I get to Barbara's house, she is laboring in bed, surrounded by her church members. It is a surreal scene. The men of the church all are wearing polyester suits with gold chains and gold jewelry. The women are subdued and dowdy and wear kerchiefs covering their hair. Husband Ron introduces himself. He has a pencil-thin mustache and slicked-back greasy air. Susie cuts me a sideways glance, as she knows this is the exact prototype of men that I detest.

The church members seem a little irritated that we are here. Perhaps they feel we represent medical interference. How ironic!

Every time Barbara has a contraction, the church members say in unison, "Praise the Lord! Another pain over and done with!"

Susie mutters under her breath, "Jesus, a whole nest of PTLs."

Susie and I try to remain unobtrusive. I can tell that Barbara is grateful for our presence, but she certainly has all the support system she needs. We hang back and observe. Except for monitoring the heart rate, we make ourselves fairly invisible until the actual delivery. The labor is smooth and slick and surprisingly fast for a first baby. Barbara does a great job, pushing for less than twenty minutes. She births her daughter easily without a tear. The baby is an average size and seems healthy. She checks out nicely in the infant exam, which I do.

As usual, Susie and I stay for a couple of hours postpartum to make sure both mother and babe are stable; then we decide to leave, as it is congested with their whole congregation. Before we leave, we do our usual routine of reminding the parents to have their baby checked out by a family doctor or pediatrician within twenty-four to forty-eight hours. They say, in no uncertain terms, that they absolutely will *not* have anyone see their child, as her health is now in the hands of the Lord.

I say I will call them in the morning.

As we walk out the door, Susie says, "Look."

She points to the phone numbers that we always request be posted by the phone in case of emergency. In this case, all the numbers have their local three-digit exchange followed by "LORD."

Susie says, "I hope the Lord is on call tonight."

I stop and look at her. "Why did you say that?"

She says, "I have no idea."

Early the next morning, before Ken and I have even crawled out of bed, the phone rings, and it is Barbara.

She says, "Hi, Carol. I just woke up and found my baby dead in her crib."

What? I sit bolt upright, pinching Ken awake. I don't even know what to do in this case. This has never happened before; we have *never* lost a baby. My heart is pounding, and I start to breathe too deeply. Ken says they should notify the authorities. I tell her that and say I will be there as soon as I possibly can.

After I hang up, I start running around the house in a blind panic, unfocused. I am trying to get dressed but can find only mismatched cowboy boots. *Holy Mother of the Gods!* What has happened? That baby seemed fine to me! All the way to her house, I review the birth for any possible explanation, but I come up blank.

When I walk in the house, the police are already there, and the baby is gone.

One big guy starts interrogating me. "So, you're the one who delivered the baby?"

"Right." I try to ignore his sneer.

Then he starts asking for my credentials. For the first time, I realize how important it is that we are legally recognized and sanctioned by the state. I tell him to contact the Department of Public Health if he wants a quick synopsis of requirements for the practice of midwifery in New Hampshire. I move on to find Barbara.

Barbara is seated in the kitchen with family members. We hug each other, and then I gently ask her what happened.

She says she really doesn't know what happened. She had been up all day with her church members, who were helping her with breast-feeding. By evening, she was exhausted and wanted to rest, so everyone left. When she fell asleep, Ron was walking the baby around the house because the baby was fussy. When she woke in the morning, she realized the baby hadn't woken in the night to nurse. She went to the crib to get her—and found her stiff and cold.

Then she says, "I'm doing fine. It's Ron I'm worried about. This is the third time this has happened to him!"

What? Oh, my god, this is going from bad to worse!

I try to lower my voice, "What do you mean, the third time?"

She whispers, "The two daughters that he had eighteen and twenty years ago—they both died like this, within a couple of days after birth."

Holy shit! Now I really feel like I can't breathe and may pass out. I must have missed something *major* in the infant exam, some congenital anomaly passed down through Ron's genes, possibly an inherited heart anomaly that caused the other two girls' deaths as well—and I didn't pick it up! My head is spinning with all the potential chromosomal fuck-ups and syndromes. *I must have missed it, and now the baby is dead!*

The big cop with the belly bulging over his belt comes over to me and says, with disgust, that since I was the "doctor" in attendance, I need to go to the hospital morgue to identify the baby for the death certificate. I try to compose myself while driving to the morgue. I have never even seen a dead baby, let alone one I held in my hands less than twenty-four hours ago! This is terrible; I don't know what to expect. My head is pounding.

When I see the baby, I know that it is definitely Barbara's child. She looks exactly the same, except now she is a dark purple and mottled. I can't help it; she looks so sweet and alone that I pick her up and hold her close to me, as though somehow I can return warmth to her cold body. I see two nurses elbow each other.

The morgue physician says, "Um, yes, well, thank you very much." He takes the baby from me and replaces her on the table.

I realize that I am about to break down in a major way, I can hear white noise in my head. I turn and start heading for the front door.

Out of the corner of my eye, I see an efficient nurse marching briskly in my direction. Oh god, now what? I hope that if maybe I don't look directly at her, she might go away. No such luck; she is definitely after me.

I think, *Mother have mercy! If this woman tells me that the reason this baby is dead is because she was born at home, I'm going to lose it entirely, and it's not going to be pretty.*

Instead, the older woman touches me gently on the shoulder and steers me into her office. She introduces herself as Mrs. So-and-So, head emergency room nurse.

I sag into the chair, feeling suddenly exhausted beyond repair. I think, *God, I hate hospitals.*

Then the nurse says the most astounding thing: "You're thinking you missed something in the infant exam and that's why it died, aren't you?"

My eyes well up with tears.

She says sweetly, "This always happens to health-care

providers. The guilt is tremendous. Everyone is understandably concerned for the family, but no one takes into consideration the emotional drain on the attendant involved. I, for one, am absolutely certain you did everything in your capacity to ensure that that baby was healthy and safe."

I lean my forehead on the edge of her desk and shake with silent sobs. I've never felt more wrung out in my entire life. She stands next to me, lightly rubbing my back, communicating her concern through her fingertips, giving me her strength. What a wise and knowing woman. I am grateful to her beyond words. I keep her wisdom with me for a long time afterward.

The funeral for the baby is a couple of days later. The coroner's preliminary autopsy report will be available at five o'clock this evening. Susie and I ride through the cemetery with Ron and Barbara. Ron is driving his canary-yellow Cadillac, and Susie and I sit in the back. I try to reach out to Barbara in her pain, but she is stiff and unresponsive. I look at Susie, questioningly. She frowns. It is a sad and silent ride.

When we get to the gravesite, there is a tiny white casket and all the other church members. Susie and I are the only ones who have brought flowers; we put them on the little casket. Barbara tries to reach out and touch the casket to say a last good-bye to her daughter, but her people prevent her. They say that the baby is with Jesus now, and that she is happy because Jesus has chosen her and called her back.

At some point, this event begins to take on a sinister tone for me—the lack of tears and normal grieving; the almost festive atmosphere of celebration now that the baby is hanging with Jesus.

I whisper to Susie, "Hm-m, what is wrong with this picture?" She says, "Right. This is downright creepy."

In the evening, Susie and I wait in the office for the coroner to call us with his report. I look at her affectionately; we've been through the wringer, I can tell. We are both wearing our stressed-to-the-max symptoms—Susie's face has broken out, and I am sporting a humungous new herpes sore on my bottom lip.

A little after 5:00, the phone rings; it is the coroner.

He asks me bluntly, "Did you girls do a forceps delivery on that baby?"

I am stunned. "Excuse me?"

He continues, "That baby died from a massive, 50cc subarachnoid hemorrhage, from a major blow to the brain."

I can't speak. Susie can tell by my face that something is not right; she is mouthing, "What? *What?*"

He asks again, "Are you sure you didn't do an instrument delivery?"

I finally find my voice. "No ... *no!* That baby slid out slick as a bar of soap!"

"Yeah?" he growls. "Well, that baby suffered massive trauma to the brain."

"Hey, wait a minute!" I am almost shouting now. "I've already talked to you about this before. This is the third time that this has come up in this guy's history. How do you explain that?"

"That's anecdotal information, sorry. We don't have a forensic pathologist here, so this is going down on record as cerebral hemorrhaging resulting from birth trauma."

"But listen to me—that's impossible! That was a straightforward, spontaneous vaginal delivery, with hardly any crowning. This can't be a birth injury!"

He concludes, "Yuh, well, that's what we got here. The final lab results will be in in six weeks. Maybe they'll be more conclusive, but I doubt it." He hangs up.

I turn to my partner. "Brace yourself, Sue Bee. You're not going to like this."

I tell her what the coroner has just said.

"Oh, for chrissake! That's ridiculous! If babies could die from births like that, the whole human race would have been wiped out in the first two generations! The entire species would never have survived its own debut. Birth trauma, my ass. It just doesn't happen that easily."

"OK, look, they're saying that this baby died from a massive blow to the brain, and we're saying the baby was born without a Come-along, so how could a baby sustain an injury like that?"

"I don't know. It's impossible."

"Well, what do you think happened?"

"Oh god ... *holy shit!*"

"Right. The third time."

Six weeks later, the final autopsy report is in. It goes down on our record as a neonatal mortality due to birth trauma. It is the *only* mortality we ever have in all our years of practice. I still don't know what happened, but even after all these years, I feel sorrow remembering the perfectly beautiful little girl I held close to me. It is a lesson for me in the incredible capriciousness of life.

Barbara calls us a year later and is ecstatic that she is pregnant again. She wants us to assist her again at home. I tell her that a prior unexplained newborn death is a contraindication for a home birth. I say that I'd be more than happy to go with her to the hospital to run interference and to make sure her experience is positive and safe.

She refuses. She says that now she'll be forced to deliver with only her church members. I put her in touch with Stussy, a midwife friend of mine who has the reputation of being somewhat of a renegade and who definitely goes by her own rules. I love Stussy; as wild as she is, she is very skilled. I know she won't turn Barbara away.

I call and tell Stussy the whole story.

When Barbara gives birth to her second child, Stussy moves in and stays with the family for three weeks, bless her heart.

This baby survives.

We will never know.

In the late summer of 1982, Ken and I start construction on our new house. We have finally found the right piece of land after looking for years. I have stumbled upon a long narrow strip of land at the top of Dimond Hill in Hopkinton; just minutes away from Merrimack Valley Hospital, so Ken won't have a long commuting time. The land is overgrown farmland. It is two fields surrounded by old stone walls and a wood lot. It is a tangle of wild flowers and native raspberries and blackberries and has a small stream.

I track down the elderly owner through the town tax maps. He is delighted that we love this rambling piece of land. He has loved it, too, but none of his family is interested in living in the country. He gives us a very fair deal. We put in a long gravel driveway, and Ken names our land "Longmeadow Farm."

We have been fantasizing and designing our home for some time. We have a whole folder full of clippings and pictures and ideas that we admire. The result is that we design a passive solar home, with a glass solarium oriented due solar south, to take full advantage of the sun in the bitter New Hampshire winters. The house is not a contemporary as much as an interesting traditional New Englander.

We find a father-and-son team to do the construction. We like them immediately and trust them implicitly. Many people describe their experience with house construction as a nightmare, but our builders are knowledgeable and respectful. They deliver our project in nine months.

Susie gives me a three-month "maternity leave," so I can paint and paper the entire interior myself. I love building. This is a great experience, although in retrospect, I'm sure I drove the builders crazy.

Ken designs his dream kitchen, as he does most of the cooking.

He takes pieces of scrap wood and mocks up the kitchen to see how traffic will flow. He invents a rollaway island for entertaining and installs an enormous, black, Garland restaurant gas range. This is his pride and joy; he loves to tell visitors that the door of the oven can support 150 pounds. Why this is a selling point, I will never know.

The kitchen is built of red oak, and the windows overlook the back field and the vegetable and medicinal herb gardens. I paint the exterior of the house a color I have made to match my favorite shorts. It is a light plum color, but Ken thinks it is gray, so that's good. We name it "compromise." We restore the fields to pasture land and plant perennial flower gardens and fruit trees. We create a beautiful haven, protected against the stresses of the outside world. Longmeadow Farm is a sanctuary for wildlife, too, including deer, wild turkeys, coyotes, and pileated woodpeckers. My brother's children will be born here.

In the fall of '82, I go to Boulder, Colorado, to join the founding mothers of the Midwives Alliance of North America (MANA) and twenty other midwives for our first business meeting. We hammer out the bylaws and articles of incorporation for MANA—in essence, creating the structure of the organization. Committees are formed, and the first officers are drafted.

A licensed midwife from the state of Washington, Teddy Charvet, is volunteered as president because of her impressive organizational skills. She has been instrumental in putting together the Seattle Midwifery School.

Ina May Gaskin, practicing midwife from Summertown, Tennessee, is vice president; she is well known for her grassroots following and her folksy wisdom; plus, she has celebrity status.

A certified nurse-midwife from California, Susan Leibel-Finkle, who is a former board member of the American College of Nurse Midwives (ACNM), is secretary and will keep us disciplined and on task. (She is the midwife who recruited me in Utah.)

I am officially appointed to remain as treasurer, as I have made a concerted effort to actually keep the books. I am also shanghaied to coordinate MANA's first national conference in Milwaukee, Wisconsin, for the following fall.

The Colorado midwives host the work meeting. They have rented an antique and historic Boulder building. They keep a white candle burning on the mantel the entire time, its bright flame being symbolic of the clarity and purity of the work we are doing. I am euphoric, being with all these strong-willed and intelligent women. We get a tremendous amount of work accomplished. MANA is drawing midwives from out of the woodwork and out of the hills to come together to create a professional organization woven of all of our collective needs and desires.

~ Philosophy of MANA ~
We believe that cooperation and strength among midwives will assure the future of midwifery as an established profession, thereby improving the quality of health care for women and their families. Midwives provide comprehensive care and education for women and their families, encompassing their physical and emotional needs and fostering their self-determination.

I sleep on the floor of the mansion in a sleeping bag, with Dorothea Lang as my roommate. I can never picture Dorothea sleeping on the floor, but she does. This shows how great is her belief and commitment to this upstart organization. Dorothea is an ex-president of the ACNM and is currently the North American representative for the International Confederation of Midwives (ICM), headquartered in London.

Dorothea looks like an aging Marilyn Monroe. Her blonde hair is never mussed, her makeup is always perfect. We secretly wonder just how old Dorothea really is; like Dick Clark, she is ageless. She is a permanent fixture on the scene, and she never seems to change. She is always there to gently guide us with her unfailing enthusiasm and vision.

On the last night, I am in a teepee in the mountains with several of the Colorado midwives. They teach me many songs, including *Sisters on a Journey*, which becomes MANA's anthem. This is sung at the closing ceremonies of all future annual conventions:

> *We are sisters on a journey,*
> *Singing now as one.*
> *Remembering the Ancient Ones,*
> *The women and the wisdom,*
> *The women and the wisdom.*
> *We are sisters on a journey,*
> *Shining in the sun.*
> *Shining through the darkest night,*
> *The healing has begun, begun,*
> *The healing has begun.*

~)(~

Mrs. McTavish's Normal Birth

As I have said, a vast majority of births are straightforward and uneventful, although all births are remarkable and a mystery. Some births just remain in sharper focus, due in large part to the memorable women themselves, their personalities, their foibles, and their strengths.

One such woman is Lenore McTavish. I believe I recall her story so fondly because she is a transplanted Brooklyn rendition of Bette Midler; in short, she is a wonderful nut. Lenore McTavish contacts me to assist her with her second pregnancy, as her first birth in the hospital had been a nightmare.

She tells me that she and her husband are "wild things"

somewhat, they conceived their first child, standing up in a gas station restroom, while hitchhiking across country. Even though the child is obviously a surprise, they are delighted and plan their birth with an obstetrician and hospital in Manchester. When Lenore arrives at the hospital in good labor, their obstetrician listens to her belly for quite some time with a fetal monitor, trying in vain to locate a fetal heartbeat. After several more attempts at repositioning and still no familiar rapid beat, the physician tells them that, unfortunately, their baby is dead.

Lenore and her husband are devastated. Lenore spends the next eighteen hours laboring in desperation with what she believes is a fetal demise. In engulfing sorrow and grief, she brings forth her little one who proceeds to wail lustily at birth. Their gas-station–begotten son, Trevor, is very much alive.

The physician looks perplexed and upon investigation, it is discovered that the fetal monitor he was using is defective. He had not attempted to auscultate with any other means. The man does not apologize to the McTavishes for the disaster, nor does he mention it again. The McTavishes are understandably furious with this lack of caring, and they use a lot of choice, spicy, X-rated language to describe their experience. I'm surprised the obstetrician didn't spontaneously combust.

Their rationale for choosing a birth at home with their second child is obvious. Lenore goes into labor a couple of weeks before her due date. When I get to the McTavish home in Goffstown in the middle of the night, little gas-station Trevor is awake. Milan takes him aside to read to him. Their house is ship-lapped wood inside and cozy, with a wood stove and quilts and the stained glass windows that Lenore makes.

It is my usual practice to listen for the baby's heartbeat with my regular old Littmann stethoscope, because this gives me much more information, including the baby's position, as Dr. Brown taught me. I usually only resort to using my handheld

Doppler ultrasound when the positioning is awkward and the pulse hard to locate, as in squatting for second stage.

But in Lenore's case, I use the Doppler exclusively, as it comforts her to hear her baby's steady rhythm throughout the entire process. Her baby is posterior; I can tell by the way Lenore is behaving and fussing about pain in her back. I'm not surprised when she chooses to deliver on her hands and knees. This position is the best for getting the baby to rotate properly. It takes a bit getting used to, as now all the hand maneuvers are reversed—that is, the perineum is now above and the clitoris is below. A little dyslexia comes in handy.

The way the baby's head looks when it is born in this position always cracks me up. It is hanging in midair, with its fat little cheeks and squished sweet face looking up at the ceiling, squinting, waiting, biding its time, frozen in space until it slides free into this world.

I make it a point to do the newborn exam right there on the bed. I explain what I am looking for as I go along, so everyone can participate. Milan and Trevor are playing with newborn Seamus's grip reflex, getting him to wrap his tiny fingers around theirs. I notice that Seamus still has copious clumps of thick white vernix on his skin, as he is a bit early. I secretly steal some of it and rub it under my eyes. This is a superstition I have. I figure if the vernix can prevent a baby from getting wrinkled during nine months submerged in water, then it can certainly prevent me from developing any more crow's feet around my eyes. It's worth a try. Milan informs me it doesn't help, but I think I have stumbled upon the world's first beauty secret.

The McTavishes are pleased, shown by a duel sigh of relief. This is the way birth should be, they say. They settle down to raise their two boys.

Milan is growing up. He is thoughtful and funny and is the apple of his second-grade teacher's eye. Sometimes his teacher "borrows" Milan for an afternoon when I am away at births, just to spend time with him. When Milan is seven, he is interviewed for our local paper, the *Concord Monitor,* as the kid who should be in the Guinness Book of World Records for seeing the most births. I am not present for the interview, which I later learn goes in part as follows:

Reporter: Have you ever pulled a baby out?
Milan: Me? No. I used to hold the flashlight. Now I wash the kits. There's these scissors and these tweezer things and a bulb syringe.
Reporter: And your mom pulls it out?
Milan: Correct; she catches it sometimes.
Reporter: Do the mothers make a lot of noise?
Milan: Some. Mostly they scream or cry; that's about it.
Reporter: How do you think a woman feels when she's having her baby?
Milan: I think she feels happy that she's having her baby.
Reporter: Do you think that small babies are people?
Milan: Yes, because when it's all calmed down and in its blanket, my mother's talking to it, like how she does because it's so cute or something, and the baby's lying there, and it's trying to talk.
Reporter: How can you tell?
Milan: Because it makes like a cooing noise.
Reporter: What's it trying to say?
Milan: I don't know; it's just trying to talk. It wants to talk to my mother.
Reporter: Could you compare watching a birth with watching TV?
Milan: Watching TV is definitely more fun. There's more exciting stuff. Mostly at births, there's no place to sit, practically. If

there's a lot of people there, I look for a seat all over the place. At home when I watch TV, I get a whole bed to lie in.

Reporter: What do you like most about going to a birth?

Milan: M-m-m-m, at the end I love it. The celebration, all the nice ladies who are there, the friends—that's the best part.

Reporter: What do you like the least about it?

Milan: I get bored a lot. Sometimes I don't want to watch it, and sometimes the woman doesn't want kids watching. They send us downstairs.

Reporter: Why do you think your mom takes you along?

Milan: I guess she wants people to meet me.

Reporter: Why would she want that?

Milan: Don't ask me. Likes me too much.

Reporter: Your mom likes you too much?

Milan: Yeah, and there's another reason. She can't find a baby-sitter for that long.

Reporter: Have all the four hundred births you've seen looked the same?

Milan: No.

Reporter: How many births do you think you're going to see?

Milan: About eight thousand, maybe—eight or thirty-five.

Reporter: Do you ever tell your friends about seeing the births?

Milan: No, they might get grossed out or something.

Reporter: But you don't mind? You'd like to see all of them?

Milan: Yes.

Reporter: Just for the celebration?

Milan: And for the people who are there. They do stuff with me; they give me candy.

Reporter: Would you like to be a midwife?

Milan: No, I'm being a dentist. I never heard of a boy midwife.

Reporter: Do you think you know everything about birth?

Milan: No, but my mother does.

CHAPTER NINE

LION'S HEART, 1983

The babies are being born fast and furious. More often than not, Susie and I are tripping over toddlers playing with stack of toys in our waiting room, conducting the prenatal clinic by day, and sitting sleepless at someone's bedside by night. The babies are all good, and some have crazy names—heavy on the Z names, for some reason. Some of the more creative nomen—all for our New Hampshire babies—are:

Acacia Alice, Aja May, Al-Debaran Eagle, Alaya Morning, Amaziah, Auralee Bliss, Autumn Snowflake, Bevin, Bobbie Vinton, Brook Trout, Cabrie, Calista, Carmel, Chandra, Chane, Colter, Crystal Gale, Daigen, Dakota, Danica Dawn, Dawn Shizuka, Deo Donne', Doran Zeb, Elvera, Flora, Fritha, Gemini, Graziella, Hyacinthe, Jada Rae, Jaimal, Jamaica, Jeb, Jehiah, J.W. (doesn't stand for anything else), Kachina, Kamika, Karisma, Kasen, Kierra, Kindreth, Krishna, Larkum, Laveda, Le Fay, Liara, Lightner, Love Sprout, Luna, Paxton, Petrova, Makiah, Maori, Marzieh, Mehra, Meir, Missy Mae Peace, Mylan (inspired by my son), Nataya, Navarra, Onnie Blue, Sadie Sunshine, Saira, Shalom, Shamshi, Shayman, Shonas Maize, Shoshana, Shulamit, Sierra Dawn (born at the Epsom traffic circle), Sihaya, Sonshine,

Sophia Solaria, Sumner Danae, Talia Kae, Tatum, Tesha, Tulsi Darcey, Ursli, Wilder, Willow, Winter, Yarrow Deva, Zacharia, Zebediah, Zelinda, Zephaniel, Zeth, Zoey, Zuleika, and Zurich.

Whatever potential future insecurities these names may engender, the children all seem to be very confident and well-adjusted. We attribute this to the fact that they have never been apart from their mothers since birth and, therefore, have never suffered separation anxiety.

A SIDS BABY

There is an insidious and disturbing tendency to place some of the blame for victims of sudden infant death syndrome (SIDS) on the mother, subtly implying a lack of vigilant care or some other horrific accusation. This is a tragic mistake that creates a burden much too heavy for the mothers to bear. This attitude stems from gross ignorance and must stop. I'm sure the mothers punish themselves in ways too numerous to know, without the added insult of whispered accusations regarding their parenting skills. The focus, instead, should be on helping the mothers to heal from their grief so they can become whole again.

Koyo Lennon is a beautiful Japanese woman, newly married to an American serviceman. She speaks almost no English. She has left her family in Japan to birth her baby in the U.S. How she got to me, I haven't a clue, but there she is, walking up the walk to my front door in a snowstorm. The only Japanese word I know is "arigato," which means "thank you," which I say to her when we are introduced and it makes her laugh. She is willowy and slender and appears to be far less pregnant than the seven months she claims to be.

It is with some concern that I learn that she has been practicing the Japanese custom of belly binding. The binder is cinched so tightly around her abdomen that I am worried that it may have inhibited the proper growth of the baby. This also makes her laugh. When she unwinds her belly band, there is a very healthy, normal-size baby residing in her deceivingly tiny body. She says it is tradition that her family practices belly binding during their pregnancies, as her ancestors did. They believe it keeps the baby in the proper position for birth. I find this fascinating. Her baby is obviously thriving, so I ask her to show me the technique for future reference.

One word that I think of to describe Koyo is "inscrutable"; she also is classically unmovable and silent. She births her baby with hardly a grimace. I guess the belly band works, because Koyo elegantly delivers an eight-pound-girl—head first, without a snag, and with a thicket of incredibly lustrous black hair— which seems nearly impossible from her slender frame. The baby appears almost as big as her mother.

I had been concerned that Koyo might be too small to deliver, but she brings the babe in with such ease that this time when I say "arigato" to her, I mean it.

A month later, they come to see me for Koyo's four-week postpartum checkup. They are also going to take their baby, Shizuka, to her pediatrician for her DPT [Diphtheria-Pertussis-Tetanus] immunization. The new family seems fine and in good spirits. When they ask me to recommend a good restaurant to dine in after Shizuka's shots, I tell them the name of my favorite local health-food eatery.

Within twenty-four hours, however, they find Shizuka convulsing on her futon cot. I get the frantic, bereaved phone call that every midwife dreads. I drive to them immediately. They tell me that they had actually discovered their daughter in the midst of the episode, convulsing and turning blue, but by the time the paramedics arrived, it was too late. A horrible, horrible ordeal.

Several days later, at Shizuka's funeral service, Koyo is very agitated and upset. Koyo is a strict macrobiotic vegetarian and studies under a famous macrobiotic proponent who now resides in the Boston area. Apparently, her macrobiotic guru has told her that the crepe she ate at my local restaurant contained an egg, and when Koyo breast-fed her daughter, the egg killed her. The man is placing the blame on this vulnerable mother; I find this to be the most unforgivable, outrageous thing I have ever heard. Shame on that chain-smoking, judgmental twit!

Koyo is beside herself with guilt and remorse, and no amount of reasoning can relieve it. She has no family members here to fall back on for support—or even to speak her own language.

Shizuka's body is laid out by the undertaker before the service. When Koyo sees her, she begins squeezing and molding her daughter's cheeks to resemble the way she remembers them. Speaking in Japanese, she says, "This is not right. This is not how she looks."

Frantically, she begins to yank the stuffing out of Shizuka's mouth, trying to restore her face to what she knows. I cover her hands gently with mine and shake my head sadly. Koyo envelops her daughter's body with her own and weeps from the depths of her soul. I know her heart is breaking.

Months later, Koyo and her husband visit me and bring me the book *DPT: A Shot in the Dark,* which correlates the increase in SIDS-related mortalities—about six per one thousand live births—and the DPT immunizations that are all but mandatory and are certainly considered the standard of care. The book claims that the strength of the pertussis (whooping cough) part of the DPT vaccine is hard to regulate in the laboratory, sometimes resulting in pertussis bacteria levels of a lethally toxic dosage. Many parents who have lost children to SIDS have tracked the performance of this vaccine. They have found that an unusually high number of children die from SIDS within twenty-four to forty-eight hours after their immunizations.

The parents bring this to the attention of the U.S. Congress, but the pharmaceutical companies refuse to cooperate and block an investigation of adverse reactions and long-term damage.

They claim it is "hysteria"; in response, the SIDS parents publish this impressive book to alert the public to the possibility of vaccine-damaged children.

Koyo and her man are convinced that this, indeed, is the culprit in their case. I am just thankful that Koyo feels exonerated, whatever it takes.

Two years later, they call me from Colorado to say they have just given birth to a baby boy. There has been a terrible snowstorm that has blocked the passes, and their midwives were unable to make it in time. Koyo's husband catches the baby, and it is breech! This is frightful, but the baby is born easily, and he is beautiful and healthy.

At the end of our conversation, Koyo tells me, in halting English, that for this pregnancy, she did not bind her belly.

MANA's 1983 spring board meeting is held at the swank Biltmore Hotel in Los Angeles, again during the ACNM's annual convention. We have a posh executive suite, but Ina May and I are delegated to sleep on the floor. We listen to the police kicking the bums out of the park across the street all night. There are a lot of nurse-midwives, who first were apprentice-trained midwives, packed in our suite. They call themselves the "Bridge Club." They are helping us flesh out MANA's goals and philosophy. It is five long days of listening to articulate and intelligent women discuss language and intent. We all work tremendously well together, and MANA's long-range goals are finished by the end of the meeting.

At one point, one of the old-guard nurse-midwives from the board of directors of the ACNM, a woman named Cat, comes to call on us. She pretty much throws down the gauntlet. She implies that she feels MANA is an upstart fledgling organization that will not survive its infancy.

Cat says, "Let me remind you that MANA was conceived in the bosom of the American College of Nurse Midwives."

I think wryly, *So that's what they're teaching these nurse-midwives? That conception happens in the bosom? We have a serious problem here.*

I am feeling feisty this day. Instead, I shoot back, "Well, then, Cat, I think we may have to nurse a little while longer, at least until we are safely into toddlerhood."

She winces. I think she wishes we will just go away.

On the last morning of the meeting, I am sitting on a couch with the working group, feeling pleasantly exhausted from thinking so much. I am staring at a potted philodendron plant on the fireplace mantle. I watch as it slowly begins to slide down the mantle, which is listing to the right.

I confess, I have been schmoozing and partying with my new midwife friends and colleagues. My first thought is *Yikes, this is one humdinger of a hangover.*

It is when the plant slides all the way off the mantle and hits the floor that my compatriots jump up, shouting, "Earthquake!"

My mouth drops open in unbelieving surprise. I am from the East Coast, so I have never encountered this. I decide that I don't like it one bit.

The veteran Californians have us all cram together in a doorway for protection. This seems like a pretty measly and pathetic defense, if you ask me. We are on the eleventh floor, and I can still definitely feel the earth's tectonic plates shift under my feet. This leaves me feeling very disoriented and unstable.

I begin to get that familiar, hyperventilation, anxiety-triggered dry mouth and numb lips, reminiscent of the old, bad drug days of the sixties. I know we are doing earthshaking work, but this is ridiculous. It is time to go home where the terra is firma.

On my way to the L.A. airport, outside the hotel on the hot

sidewalk, I find the biggest dead cockroach I have ever seen. I later learn that this is actually a palmetto bug, but I am a country girl and this looks like the most unbelievably huge cockroach in the world—at least two inches long. I pick it up and wrap it in a napkin to show Ken, because he says I always exaggerate. I want to prove to him the size of this giant cucaracha.

Ken picks me up at the airport in Boston and takes me to dinner at a very upscale restaurant, Lillie's, in Haymarket Square. I am really happy to see him and spend the time excitedly filling him in on all the work MANA is doing and all the gossip. I forget all about my specimen until the end of the meal.

When I remember the insect, I secretly unwrap it and push it under the side of Ken's plate when he's not looking. I feign innocence.

There is silence for a moment, then Ken says, deadpan, "That's very impressive, sweetie, but look …."

I look at him and see that he is trying to suppress a smile, but his eyes are dancing.

I look down at the cockroach and to my horror, I see a mass of wriggling maggots have crawled out of the dead bug and are now inching across the table.

I scream.

First the waiter and then the manager come rushing to the table. They are very concerned and apologetic and solicitous. They offer to give us our meals for free to cover their embarrassment. Of course, at this point, I can't tell them that *I* have put the offending roach there in the first place. We graciously accept their generosity.

As we are leaving, Ken whispers, "Way to go, kid! That was a *great* trick!"

THE POPULATION OF WATERVILLE INCREASES SUBSTANTIALLY

A very cute, wholesome, and athletic couple arrange with me to assist them with their birth in the northern ski-resort town of Waterville. They are both ski instructors for the local ski area; she leads cross-country ski expeditions at the Waterville X-C Ski Center, and he teaches freestyle ballet skiing. He eventually takes his team to compete in the Winter Olympics in Japan.

They practice their maneuvers in the summer by skiing down a chute and twisting and flipping in the air before landing in a pond. They own a great old, funky country inn, the Mountain Faire Inn, that they run as a bed-and-breakfast for skiers in the winter and hikers in the White Mountains in the summer. They are charming and pretty and very physically fit.

Linda is due with her first baby in the late fall, when Ken and I like best to go hiking in the Whites. On a beautiful Indian summer day, Ken and I plan to hike up Mount Chocorua. I call Linda first to make sure she isn't getting active; it doesn't sound like much is happening. She jokingly assures me that if something does develop, her husband, Chuck, will come get me, as the mountain is close by.

Ken and I set out up the Piper Trail, which is very scenic. We make it to the summit in a little under three hours, which we think is pretty good time. The top of Chocorua is vast, bald rock that commands a spectacular 360-degree view. We are bushed and sweaty from the exertion. We find a cranny of rock out of the wind, eat our picnic lunch, and fall asleep in the warm October sun.

I am in a sound sleep when Ken wakes me by saying, "What's that funny sound?"

We can hear a rhythmic clicking sound, accompanied by bells. As it gets louder and definitely closer, I stand up and see a shirtless Chuck, effortlessly trotting up the trail with two ski poles that have bear bells on them. I shout and wave. He grins and gives me the sign that it is time to go. Ken and I pack up and start to scramble down the mountain after him. Chuck tells us it has taken him thirty minutes to get to the top. It takes Ken and me two hours longer than that just to get down.

Linda's birth is lovely. She has a couple of women friends present, who are very supportive and doting. Ken hangs back for the most part, comfortably reading a cheap murder mystery in front of the blazing fire in the inn's great room. At the actual delivery, he sits quietly on the edge of the bed next to me, in case I need a hand. His eyes are glinting amber-green, and he has a slight shy smile, so I know he is enjoying it all immensely.

Chuck and Linda have a baby snow-bunny, whose thick hair sticks straight up in the air. Very cute. When it comes time to leave, Chuck recruits Ken to help him change the sign at the entrance to town. The large sign welcoming people to Waterville has a smaller sign above it that reads "POP. 199." The two men hoist up a ladder and change the little sign with Chuck's homemade one so that it now reads:

WELCOME TO WATERVILLE ~ POP. 200

A couple of years later, this couple hires me again. Because Linda's first labor was fairly brisk, and I am concerned about my driving time, they also enlist the aid of a family friend of theirs, who is a retired general practitioner living near the ski resort, in case I don't make it in time. This turns out to be an excellent idea.

I drive like a bat out of hell to get to them in the middle of the night. When I walk into their room, Linda and Chuck are calmly lounging in bed. The GP is sitting in a chair, chatting with them. I think I have driven like a mad woman for false labor. Great. I try to still myself from the driving frenzy and am sharing a little small talk with the friendly doc.

Linda says, "Well, did you see her yet?"

Her, who? Then I look down and see the newest little snow-bunny cuddled between her two parents. A new downhill racer in the making.

This time, Chuck and the elderly doc haul out the ladder again and change the sign:

WELCOME TO WATERVILLE ~ POP. 201

⌁

Susie and I are driving home from a birth on the Seacoast very late one night. We are heading west on Route 4 when we come up behind a white Ford Pinto. The Pinto is swerving all over the road. The driver is obviously severely impaired.

I say, "Probably some party-hardies from the university."

Susie says, "Yeah, but slow down. Don't get too close behind them; they're a disaster trying to happen."

Just then the car takes a large sweeping swerve into the left lane.

"Jesus, what assholes. Wonder if we should try to flash them and get them to pull off the road or something?"

Both of our sons are still young enough that Susie and I are able to be self-righteous and judgmental. Suddenly, the car's taillights fly off the road to the right and into the woods.

"Oh, christ, now they've done it!"

We pull over and run into the woods, looking for them. The little car has flipped over on its side. We can hear bottles clanking and bodies scrambling around inside. Susie hoists me up so I can pull open the door, sideways, pushing it up in the air. When I look in, a fresh-faced, bleary-eyed, stoned kid looks up at me.

He says, "Oh, wow, are you an angel?"

Oh, shut up!

Miraculously, they are unscathed, potentially due to the amount of anesthesia they have consumed. We get them taken care of.

Susie says, "God, what a bunch of yahoos."

Obviously, she and I are blissfully unaware of the trials and tribulations of young manhood that are yet to come for both of us.

THE WORST BLEED

Every midwife dreads a bad bleed. Even though we are trained and prepared for hemorrhaging, a heavy bleed always gets our adrenaline going like no other complication. We carry the same medications and equipment that are available in a standard hospital birth. Severe hemorrhaging is very rare in a properly nourished, screened, low-risk woman, but it does happen once in a blue moon, and it is not fun. I have a midwife friend who is superstitious; she won't wear red to a birth, lest it be bad luck and "turn on the faucet."

Elizabeth comes to Concord Midwifery Service for her second baby, hoping for a vaginal birth after a cesarean section. She is upset about her previous cesarean section because she feels she was not given a fighting chance at a normal birth. It's the same old story—she was induced with Pitocin for one trumped-up reason or another, and her body was not ripe or ready to open up. Her physicians let her labor for the requisite amount of time—until they get bored waiting around and then announced she needed a section because she was in arrested labor. They did the surgery, charged her a few thousand dollars extra for it, and they were pleased with their "good outcome." Elizabeth is understandably livid; she says she feels cheated and mismanaged. She had not gotten anywhere close to full dilation.

Midwives in New Hampshire have not been given official permission by the state to attend VBACs at home yet. We arrange to see Elizabeth for her prenatal care. In labor, we will go with her to the hospital and co-manage the birth with Ken. Everything with her pregnancy is hunky-dory, so we are not particularly concerned with her history. We plan to treat her like any other woman having a baby.

Elizabeth calls a few days after her due date and says she has been contracting "on and off" for several days. Her greatest fear is getting to the hospital too early and encountering the slippery slope of intervention, with the same resulting fiasco all over again. She wants to wait until she is in good, strong labor before she goes in. I ask her to come into the office. We'll check to see if the contractions are making any cervical change, and we'll make a plan from there.

When she arrives, Susie and I are with another client. I can hear Elizabeth breathing loudly in the waiting room, huffing and puffing like an old locomotive. I say, "This sounds pretty serious!" I bring her into the other exam room.

When I check her, it is just as I suspected by her disheveled appearance—she is fully dilated and ready to go. She has spent her entire labor sitting by the phone, wondering whether or not it was the real thing. I grin and congratulate her, and I tell her I don't think we're going to make it anywhere else in time.

Elizabeth squats on the floor of our office and mightily pushes out a nine-pound baby boy. The placenta separates about ten minutes later and is born easily, without any cord traction. Her fundus feels firm and well contracted.

We get her comfortable and nursing her son, Alex, on our exam bed. Susie gives her a slice of pumpkin bread that a client has made for us. I am boiling water—for tea.

Then I hear the dreaded sound.

Oh, Blessed Mother!

I whirl around and see a torrent of blood, the kind you don't mess around with for a second. Susie and I have a code word for this and we know all too well what it means.

I say, "Geyser!"

We go into automatic action. Susie draws up the first of the oxytocic drugs, some Pitocin, and injects Elizabeth in the thigh. I try to get her uterus to contract by massaging the fundus externally through her belly wall. The red river is not to be appeased this easily, however, and it continues way beyond our comfort level. Susie gives her a second injection, some Methergine, and I begin bimanual compression. Susie checks Elizabeth's vital signs, including her pulse rate and blood pressure, which are elevating and dropping, respectively.

I slide my hand gently into Elizabeth's vagina, then close it to form a fist. I push up in the direction of the anterior fornix. At the same time, my left hand, outside on the abdominal wall, pushes down behind her uterus, pulling it forward over the symphysis pubis. Then I press my two hands together firmly, cupping and compressing the uterus between them and—I hope—the placental site. But her uterus does not contract adequately; it remains boggy. The blood loss is becoming alarming.

As I maintain pressure on the uterus, I am talking to Elizabeth quietly, trying to keep her present. Susie gives her another injection of Methergine, then starts an IV in the crook of Elizabeth's arm. An apprentice midwife calls the Concord Fire Department paramedics. We begin giving Elizabeth oxygen and an IV solution of lactated Ringer's, which is a volume expander and is used to balance electrolytes.

Elizabeth is beginning to exhibit the first signs of shock, just as the ambulance pulls into our driveway. Her blood pressure is low, her pulse is weak and thready, and she is starting to get confused about what is happening. Of course, on the short trip to the hospital, she rallies remarkably and is fairly back to normal. She is actually chipper when Ken meets us in the emergency room.

Ken does a pelvic exam and says that her uterus feels normally involuted for the time frame and that she is dry. I tell him that we have given her enough oxytocin to shrink her unit down to the size of a raisin, for godsake. He is concerned about the blood loss and suggests that he do a D&C to make sure that there are no retained placental fragments. Elizabeth refuses, saying she feels great and wants to go home to be with her baby and her man. Her blood-iron levels are checked, and it is found that she has bled significantly enough to make her very anemic. Her hemoglobin values have dropped to 7.5 grams, so she is given two units of blood before returning home to make her recovery easier.

I look at her placenta the next day, which had been put in our office refrigerator during Elizabeth's transfer. I think it looks normal to me. I examine it carefully. I don't see any abnormal looking vessels running off to the side, which could indicate a lost lobe, or any missing chunks or holes to speak of. I breathe a sigh of relief. I am grateful that everybody has been so cool and efficient and handled the emergency with aplomb.

But a month later, Elizabeth's husband calls me at home in a state of panic. He is almost shouting. He says that Elizabeth was taking a hot bath, and when she got out of the tub, blood started gushing everywhere. He sounds really shaky. I try to calm him down to get an assessment of how bad it really is. I ask him to go back into the bathroom to see what the status is.

When he comes back, he is hysterical. He yells into the phone, "It's coming out in spurts! Like with her pulse!"

Bloody Mother! This is life-threatening! Trying not to yell myself, I tell him to call the rescue squad immediately. I will meet them in the emergency room at Merrimack Valley.

A couple of my friends are the ER nurses on duty this night. I tell them what is coming in, so we are prepared and waiting.

The EMTs are white-faced when they come running in with the stretcher. I can tell by the rescue squad's expressions that they are scared shitless, which is not a good sign. When I lift up the blanket covering Elizabeth, the clots between her legs look to be about the size of six placentas.

Ancient Mother, be with us now; this woman is dying.

Elizabeth's face has a grayish pallor, her skin is cold and clammy, and she is unconscious. The ER nurses can't get a blood pressure reading, and her pulse is absent. The nurses fly into action. Somehow, they get an IV going in both arms, despite collapsed veins.

I hold Elizabeth's face between my two hands. I put my face very close to hers, and I say firmly in her ear, "Don't you leave, Elizabeth. Don't you *dare* leave like this. You come back now, do you hear me? Don't you leave like this! I'll be so pissed at you! Talk to me!" I repeat this over and over.

Elizabeth's eyes flutter and roll up. She tries to make a sound. Later, she says she could hear my voice faintly; that it sounded tinny, as if coming from a long, long tunnel. But she knew it was me, and she was struggling to come back to tell me she was OK. She didn't want me to be pissed at her.

Ken does a D&C in the operating room, and he finds the culprit. He removes a retained placental fragment, probably a cotyledon, about the size of a cherry. I am astounded this could have remained in her uterus for a full month, waiting to wreak havoc. And that something so small could have killed her! Elizabeth has lost a tremendous amount of blood. Her blood values come back exsanguinated at a 6 percent hematocrit and a hemoglobin of two grams—this is about as low as you can go without being ... well ... dead.

Elizabeth is given blood-replacement therapy until she stabilizes, and she is able to go home in a few days and feels fine. I am so grateful for Ken's gentleness and skill and for the

ER nurses' crackerjack expertise. What a blessing. What a close call.

The day after Elizabeth's admittance to the ER, the principal of Milan's school calls to tell me that Milan was rough-housing with friends on the playground. He has fallen, and his upper front tooth bit clean through his bottom lip. I need to pick him up to get his lip stitched.

On the way to the hospital, Milan tells me in no uncertain terms that he doesn't want stitches. I look at the clean, round hole piercing his bottom lip.

I say, "OK, sure, we can just put a straw through your bottom lip permanently so you won't have to bother with drinking out of a cup and leaking."

This makes him laugh. He agrees that maybe a little patch job might be a good idea.

The same crew is in the ER from the day before. We trade some chat about Elizabeth's well-being. A very nice Ear-Nose-Throat doctor comes in to stitch Milan's lip. I am calmly watching this when I begin to get prickly hot and dizzy. I feel sweaty and as limp as a rag doll. I start seeing spots. I realize I'm about to faint. I feel sick. I lean over and put my head between my legs.

My friend, Pam, the ER nurse, catches me in time and puts a cold washcloth on my neck.

She says, "Don't you *dare* pass out on me. Do you hear me? I will be so pissed at you!"

Wisenheimer. The nurses think this is hilarious. They say, "Yesterday, you come in here with a practically bled-out cadaver and you're a machine. Today, you're in here with a little kid who needs a couple of stitches and you tank. What a pussy!"

Ah, the wonders of motherhood.

In the early fall of 1983, I coordinate MANA's first national conference in Milwaukee with another midwife who lives in Wisconsin. It is an overwhelming success but not without its challenges. The most notable confrontation comes at the Open Forum, when many of the midwives attending express fear and concern about MANA's attempt to define standards of practice for all midwives. They are worried that we will be elitist or exclusionary somehow, and it will restrict their practices.

The irony of this, of course, is that this is the antithesis of what we intend, but they don't know that yet. The angriest group, by far, are the midwives from West Virginia. Do they ever have their knickers in a twist! They are madder than a bunch of wet hens.

They say, "Who the hell are you to try to tell us what to do?"

I can see that they are just sick of being overlooked and disempowered—that causes them a lot of pain. We invite them to get involved, to join the practice committee where their input will be heard and incorporated. I think a couple of these West Virginia hotheads are still on the board today. Their cranky voices have been invaluable over the years.

The keynote address is a call for midwives to reclaim the art and science of midwifery, to create a separate generation of knowledge and language by midwives, different from the medical model. It is a challenge for us to free ourselves from outside domination and oppression and for us to define who we are in such a way that we can't be dismissed. We will overcome the Burning Times of the past, and in so doing, we'll create the unity that we so richly deserve.

My fondest memory of the Milwaukee conference is meeting Elizabeth Davis for the first time. She is sitting on the edge of the indoor pool in a neon-purple bathing suit, daintily dipping her toe in the water. She is slated to be an inspirational speaker, as she wrote *Hearts and Hands: A Midwife's Guide to Pregnancy and Birth*, which is pretty much the bible for student midwives. I have been very impressed by the power and beauty of her writing.

We immediately dive into a profound, philosophical discussion about how midwifery is a way of life and is both grueling and transformative; how it works a woman on all levels, either disintegrating her and bringing her to her knees or elevating her to her essence. I am spellbound by the depth and clarity of her thinking. These passionate, enlightened conversations become the hallmark of our times together. Years later, we will write a book together, *The Women's Wheel of Life: Thirteen Archetypes of Woman at Her Fullest Power.*

I also am amazed at how unbelievably *feminine* she is—an aquamarine-eyed, blonde Barbie doll, with a razor-sharp brain. It is West Coast valley girl meets East Coast cowgirl—or, in retrospect, more appropriately, Gloria Steinem meets Bella Abzug.

SIBLINGS AT BIRTH

Kids are wonderful at births. They are always welcome and are a real and unfailing joy. We encourage the siblings to participate in their mother's pregnancy and to come to the prenatal visits so they will be comfortable with Susie and me. When kids are at the visit, I like to draw the exact position of the baby on the mom's belly with a magic marker. I consider myself a bit of an artiste; I find my renderings are quite lifelike and surprisingly accurate.

First, I palpate the belly and find the exact location of the feet. I draw two chubby legs with kicking feet, then a chubby torso with the back true to its position. The head is (I hope) down in the pelvis, with a little face looking one way or the other. I show the child that his brother or sister may have hair already, as I point to the little tufts of their mom's pubic hair that now appears to be on top of the baby's head. This always cracks them up.

I usually draw the baby sucking its thumb, because it does. Then I draw a little heart in the spot where the heartbeat is heard the loudest. I show the child how to listen to the baby's heartbeat through an empty cardboard toilet-paper tube. The secret is to lean gently on the tube with the ear and without using hands. This way, the pulse is clearly audible, and the child will know how to listen for it at home. These activities get the children involved and excited about their coming sib.

When children are prepared for birth—the sounds, the smells, the blood—they usually handle it a lot better than some adults, as they don't have any preconceived beliefs about birth; no fear, just normal curiosity. We explain to them that the blood is "good" blood that has been feeding the baby and keeping it alive; that it isn't "hurt" blood. This always seems to satisfy that question. There are some fine books available to prepare children, like *Mom and Dad and I Are Having a Baby*, with great drawings, from a child's perspective, in living color.

Because children's attention spans are so unpredictable, we always request that one adult be assigned to track the child's reaction. If that means they have to sit out the birth, then so be it. If the child is high energy or is demanding attention from his mother, then perhaps it's better to read or play with him elsewhere. Then, he can come in immediately after the birth, so the important bonding window is not missed.

Older kids often want to be helpful; they make great "go-fers" and assistants—that is, until the baby's head is visible on the perineum. Then the kids have their nosey little faces in there so close, inspecting the amount of hair—or lack thereof—on their new sib. Often, we have to gently move them aside for a little elbow room.

Kids seem to tolerate the intensity of birth just fine. Having stated that, of course, perversely, this brings to mind one child who didn't fare so well.

Sweet little Jackson had been born at home with us attending. When he is four years old, his mom, Zelda, becomes pregnant again. Zelda is a craftsperson who makes fabulously gorgeous hats of all kinds—sophisticated hats in rich velvets, bright silks, and elegant brocades, with feathers and plastic grapes, lizards, and lobsters, and junque vintage jewelry scavenged from flea markets.

Her hats are famous and are all the rage in Manhattan, so she has hired several townspeople to sew for her. I am paid completely in hats for Jackson's birth, and as I am a hat person, I think this is stunning.

When Zelda is in labor with her second child, Jackson is wonderful with her. He has gone to childbirth classes with his parents. He knows how to help his mother relax. He does light effleurage on her belly and breathes with her through contractions. I am watching carefully to see if this is inhibiting Zelda, but she seems truly comforted by his presence; his touch is genuinely light and knowing. I smile to see that Zelda's "baby" is still outlined on her belly. I must have used permanent marker.

When Zelda is in the thick of hard labor and becomes pretty vocal, Jackson's eyes widen with concern. His eyes search mine for assurance that this is normal. Susie and I smile at him and mug back and generally let him know all is well. After a particularly whopper contraction, I look at him and roll my eyes, as if to say "Wow!" I wink at him. He grins back.

Jackson is at his mother's head, holding a cool washcloth on her brow, when his brother, Mikey, is born, weighing a hefty ten pounds. Jackson is very, very happy to see his baby brother—probably more so now that his mother is no longer in pain. He has been keenly protective of her.

When the placenta is born, there isn't a bowl within reach, so I just deliver it into a handy garbage bag. I forget about it for the time being. Susie and I bustle around, tidying up. We get newborn Mikey muckled on the breast.

In all this commotion, no one is paying particular attention to Jackson. I look up and notice he looks green. I ask him if he feels sick, and he nods miserably and says, "Placenta."

Just then his little shoulders start to heave. I know he is about to lose his lunch. Without thinking, I grab the garbage bag for him to retch in. I have forgotten that the offending placenta is in there. I hold it open under his chin, he takes one look inside, and this pushes the poor little guy over the edge. When I realize what I have done, I feel so sorry for torturing him like that. Dang, what a sweet and serious little kid.

Susie says she thinks some of his reaction was a release due to the stress and responsibility he took on as head coach.

Each child is an individual, and *all* are wonders.

———

In the late fall of 1983, Susie has the great idea that we should enter a float in the competition in the Warner Fall Foliage Festival parade. She has somehow finagled the Kearsarge Reel Company to donate one of their long flatbed trailers to us for the event. The theme for our float is *The Wizard of Oz*, and a bunch of us, apprentices and our families, spend days transforming the flatbed into Oz. I want it to be called *The Sorceresses of OS*, but that doesn't fly.

We paint an Emerald City, with a yellow brick road running the length of the truck. One of our apprentices is an Amazonian Dorothy. She is perfect, with her hair in long, dark braids tied with ribbons; white knee-highs in spray-painted ruby slippers; and an innocent, flouncy, gingham-checked dress with a bib front. (Where she unearthed this little number, I will never know.) She even has a real Toto—a horrible, yappy little Yorkshire terrier someone has lent her for the day—in a picnic basket. She is the quintessential Dorothy—except she is six feet tall.

Milan is the wizard, of course; he is way into wizards at the time. His wizard is more Merlin-esque, but he looks great and wise with a long gray beard and bushy eyebrows glued on with spirit gum. He takes this role very seriously.

Susie gets to be Glinda, the good witch, which means, obviously, I am relegated to being the Wicked Witch of the West. I ask her how this happened, and she says it is typecasting. I don't argue, because it's true.

Susie has on a frothy, white ball gown and a glittery tiara and wand, rented from a local costumer. It is a size-five dress, and Susie is a size ten, so we pin the back closed with diaper pins. One little girl says to Susie, in awe, "You look beauty-full."

I have fun with my character, even though she's so blatantly stereotypical of all powerful women in myth who are depicted as "evil." Though it belittles my religion, I do the expected frightening look, with peaked, conical hat; long, black, scraggly hair; long fingernails; standard warty nose; and great, striped stockings with cowboy boots. After three layers of black eyeliner, the effect is intimidating.

I practice my one line: "I'll get you, my little pretty!"

We invite all the little kids from the Warner area who have been born at home to ride on the float with us as Munchkins. On the day of the parade, the children arrive in varying degrees of darling Munchkin-ness. We give them all large cardboard swirled "lollipops" to carry as a souvenir. The kids turn out in droves. It is a raw, blustery day, and all the Munchkins are shivering. Some organized parents have the foresight to bring huge thermoses of hot chocolate for the residents of Lollipop Land, so everyone remains happy and excited about being in a parade.

There are about fifty kids on the float with us, all waving and licking their "lollipops." When we hit Main Street, the Munchkins throw out balloons to the crowd that read "*Concord Midwifery Service, For A Special Delivery.*" Below the float, people are scrambling for the balloons.

As we pass the judges stand, the master of ceremonies reads over the loudspeaker the banner that is printed on the side of our float:

"THERE'S NO PLACE LIKE HOME!"

We win first prize.

CHAPTER TEN

LION'S HEART, 1984

The state of New Hampshire kindly does a survey of the families who opt for home births, and they publish their findings in 1984. I believe they are half expecting to find that most people who choose an out-of-hospital birth will be the lunatic fringe, but instead, to their surprise, they find quite the opposite. The profile of a typical woman having a baby at home is a twenty-seven-year-old with two and a half years of college. She is in the middle-income bracket, and about 80 percent of these women have taken childbirth preparation classes. She will deliver a child that weighs eight and a half pounds, about a pound larger than the national average. The average fee for a home birth with a midwife attending is six hundred dollars (and a good barter is always acceptable.)

A NUCHAL CORD

Nucha means "nape of the neck." A nuchal cord is when the umbilical cord is coiled around the baby's neck at birth. The cord being around the neck is rarely a complication. The cord *is* around the neck about a quarter of the time, and it's fine—it's normal. It is not an emergency situation. Because the cord itself is usually more than two feet long, the baby can slide out without removing it and still not get hung up. The baby's neck actually protects the cord from being compressed during delivery; it just ends up there as a result of intrauterine fetal movements.

After the baby's head is born and I gently wipe the face, I check to see if the cord is around the neck. If I can feel one or more coils, then I draw out a loose loop of cord, which usually slips easily over the baby's head. Then the baby's body should slide free with the next contraction. It is extremely rare that the cord will be so tightly applied to the neck as to cause a problem. I can count on one hand the times a nuchal cord was of any consequence, and a couple of times I sensed it in advance.

One night, I am on the phone chatting with a good girlfriend, when the answering service interrupts the conversation and patches through a call from an anxious father, who asks me to hurry to Manchester. Previously, his wife had a precipitous labor, and he caught the baby before I arrived. This night, his wife wakes up and immediately feels "pushy."

I throw on a Japanese kimono, step into some flip-flops, and run out the door. I drive above the speed limit to get there, thankful that my plates read MIDWYF, which usually prevents me from getting stopped.

When I arrive, Linda is on couch cushions that she has piled in a nest on the living room floor. She is straining, the head is just barely becoming visible.

Her husband says with a relieved smile, "Well, this time the baby waited for you to get here."

I turn and look at him. "Oh?"

Just the way he says those words alerts my antennae. I watch Linda push. I think, *This really is different from the last time.* Something is going on; I get my equipment laid out within easy reach. I squat on my haunches, waiting.

The heartbeat is steady and fine. There are no other

indicators that anything is amiss, except for that one statement from the dad. I don't know what is coming exactly, but I am ready for anything. When the head is born, there are several loops of cord—the tightest I have ever felt. I can't budge the noose even a millimeter. It truly is a stranglehold. The baby's face starts to get suffused and dark. Because I already have the two hemostats and scissors in my hands, within seconds I clamp the cord in the vagina and cut between the hemostats—and the baby is free. She is fine, Apgar 9.

The father says in a quiet voice, "Man, I'm sure glad you were here to do that."

I say, "You knew, didn't you?"

He asks, "Knew what?"

"You knew that your daughter was waiting because she was going to need help."

"What? I don't know what you're talking about."

I don't elaborate.

"You and this baby are very, very connected. Trust me; you two are more connected than you will ever know."

—

The Midwifery Advisory Committee to the Director of Public Health has been meeting weekly and working diligently to develop the rules and regulations for midwifery practice. We are finally finished and are satisfied with the final draft, which is now sent to the Joint Legislative Committee on Administrative Rules—the last step before being implemented and becoming law. The draft has been sent to health-care professionals for review, and this hearing is the last chance for input from others.

There are three criticism and recommendations from physicians who have opposing points of view. They feel that as midwives, we should not be allowed to carry medications such as oxytocin to prevent hemorrhage, that we should be required to have signed physician backup, and that we should carry mandatory malpractice insurance. The last two points being a virtual impossibility for a majority of midwives practicing in New Hampshire.

Most physicians will not engage in a formal backup arrangement with midwives. Even though they may be friendly and work together informally, physicians fear *their* malpractice insurance costs will rise due to increased exposure to liability. At this point, malpractice insurance is unavailable to independent midwives, except at a rate so ridiculously exorbitant that it is approximately triple a midwife's annual income. To be made to practice without the benefit of oxytocin for third-stage hemorrhage is not only absurd and without any sound rationale, it is also irresponsible and potentially dangerous.

In short, all of this is a poorly disguised attempt, at the last hour, to regulate midwives out of existence by legislating requirements that are unattainable.

We are told that these three conditions are a fait accompli. The midwives are grieving, for they believe they hear their death knell. The New Hampshire Midwives Association meets the night before the hearing to prepare our testimony. I am hoping we can turn this attitude of hopelessness and despair around.

The midwives end up making an amulet for me to wear while speaking to the committee. It is filled with a token from each midwife, for protection and justice and equality for our profession. Several of the midwives bring garlic to ward off ill intentions. Another contributes a paper eye, cut from a magazine to represent the "eye of justice." Others bring herbs, such as sage for wisdom and clarity. We infuse this amulet with our strengths and our dedication to the health and well-being of our mothers and babies.

The next morning, I sit in the hearing with the bulging

amulet tucked in my bra under my best white Lord & Taylor silk blouse. Unfortunately, as the charm warms up from my body heat, it starts reeking of garlic. I begin to smell like an Italian restaurant.

Many of the same old duffers who heard the original arguments for and against midwifery several years ago are on the committee. Eugene Daniell is still here, bless his Yankee soul. He reads the three recommendations from the medical society.

He stands to speak, but he turns to me. He asks simply, "Is this what you girls really want?"

I answer, "God, no!"

He says, "Yuh, didn't think so. The original rules and regulations, as drafted by the advisory committee, look fine to me without this added rigmarole. If it ain't broke, don't fix it, I always say. I move that these regulations be adopted as is."

The other committee members nod in agreement and that is the end of that—meeting adjourned, done deal.

As we are leaving, I thank him for his foresight once again. He invites me to lunch in the State House cafeteria.

He says, "I don't know what's come over me. I'm famished! How about a pizza?"

This year, MANA's spring board meeting is in Philadelphia. The main focus is on MANA's membership bid in the International Confederation of Midwives (ICM), which works with the World Health Organization in developing international maternal/infant health-care policies. Dorothea Lang has been pushing us hard in this direction for some time now. She insists that it is imperative that we have a voice equal to the ACNM in representing midwifery in North America to the international community. MANA must protect and honor the various traditions of midwifery and bring credibility and recognition to indigenous midwives in the United States, Canada, and Mexico.

This means that MANA has to adopt the International Definition of Midwifery. This is a controversial topic and is hotly debated, but it is passed.

The International Definition of Midwifery

A midwife is a person who, having been regularly admitted to a midwifery education program fully recognized in the country in which it is located, has successfully completed the prescribed course of studies in midwifery and has acquired the requisite qualifications to be registered and/or legally licensed to practice midwifery.

The midwife must be able to give the necessary supervision, care, and advice to women during pregnancy, labor, and postpartum periods; to conduct deliveries on her own responsibility; and to care for the newborn and the infant. This care includes preventive measures, the detection of abnormal conditions in mother and child, the procurement of medical assistance, and the execution of emergency measures in the absence of medical help.

The midwife has an important task in counseling and education—not only for patients/clients but within the family and the community. The work should involve antenatal education and preparation for parenthood and extends to certain areas of gynecology, family planning, and child care.

The midwife may practice in hospitals, clinics, health units, domiciliary conditions, or any other service.

~ International Confederation of Midwives, 1972

I consider myself to be an indigenous midwife, as I am a product of my environment and my community, *and* I am legally recognized to practice midwifery in my state. I am elected chairwoman of the international section of the ICM, and Teddy Charvet and I are to go to Sydney, Australia, in the fall to bring MANA's membership bid to the floor of the World Congress for a vote.

A SENSUAL BIRTH

Dr. Michel Odent is a French physician and surgeon who practices in a state hospital in the small town of Pithiviers in northern France. As head of the Pithiviers Maternity Unit for twenty years, he is a pioneer in active, natural childbirth practices and has created a minor revolution in modern obstetrics. His book, *Birth Reborn*, is published in 1984; in it, he champions the use of midwives and very little obstetrical intervention. His maternity unit boasts some of the lowest perinatal mortality, cesarean, and episiotomy rates in the world.

As luck would have it, by a long, convoluted, and fated journey, Dr. Odent ends up doing grand rounds one day with Ken at Merrimack Valley Hospital.

I am delighted to meet him. Dr. Odent is a tall, attractive man who has the appearance of a sleepy hedgehog being startled in his den. His silver-gray hair is thick and sticks up, and he squints and blinks as though adjusting to the sun. He has the casual, rumpled look of an absent-minded professor. And, oh, that accent! That very thick, sexy French accent, reminiscent of Maurice Chevalier. All in all, a very nice package of a man who is confident yet humble.

He trails after Ken down the halls of the labor and delivery unit. Ken proudly shows him the new rooms and the progress MVH has made toward family-centered birthing. The two men understand each other immediately. Even with the language barrier, they talk the same philosophy—that by simply listening to women and providing what they intuitively desire in labor, the outcomes improve significantly.

Just as they finish up their tour, my pager goes off. It is one of the apprentice-midwives; a born-again Christian couple is in labor down the street in the city. I spontaneously ask Dr. Odent if he would like to observe a New England home birth. He is delighted, and the couple say they are fine with having a spectator.

When the two of us arrive at Chrisanne and Doug's house, she is already pretty active. Chrisanne is a week past her due date. She is sick and tired of being pregnant, so she and Doug have made love to get her labor going. Orgasm triggers the release of oxytocin, the hormone that causes contractions. They are still mushy from the postcoital glow. They are being playfully affectionate and sensual with each other, even though Chrisanne is definitely working with her contractions.

Chrisanne is naked and leaning back against Doug, who is wearing only a pair of shorts. Doug is still doing nipple stimulation, although this has produced the desired effect some time ago. As the intensity of Chrisanne's contractions increases, she and her man kiss deeply for the duration of the pain, then look steadily into each other's eyes. They are clearly in love and in this thing together. It is very nice. I am enjoying their tenderness immensely.

As things get heated up, I look over at Michel and see that he looks uncomfortable. I am surprised. I talk with him in another room.

He whispers, "This is their intimate life. I am a stranger in their home, and I do not want to inhibit this couple in any way."

I realize with astonishment that he is *shy!* This is so sweet, so *French!* How endearing.

I have attended Chrisanne twice before, so I can assure him with certainty, "I don't think they're aware of anybody else at the moment."

I do appreciate his being so considerate.

His comment makes me watch Chrisanne's labor with heightened awareness. It's not that I am inured to the sexuality of birth, nor am I a voyeur. I have come to take for granted that there is a certain amount of sexual energy during birth; I feel it is almost necessary for true opening up. I watch Chrisanne as the thin line between pleasure and pain becomes blurred for her. Her sounds at the approach to pushing are distinctly, heavily sexual. Her mouth is nice and loose as she opens to her child. She groans as the child begins to move down. Chrisanne is surrendering to the process with abandon.

As I watch, I realize that childbirth is one of the great initiations into women's blood mysteries, along with menarche and menopause. These milestones are the source of our true power, and women need to experience these to the fullest in order to create wholeness and a sense of completion. Even in the throes of the deepest surrendering comes woman's greatest triumph.

Chrisanne opens to the powerful forces guiding her body as she becomes the gateway for her child to enter this world. Her sounds now are intense and unmistakably climactic. Her daughter, Rose, is born at the peak of this orgasmic birth. I have to admit that my own breathing is a tad more rapid than normal.

I turn to grin at Michel. He has been watching with keen curiosity but has graciously remained respectfully invisible.

With Chrisanne glowing and satisfied and welcoming her newest family member, Michel says his congratulations and "Au revoir!" He has a plane to catch in Boston.

It is a fair trek to the airport. The apprentice-midwife has enthusiastically volunteered to drive Dr. Odent to the airport, as he is one of her heroes. The thought of an exclusive hour-and-a-half chat time with him is almost more than she can stand.

I smile as I wave good-bye to the famous French physician,

who is going down the street in a little orange VW bug in the
rain.

━━━

Every once in a while, local woodsmen or kids banged up from
skateboarding come to me to stitch them up. The woodcutters,
having wrangled with the wrong end of a chainsaw, show up
on my doorstep, as they don't believe in going to doctors or
hospitals. I think this is probably because they don't have health
insurance and can't afford the ER.

The first time I repair a chain-saw gash in a timberman's
forearm, I stitch him up on my kitchen table. I can't believe
how tough his skin is. I am used to soft, pliant, sweet little
perineums, not the thick lizard skin these guys manage to rip
up. It practically bends my suture needle. I am usually paid for
this service with cordwood or snowplowing.

The best deal ever, though, is a local carpenter who
accidentally stabs himself in the thigh with a utility knife. After I
close the wound, he is so grateful that he asks if there is anything
he can build for me. I say that a simple arbor over a patch of
wild Concord grapes that are growing out back near the potting
shed would be swell. This skilled man commences to build a
large, latticework pergola where the grapevines grow in obscene
abundance and hide the interior of a little outdoor room.

Ken and I suspend a swinging bed with a double-size air
mattress from the cross pieces of the pergola. We cover this
with mosquito netting and call this our outdoor bed. We sleep
outside in the summer as much as possible, rocked by a gentle
breeze. I plant night-scented stock around the pergola, so the
heady smell of jasmine wafts seductively over us at night. With
fireflies blinking in the field, it is shamelessly romantic.

A PROLAPSED CORD

There are occasional moments at births when I know for certain that I have been blessed and guided by divine intervention. This is the case in little Sissy's birth, an instance of an unrelated maneuver causing a red flag that alerted me to a completely different complication.

Sissy's mother, Delores, is a close friend of mine. She is in my women's group that meets on a monthly basis. When she is thirty-one weeks pregnant, Delores calls to tell me that she has just broken her water. I have attended her twice before with no problems whatsoever. I assume she must have sneezed or something and that it is just urine she's feeling. I tell her my educated theory.

She gets quite snippy. "I guess the hell by now I should know what amniotic fluid looks and smells like, for godsake." She growls, "This 'urine' has white flecks floating in it, and it smells sweet, like birth. Now get your know-it-all skinny butt over here!"

Driving to her house, which is not far from mine, I try to think of other things that could possibly be going on besides severe prematurity. I am hoping for another explanation, but that doesn't happen.

Delores lives beside a stream in a tiny, antique Cape that has a greenhouse, where she grows flowers and field-dug pansies to sell. She also grows herbs to make into commercial botanical body-care products. Her yard has lush, verdant growth everywhere; it always has an unruly, wild, "Martha Stewart on acid" look to it.

When I walk into her living room, she is lying on a vintage couch in front of open French doors, with a towel between her legs. Her husband, Julian, is very concerned, but I say to him that it's probably just a "high leak" that will seal up and be of no more concern.

To my dismay, I don't even have to do a sterile speculum exam. Delores's water is gushing out in copious amounts. I put a piece of nitrazine litmus paper in the pooling fluid, and it turns dark purple, confirming my worst fears. It is definitely amniotic fluid, no doubt about it. Damn! This certainly has not been on the screen for this pregnancy.

I consult with Ken, who says that Delores needs to go straight to Hanover, where they are better equipped to deal with a very early baby like this. I watch as Delores gets ready to go to the neonatal intensive care facility by wrapping her mound of dreadlocked, henna'd hair on top of her head and tying it up with a fringed silk sash. She puts on a vintage Chinese-silk dressing gown with her best cowboy boots and rhinestone earrings shaped like peacocks. I wonder if Hanover is prepared for this.

The upshot of Delores's visit is that she stays for five days while they monitor her temperature and white blood cell count to make sure she isn't developing a uterine infection. Otherwise, they are just buying time so the baby's lungs can get a little more mature before being born.

Delores soon gets bored. She announces to the high-risk guys that she is going home, that her midwife can do the same things they are doing; she goes AWOL. My guess is that she was making life a living hell for everyone involved in her care. The docs call me and tell me which tests I should be running to assume her care. They are very considerate and informative and treat me with respect, as though consulting with another colleague.

My bet is that they are glad to see her go and are relieved that someone else will have to deal with such an opinionated, mouthy wench. They say as soon as she starts contracting, she should hightail it back up there.

I find myself obsessing about this ridiculously high-risk case. I drive to Delores's house twice a day to draw her blood for a white blood cell (WBC) count and to check her vitals and the baby's heart rate. This goes on for a week and a half, with Delores gushing on her funky couch. Everything remains stable until the morning when there is a moderate amount of pinkish blood in the fluid. This is the signal that her cervix is silently dilating, even though she isn't aware of any contractions.

I say I believe this is the day of reckoning. We need to gear up for the hour-long drive back to Hanover. I palpate Delores's belly and distinctly feel a little head up in the fundus. This baby is breech. I tell Delores that I will try a gentle version to get the baby flipped to vertex so the birth will be easier and safer for her. I don't anticipate that there will be any difficulty with this, as the presenting part is high, and the baby is still tiny.

I am holding my Doppler to Delores's belly to monitor the baby's response to the maneuver. As I begin the pressure, I hear the baby's heartbeat cut out completely for a couple of beats. *Completely gone.* Then it recovers. I have never heard anything like this—it is almost as though there is a short in an electrical cord. I try for a second time to move the child; it happens again—a complete bottoming out of the heartbeat.

This is not a good sign. My hands begin to shake as I put on a sterile glove so I can check to see what is going on. I'm pretty sure I know the only thing that could cause it to sound so bad. Sure enough, as Delores's cervix has begun to dilate, the cord has slipped through ahead of the baby. Now I feel the cord sitting in her vagina, pulsing away.

Oh, Blessed Mother! Have mercy on this child!

I feel Sissy's buttocks beginning to come down into the mid-pelvis. I push her bottom back up as much as I can with my fingers to prevent her from compressing her cord.

Now I am in overdrive. I try to calm my voice as I begin giving orders.

Julian dials Ken. I tell him we are coming in with a preemie with a prolapsed cord and for him to be ready to do a STAT section. We'll be there in less than fifteen minutes. Forget

Hanover—too far away. Forget the rescue squad—they are farther from us than the hospital and in the wrong direction.

Julian, in a panicked Herculean feat, picks Delores up bodily, with me trailing beside her with my fingers still in her vagina, and carries her to the car. In the backseat of their old Volvo, Delores gets in a knee-chest position to help stop Sissy from descending any further. I am still holding Sissy's butt up out of the pelvis with my fingers pushing counter to the force of Delores's contracting uterus. I am listening to Sissy's heart's response to all this with the Doppler. She sounds great—so far.

Julian drives like a madman down bumpy country roads, speeding to the hospital. I am talking calmly to them both— even though I am very frightened myself—telling them that Sissy sounds great, that she is strong and is going to be fine.

Delores, with her face buried in the car seat, says, "I can feel her. She's all right. I can feel that she's OK."

When we get to the ER, they put Delores on a stretcher, keeping her in knee-chest position, with me running alongside her, still pushing up on Sissy's bottom. We run down hallways until we get to the operating room, where Ken is waiting. One quick incision, and I swear I can feel the scalpel graze my fingers. Sissy is out and healthy and squalling in outrage at her unexpected new surroundings.

She only weighs four and half pounds, but Sissy is a true scrapper, and she nurses right away. She has no breathing problems. Some of this is due to the fact that the membranes were ruptured long enough to elevate Sissy's surfactant levels, so her lungs are more mature than expected.

After it is clear that everyone is healthy and happy, I go outside for a little downtime. I thank the Divine Mother from the deepest place in my heart for being so direct and clear with me, for giving me such an obvious message. I clearly know that if I hadn't attempted that version with the resulting discovery of the prolapsed cord, Sissy would have died on the hour-long trip back to Hanover.

—

In September of 1984, Teddy Charvet and I fly to Sydney, Australia, to represent MANA in the membership bid into the ICM. Teddy and I meet up at the airport in Vancouver, British Columbia, as she lives in the Pacific Northwest. Our plane taxis down the runway for takeoff, but it suddenly stops and turns around. There has been a serious malfunction, and we have to sit in the plane while mechanics replace the entire engine.

Flight attendants go up and down the aisles for hours, plying the captive passengers with unlimited wine, as a form of apology and, I suppose, anxiety relief. Due to this hospitable delay, I sleep the entire twenty-four-hour flight to the Land Down Under. I arrive only slightly hung over and ready to take on the daunting task of gaining international recognition for North America's midwives.

Our membership bid is controversial because we have members, like me, in the international section who are not nurses. While this is true, we still meet the criteria of the International Definition of Midwifery. Our members are duly recognized in their states and are legal.

I get into a quasi-friendly, verbal fisticuff with the president of the ACNM at a wine-and-cheese reception. She states that her opposition to us is that some of our members are apprentice-trained and lack formal schooling. I say I will defend to my dying day the validity of hands-on apprentice training as equal, if not superior to, theoretical, didactic book learning. I remind her that the United States was founded on the apprentice model, where journeymen learned their craft or trade through practical experience under a skilled master artisan for a prescribed period, until their trade was perfected.

She says that many MANA midwives are practicing in states where midwifery is illegal, so they are breaking the law. I say that while this is true, I remind her again that our country was founded on breaking the law, when our founding fathers felt that the laws were unjust and intolerable. The freedom to rebel is almost a tradition in the United States. I notice some eavesdropping Australian midwives nodding their heads in agreement—their entire country was founded by a bunch of convicts.

Our hotel suite in Sydney becomes a crash pad for all the indigent, ex-pat, radical midwives from around the world. At any given time, Teddy and I have to step over ten to twenty bodies of women scattered on couches and on the floor—women who have traveled from the far corners of the earth to get here; women who are recovering from serious jet lag, or malaria, or whatever virus or bacteria du jour they have contracted while working to deliver babies in some godforsaken, war-torn area where nobody else dares to tread.

These women have come because they agree with us and are giving their support. It is phenomenal what happens here. Someone brings an old, clunky typewriter and Teddy whips off our ICM speech, with the help of midwives who speak several different languages. These women have seen it all. I feel like a novice. These are dedicated midwives who envision us, globally, as being an independent, autonomous profession, able to practice without the chafing, potentially dangerous constraints of an archaic medical model.

One flaming-red-haired Canadian midwife by the name of Holiday has been working for a long time with the Punjab women behind enemy lines in India. It is a harrowing feat to attend the women who birth the babies of the outlawed Punjab warriors. Over time, Holiday has cultivated some type of jungle rot, due to damp and humid conditions, that festers and blisters on her legs. I am unaware, temporarily, of this contagious, leprosy-like skin malady. She asks me if she can borrow some of my pantyhose, as her luggage has been either lost or confiscated. She looks so professional in my stockings, so statuesque and impressive, that later, learning of her scaly plight, I wholeheartedly let her keep my stockings to further the cause.

Teddy and I present our speech in front of fifty nations. It is staggering. The ICM member nations that do not speak English have earphones through which they listen to a simultaneous translation in their mother tongues. Our argument is that North America is virtually a developing country, as far as midwifery as a viable profession is concerned. We have only recently evolved in the area of midwifery education and are laboring for mainstream public and consumer awareness and access to midwifery care.

We explain that we don't have the long and accepted history of our European counterparts; that midwives in the United States were deliberately and systemically eradicated at the turn of the twentieth century by a jealous medical profession. Even at the present time, many midwives in the U.S. are persecuted, and some have even been jailed. We are asking for their support and recognition of us, to assure midwifery in its purest sense will survive in North America.

In the end, our membership bid isn't controversial or debated at all. The only negative vote comes from the president of the ACNM in the United States. This is a tremendous success and identifying factor for MANA, which now has a voice in the ICM that is equal to the ACNM. This makes MANA visible internationally—pretty heady stuff for a country girl from New England. It is especially surprising when, after the vote, midwives from other countries come to welcome us and say they are looking to MANA to lead the way globally. Many midwives practicing in countries where the profession is taken for granted feel that their work has been co-opted and medicalized. They

see our grassroots efforts as preserving and defending the true
heart and soul of midwifery.

I call the MANA board, waiting for the word back home, to
tell them of our stunning victory. Even though it is 3:00 AM in
the U.S., there is tremendous joy and relief across the country.
This is a monumental advance for the practice of midwifery in
North America.

We have done it.

A few days later, when the festivities die down, I go to a beach
outside of Sydney to get some rest and recuperation from the
stress and excitement. I take a bus by myself to Long Reef Beach
in Collaroy. It is a sunny day, though windy, and I lie on the
beach reading my all-time favorite book, *The Mists of Avalon*,
until I become drowsy and fall asleep. When I wake, I see tiny,
colorful specks flying around some steep cliffs over the ocean,
about a mile down the beach. They are hang gliders. I decide to
go watch them, as I am interested in flying.

I have been studying for my pilot's license because I have
the fantasy of flying a small plane to the northern parts of New
Hampshire to catch babies where there are no other attendants
available. I am close to soloing, but I have one problem: I have
a knee-jerk reaction while landing. I always close my eyes tightly
right before contact with the tarmac. My flight instructor says
this is not compatible with life. So, maybe I'd like hang gliding
instead. I walk to the top of the cliffs to investigate.

There is a whole flock of hang gliders sailing on the thermals
coming off the exceptionally steep, shale headlands that run
along the ocean here. The day has perfect conditions, and
the gliders are mesmerizing and silent. There are no other
spectators. Eventually, a glider with a long-legged young man
comes in for a landing on the cliff top. A sudden updraft causes
his glider to stall and then dive straight down over the edge of
the cliff.

Holy Mother of God! Did that just happen?

For a split second I freeze in fear. I look around and realize that nobody else on the ground has seen the accident. I can't believe it; it has happened so quickly and without a sound, like a choppy silent movie. I run to the cliff edge but can't see the pilot. I start to descend the cliff face, which is very slippery; the shale breaks easily and slides under my feet. I skitter down about fifty feet until I see where the pilot has collided with the rock face. His kite is wedged in a narrow rock cranny. It is about three hundred feet to the ocean, which is crashing on the rocks below us. The young pilot is dangling like a limp rag doll in his harness, unconscious.

The crashed hang-glider pilot doesn't appear to be breathing. I can't find a pulse in his neck. I am trained in CPR, but my focus has always been on infant resuscitation, not a broken, grown man. In order to apply adequate chest compression to stimulate his heart, I have to slip underneath his dangling body and wedge my toes in small crevices in the cliff face. I brace my legs and hang onto his harness and push upwards firmly on his chest.

I am on autopilot. I'm not feeling anything, really, except an extreme focus on bringing this man back to life. It seems like an eternity (but is probably less than ten minutes) before the young pilot starts to make guttural sounds, and blood and mucus comes out of his nostrils. He has been looking dusky and funky-colored, but now his color begins to improve.

At the same time that the young man starts to make incoherent sounds, two of his flying mates slide down to us with a rope that some rescue folks, waiting at the top, are securing. Someone had been watching the hang gliders with binoculars from the beach and reported the crash. The pilot's friends tie the rope around his harness and cut the guy wires to his kite; it tumbles the rest of the way down the cliff to the ocean below.

When they jettison the kite, it drops the man's body on top of me, and I lose my toehold. I am dangling freely out over the ocean, hanging on to an unconscious man's harness, which is suspended by a rope from above. A helicopter is flying close to us but can't be of any help because of the severe updrafts. Now I'm feeling a *lot*. I have enough adrenaline surging to last me a lifetime.

The rescue workers haul the two of us up in tandem until we are safely at the top. They put the crashed glider pilot in a Stokes litter and take him to the hospital. Later, I see him briefly at the hospital, although he is still unconscious and babbling gibberish about thermals and air currents. His name is Kulen and, apparently, he's going to be OK. He is kind of cute, with dark curly hair and high cheekbones, even though these are pretty smashed up.

The rest of his hang-gliding mates are so appreciative of my efforts that they make sure I am royally entertained. I am wined and dined by them for the rest of my visit in Australia. Several days later, I am hiking the Seven Sisters mountain range with some of the blokes when I am told that the authorities in Sydney are looking for me.

I think, *Oh, great. Now what have I done?*

As it turns out, some people in Sydney, particularly Kulen's mother, want to formally express their gratitude for my heroic efforts. The Australian government wants to present me with a Bronze Medal for Bravery. I am speechless. They've got to be kidding! But it is no joke; they take this quite seriously. I go back to the hospital, where Kulen is recovering, and face a lot of reporters and photographers and Kulen's entire family, a very appreciative group.

The Royal Humane Society of New South Wales presents me with a heavy bronze Southern Cross, which hangs from a striped grosgrain ribbon, with my name inscribed as well as the words "For Bravery." I am greatly honored.

I call Ken and excitedly tell him about the rescue and my medal.

He laughs. He says, "What is this, the *Perils of Pauline?* High drama follows you around like a faithful dog, Carol. For you, this is par for the course."

After my return home, the story of the cliff rescue is published in *Women's World* news magazine, which in turn is picked up by the *Gary Collins Show*. His show flies me out to be interviewed on live TV for the segment Gary Collins does called "Greatest American Heroes."

While I am backstage, being plastered with thick, TV pancake makeup, I see the actor George Hamilton being heavily brushed with Indian Earth powder to make him look gorgeous and perennially tanned. I am impressed, as Indian Earth is the *only* thing I ever use on my face; I have been using it for years. I feel George and I are bonded in our shared preference for this mystery dirt. Before going on stage, I approach the actor to tell him that Indian Earth is my beauty secret, too, and that his secret is safe with me. He gives me a square, white, disingenuous smile. But his eyes seem full of alarm. I think he is trying to figure out if I am just a demented fan or a dangerous stalker.

I am embarrassed to retell the story of my being a hero in front of a large studio audience. But Gary Collins has a surprise; he has Kulen on the phone, live from Australia. I hear Kulen's chipper voice with his thick Aussie accent.

Kulen says, "Excuse me for being impetuous, but I am totally infatuated with you because no one has ever saved my life before!"

He says he is fully recovered and is flying again, the crazy boy. I say I will probably never become a big fan of the sport after watching a guy jump off a cliff with his measly tinfoil wings and crash. The show has managed to get a news clip from the Sydney news station that filmed the rescue from a helicopter. I am astounded to see a matchstick figure, dangling from a rope and a carcass against the ocean cliffs, toothpick white legs and a purple tank top, swaying out over the waves crashing far below.

Me. It looks much more horrifying on film than it seemed at the time.

Milan thinks the whole thing is great. He wears my medal to school for a month, singing, "I am k-k-king of the jungle!"

A DOCTOR'S BIRTH

Ken's practice occasionally is a clinical training site for medical students who are doing their ob-gyn rotations. The students who seek him out are usually a special breed of individuals in the medical field in that they want to apprentice with midwives; they want to learn a more authentic and loving approach to birth. Because of this fundamental difference in ego and humbleness, these students are almost always compassionate and sincere and interesting to be with.

One young hotshot doctor, Tina Henry, was at the head of her class at Harvard Medical School. She is blonde, athletic, vivacious, and fun. She and I become good friends. She attends some home births with me to observe, but mostly she works in the hospital with Ken. She tags after Ken for months and has the benefit of his knowledge of state-of-the-art technology in the field, combined with true gentleness and a deep and abiding respect for women.

Tina makes good use of her mentor. She goes on to become a gifted and busy family practice physician in a small rural town in the mountains of western Maine—the town's only doctor.

Tina's focus is still obstetrics, as that was her specialty and her first love. She longs to have a child of her own but has some trouble with infertility. It is several years before she is able to conceive. By the time she becomes pregnant, she has delivered hundreds of babies for the town in their small community hospital.

Tina and her husband decide that they prefer to give birth in the comfort and privacy of their own home; they ask me if I'd be willing to drive that far for their baby's emergence. I say I would be honored, as they are close friends. I am certain I will make it in time if they call me right away, as first babies are notorious for taking much longer than seems reasonable or tolerable or even fair. Most first babies take an average of twenty-four hours, from soup to nuts.

Tina has another physician, her partner, standing by in the interim. I figure I have time for a leisurely trek through the White Mountains to the northern side, with plenty of time to spare.

Tina calls late in the night and says she's pretty sure labor has started. She sounds excited but steady, and as we talk, she is forced to stop with each contraction and breathe a little deeper. I say it sounds like the real enchilada to me; I will head out and be there in three hours.

I drive through the pitch dark of wolf dawn until I cross through the pass that circles around Mount Chocourua. Here, the sun is just rising and the dawn light causes the mountain to be illuminated in a breathtaking way, like a Maxfield Parrish painting. The mountain's pyramid peak and Lake Chocourua are washed in impossible hues of gold and copper with startling clarity. I have a tremendous sense of well-being. I know this birth is going to be golden.

I drive through the sleeping little Maine town in the early morning light. When I arrive at Tina's door, she rushes at me in wild-eyed panic. She is still being a doctor; she is trying to remain objective and professional, but she is failing miserably.

"Something's wrong! Something has happened, and this is not right! This is just way too intense; I cannot do this! We've got to transfer to the hospital immediately!"

I, on the other hand, am still infused with the beauty and serenity of the mountain sunrise. I can't suppress a half-smile, as I am pretty sure I know what is going on. I don't sense any danger at all. I hear her concern, but I am also trying not to grin.

"OK, Tina, OK. We'll leave in a heartbeat, of course. But first let me check you and the baby to see what's going on, to see if we can find what the problem is."

When I examine her, she is already eight centimeters, which is what I suspected the minute I walked in the door and she flew at me like a hysterical banshee. I grin as I tell her that I think I have found the cause of her abnormal intensity.

She looks at me in astonishment, then relief, when I tell her she is dilated eight centimeters. "You've got to be joking! That means I've only been in labor for four hours and I'm already eight? Unbelievable! And I thought I was just beginning. No wonder it's so frickin' intense. This is a piece of cake!"

This "piece of cake" gets considerably fiercer as she reaches full dilation and begins to bring her son down, but now she is surging with confidence and is concentrating on her body's rhythms. Tina does a wonderful job of delivering her own child. I hold up a hand mirror so she can watch her baby's head crowning. She massages her perineum where the stretch is burning the most. Her face becomes a deep purple with each straining effort of bearing down, but she relaxes and smiles in between contractions. Her fingers track the progress in descent that her son's head makes with every push.

Tina sits up, watching in the mirror, as she guides her son out. In one tremendous gush, William's body slides free. Tina gathers him up in her arms and throws her head back with a huge howl of triumph. What a great sight—Tina, finally holding a baby of her own.

Tina's husband cracks open some Moet, and we toast the new arrival. They thank the baby for coming to them, for making them the family they have longed for. I look fondly at this woman who has delivered so many babies, who is now a mother herself.

I hold up my goblet of champagne to Tina. I say, "Well, revered and esteemed Dr. Henry, what is your assessment of childbirth now?"

Tina looks up from nursing William and rolls her eyes. "Wow, what an initiation. It really is true; there's no way to describe that, no matter how hard you try. I thought I knew, but I had no idea how much that really sucked. I guess I freaked out for a minute there. I never felt overwhelmed or like I couldn't handle it, but I did go somewhere else. This is definitely the strongest thing I've ever done in my life. I am so proud that I could do it! What an incredible experience. But I will never, *ever* make small talk or bullshit chitchat with a woman in labor again."

In November of 1984, I am elected vice president of MANA at our second international conference in Toronto, Canada. My job description is to coordinate the annual conferences, but I am also frequently asked to speak at legislative hearings, to give expert testimony in states and provinces where midwifery legislation is being proposed. There are several states considering licensing midwives at this time. These efforts are still met with the typical resistance and animosity from the medical community in the age-old territorial turf battle.

One hearing at which I testify about the safety and validity of midwifery care is heard in front of the Crown for the province of Ontario, Canada. I can not believe how rowdy and raucous the Parliament members are. They yell obscenities and blow raspberries at each other and throw spit balls across the room as though still in fifth grade. It is fabulous fun, much more chaotic and interesting than our staid, stuffy, and repressed legislative hearings in the States—although I'm not sure if the heckling is effective or if decisions are actually influenced by the rudeness.

In the end, it is pretty much the same disappointing scenario. The Toronto midwives have put together some very impressive data, which is summarily dismissed by a group of arrogant, condescending bewigged men, who don't listen for a minute to the carefully documented facts and statistics. Instead, they write silly notes to each other or stare out the windows at the black squirrels cavorting on the lawn. They yawn and look at their watches.

These hearings, along with the self-aggrandizing, upper-class, middle-aged white men who are so belittling and patronizing, make me so *angry*. Ken decides to tutor me in the fine art of keeping my cool and to hone my skills in argumentation. Every night after dinner, he plays devil's advocate, representing the opposition in an upcoming situation. He baits me. He is good at it; as a matter of fact, he is wicked good at it (after all, he *is* a seasoned obstetrician). He's heard all the unsubstantiated propaganda against midwives for decades. He knows how to manipulate the defamation to sound like established medical fact.

Whenever I explode in outrage, or respond defensively with an edge to my voice, or make a groundless, obnoxious, flip retort, he makes me do it again and again until I am composed and steely. I get so goddamn mad at him. He finally cracks up.

He says, "No good, sweetie, slow down. Take a deep breath. Don't let yourself be intimidated. You know what you're talking about. OK, let's take it from the top."

He shows me what they will say that will push my buttons and make me angry. I eventually get to a place of aloofness and reserve and confidence in my position, but this makes for some very heated après-dinner conversations. I get so pissed at him; I love him for it.

Ken teaches me how to think in algorithms or a step-by-step process for problem solving. I begin to respond to unfounded accusations with specific scientific formulae of statistics and published data and factual information. Ken is tireless. When I get discouraged by some medical expert slinging uneducated slander, he interjects a little humor for comic relief. My presentations become increasingly more sophisticated.

Ken's tutoring is put to a real test when I testify at a hearing in New Orleans for legal recognition of midwives in Louisiana. I am shocked at how sexist and condescending the puffy legislators are. My testimony is based on data compiled by the Louisiana midwives in conjunction with the state's Bureau of Vital Statistics, and I compare this with the overall national safety record.

One of the "good ol' boys," who had been picking his teeth with a toothpick, responds to my presentation.

He says, "Now, don't you worry your pretty little head about nothin', darlin'. We'll take care of everythin'. We don't need you botherin' with all these numbers and such. You girls needn't go to all this trouble and worry your cute little selves. We'll take care of you just fine, hear?"

My mouth drops open. I grew up in New England and have never been spoken to like this in all my life.

Suddenly, I imagine Ken taking on the personality of this cracker in our next debate. This makes me smile. The more I imagine Ken with a lazy Southern drawl, the more I crack up.

The legislator responds to my smile, first in surprise, then with a big, easy, greasy smile.

Oh, my god, this buffoon thinks I'm flirting with him! Jesus! The absurdity of this makes me grin all the more. I can't stop myself.

The bureaucrat flashes me a wide, oily smile and a wink. He is giving me the kooky-eye.

I don't know if this little interchange had any effect on the outcome this day, but the Louisiana midwives are successful in the passage of a good and fair program for legal practice.

My feminist girlfriends would have me tarred and feathered for the way this victory was won. *C'est la guerre!*

CHAPTER ELEVEN

LION'S HEART, 1985

There is a tree deep in the forest, standing at the southernmost edge of our property that is the most enormous bull pine I have ever seen. It looks as though two large pines have grown together to create one massive tree. This monolithic tree is in the middle of our woods, and Ken and I grow to love the peacefulness of the forest there. Over time, this tree—which we cleverly dub "the Tree"—becomes important to us, both as a place of relaxation and rejuvenation and as a comforting place to sit quietly when times get tough.

Many times, we pack a picnic lunch and amble to the Tree together for some rest and downtime, but more often, we seek out the solace of the Tree alone, when either of us needs comforting. There is a babbling creek down a mossy embankment, and the base of the Tree always has a sun-dappled, pine-needled floor. We clear an old logging road of scrub brush so we can cross-country ski along the ridge that leads to the Tree. This way, we can seek out this place even in the dead of winter.

The Tree becomes an understood healing place for us. Many times, as I watch the back field from the kitchen window, I see

Ken emerging from the woods, walking along the path from the Tree. This becomes a very comforting sight for me.

THE STORK STORY

Many times, the gravity and enormity of birth is balanced by sheer silliness. The following story always sounds impossibly silly, even to me, but I have the pictures to prove it.

It is Halloween night 1985. Susie is on call, so I am on my way to a friend's costume party, dressed in a great costume that I put together at the last minute. I think it is hilariously funny. I think it will be a grand entrance, arriving dressed as a stork (even though Susie is the one whose license plate reads STORK).

I have found a saucy, trashy, white silk teddy that is trimmed with downy white feathers in all the necessary places. I am wearing shiny white pantyhose and have found an outrageous white feather boa that I have taped to my arms for wings. I have on a white rubber bathing cap, onto which I have glued some chicken feathers. I have made a long stork bill out of cardboard painted day-glow orange, and I have attached it to my nose with heavy-duty elastic around my head. This is already giving me a killer headache, but it is worth it.

The most difficult part of this outfit is driving while wearing swim flippers, which I have also spray-painted orange, for my stork feet. Completing the ensemble, of course, is the requisite blue baby blanket, with a disturbing Cabbage Patch baby sticking out.

But the fates intervene. Halfway to my friend's house, my pager goes off and the answering service says we have two women in labor at once. Susie has sped to one, and I am to go to the other immediately. This is the woman's fifth baby, and I know that she, Rose, has a history of very quick and easy deliveries. I turn my car around to Route 4 West and fly to Northwood.

I don't even attempt to take off my swim flippers as I grab my birth bag out of the backseat of the car; I'm assuming she is very active. My wings get tangled in the straps of my O_2 tank. I step on my own feet, and I forget all about my beak until I rush into the kitchen. Four little kids look up at me in awe.

The oldest of the children calls to her mother in the next room. "Mom! The stork's here!"

Her mother laughs. "Oh, Lissie, you're so funny!"

Lissie insists, "No, Mom! I mean it—the stork's here!"

The other kids take up the refrain: "The stork's here! The stork's here!"

I flipper-walk into the bedroom. Rose's eyes get huge, and then she bursts into laughter. I am embarrassed.

I say, "Yeah, well, it's Halloween."

There isn't much more conversation, as Rose's baby intends to make a Halloween entrance as well. Rose is a veteran, and the birth is remarkably easy. Annie comes winging out. I do remove my beak for the birth. As Annie's head is crowning, which takes my full concentration, the kids are giggling and plucking out my feathers. By the time Annie has landed, I am a partially denuded stork. The siblings want to keep my feathers as souvenirs.

I have an old Polaroid picture of me, standing in their kitchen, with my wings around the kids, and a few paltry poultry feathers still remaining on my head. The pose shows long, skinny white legs and a little pot belly and my bright orange beak, looking for all the world like a geeky, overnourished, embarrassing human stork.

As I leave, I decide that, blessedly, the fledgling new baby is a whole lot cuter than that frightening Cabbage Patch baby I arrived with.

In the summer of 1985, Susie and I have the dubious honor of being the first two midwives to take the New Hampshire state midwifery certifying exam. I have been working with the Department of Public Health for years, designing the midwifery program, and I have been bragging about how smart and competent we are. Now I have to put my money where my big mouth is and prove it. It is ridiculously stressful.

Susie and I both gain ten pounds while studying for the exam together. We eat pizza every night for a month and literally put our families on hold until it is over. The test is compiled by experts and physicians and health-care professionals in the state. I think part of the intent is to trip us up by creating a ludicrously long, arduous, and esoteric test. Many of the questions ask for detailed and obscure information that only peripherally pertains to midwifery practice. We are the guinea pigs to test the test and to see how we fare with it.

It takes Susie and me *thirteen hours* to complete the written test. We have to go home to sleep and then return to the Health and Welfare building the next morning to finish the damn thing. The oral exam is the following evening. We both are wrecks by the end of it. Susie's face has erupted and my lips look like inflatable rubber tires from stress-induced cold sores.

Despite the nit-picky, mean-spirited nature of the test, Susie aces it—and I am only ten points behind her. We are incredibly proud and relieved to be the first two midwives to finally be granted certificates to practice legally in New Hampshire. Our certificates are scrolly, ornate paper documents with a gold New Hampshire state seal and signed by William T. Wallace, MD, Director.

I am immediately appointed to a review committee to process and grade new midwife applicants. My first recommendation, on which I am insistent, is that the bloody test be reduced by half for the midwives yet to come.

THE DEAD WORM

There is a town south of Concord that is a very depressed and seedy area, and unfortunately, it has more than the average number per capita of uneducated, mouthy, abusive men. We suffer more than our fair share of these guys in our practice, mostly because we are the most affordable show around, although we make sure that cost is not the exclusive reason for seeking a home birth.

Due to geography, I am working with the midwife, Roberta, with this couple. Roberta can barely tolerate the implied violence in these situations, and it certainly is a stretch for me. I feel we owe our allegiance to the pregnant women; it's not our fault if they have terrible taste in partners. At least they'll have a powerful and rewarding experience giving birth, and maybe this will increase their self-esteem. This is about all we can do about the problem. We try to ignore these surly men as much as possible, but sometimes they are so in our face, it's a hard thing to do gracefully.

Lacey comes to us in the middle of her pregnancy. She is young, just barely seventeen. We attended her new half-sibling's birth only a couple of months earlier. Lacey is typical for this area—a high school dropout, pregnant by a repulsive boyfriend, but a very sweet and naïve young woman nonetheless. Her boyfriend, Bill, is gangly and malnourished-looking, with pasty, pimply skin and shoulder-length greasy hair. He wears a huge belt buckle that reads "Jim Beam."

Bill comes to all her prenatal appointments, but he spends the time calling Lacey a "stupid bitch" and other vile names. Why he even bothers to accompany her is beyond me, unless he is afraid that she might run away and seek help. Roberta is on a slow boil due to his language and horrific sexist attitude. I find myself spending the entire time running interference and doing damage control among everyone. All in all, this is a very stressful couple for us.

The day finally comes when Bill calls Lacey a "dumb cunt," and this pushes Roberta over the edge. She storms out of the exam room seething.

I take him aside and say firmly, "Look, Billy Bob, your days here are numbered. Your role is to support and sustain your woman. If you can't be nice and loving to her in your language and your gestures, then you're not invited back here anymore."

He shoots me a dark and hateful look, but he is subdued and petulant for the rest of the appointment time.

Roberta and I drive to their rundown apartment building, which is under a bridge. Lacey is in good labor, and she actually is doing a terrific job of it, despite being a young and timid kid. She is concentrating fiercely and working hard. She has a fast and efficient labor.

I suspect that our friend Bill has been drinking in honor of the event, because he is louder and more obnoxious than usual.

He is spewing out endearing gems: "Come on, bitch! Push my son out, you stupid whore! I'm gonna put him on a Harley! I'm gonna give him some Jim Beam!"

Roberta mutters under her breath, "Jesus, what a fucking asshole. I can barely stand to listen to this guy's macho bullshit one more minute before I knock him into next Sunday."

I whisper back, "I know, but *please* just try to ignore him. She's doing such a great job, and then we never have to look at his nasty pockmarked face ever again."

And Lacey does do a great job. She gets down on the floor, squats flat-footed, and powerfully pushes out a baby girl. Roberta and I are hovering around her, giving her words of congratulations and sincere praise for a job well done.

In the background, Bill is swearing and complaining bitterly that the baby is a goddamn stupid *girl!* What the hell use is that?

What the hell is he supposed to do with another dumb bitch in the house? Jesus Christ! Of all the stupid mistakes. Lacey can't even do this right and have a friggin' boy. He goes on and on, ad nauseam.

Roberta and I get Lacey back in bed and make sure she's comfortable. Roberta helps Lacey start nursing her daughter, Tara, while I pay attention to the placenta. When the placenta is born, Bill mumbles to me that he is going to the bathroom. I don't pay particular attention to this until I hear a loud crash. I run down the hall to see what has happened.

I open the door to the bathroom and see Bill passed out, sprawled on the bathroom floor. He must have fainted and fallen backwards while he was urinating, because now he is flat on his back, with his pants unzipped and his penis hanging out of his fly. I run to the sink to put cold water on his face to revive him, but he is out colder than a mackerel. I call to Roberta to bring some ammonia smelling salts in a hurry.

Roberta rushes in and looks shocked upon surveying the scene. Once she figures out what has happened, she gasps, "Oh, my god! For a second there I thought he had gotten weird and exposed himself to you, and then you cold-cocked him! Damn. Guess that was just wishful thinking."

Then we look at each other and start to giggle uncontrollably, like two little girls hiding out in a bathroom, looking at something naughty. Roberta positions her foot and starts to flip his penis around with her socked toe. It is very flaccid and pale and shriveled.

She says, "Jeesh, I wonder if men know how ridiculous they look. This looks like a dead worm. No, really, it does. See, it's all segmented and shit."

She continues to flop it around and examine it, and I get more and more hysterical, laughing until tears run down my face.

I have a fleeting moment of guilt about this joke at Bill's

expense, but then I think, "Nah. This guy's a mean bastard. This is so fitting."

The look of pure disgust on Roberta's face is the funniest thing I have ever seen. She is flicking the escaped organ around, inspecting it scientifically, as though in Anatomy and Physiology 101, when our hero starts to come to consciousness. And he comes to, swinging. He begins flailing his arms around violently, as though trying to beat us off.

I hold him down with my foot, bracing myself up against the sink.

I say, "Whoa, now, Billy Bob! Everything's fine; nobody's trying to fight you. You're OK; you're safe. You just had a momentary leave of your senses."

He looks at the two of us very suspiciously.

We leave the birth, thankful that a new baby has been born safely, but regretful that yet another girl-child has been brought into a demeaning and belittling atmosphere due solely to her sex. How immensely sad, and there is nothing we can ever do to change that part of her future.

To blow off tension, Roberta and I go out to breakfast in that town, and we get very silly. The mere mention of penises leaves us limp with inappropriate, junior high school levity. The regular patrons look at us disapprovingly, as though they feel it is way too early in the morning in New Hampshire for this kind of graphic talk about genitalia.

Just when I think I am recovering some semblance of sanity, Roberta says, "Hey, look—who am I?"

I watch as she flicks a soft, undercooked breakfast sausage around on her plate with the tip of her finger and a look of sheer horror.

I grin. I shake my head in disbelief. "What a weenie he turned out to be! The placenta must have pushed him over the edge. So much for the manly man. As deserving as it is, if that guy heard us in his unconscious state, he'll probably never get it up again."

One can only hope.

⌐

In March 1985, the truth about the safety of out-of-hospital births, which I have known empirically all along, is finally validated. The highly respected *Journal of the American Medical Association* publishes an article in which numbers from the National Center for Health Statistics clearly demonstrate that home births are as safe, if not safer, than hospital births. The researcher breaks down the statistics into four separate and important categories:

- Planned home births with a trained midwife attending: the neonatal mortality rate is 3 per 1000.
- Planned home births without a skilled attendant: the neonatal mortality rate is 30 per 1000.
- Unplanned home births (i.e., accidental and premature births): the neonatal mortality rate is 120 per 1000.
- Planned hospital births with a physician attending: the neonatal mortality rate is 13 per 1000.

This last statistic is a skewed one, because physicians in hospitals take care of high-risk women as well, whereas midwives do not. Even so, the evidence is clear that home births are a viable alternative to hospital deliveries for healthy, low-risk women. Prior to this study, home-birth opponents had erroneously, or deliberately, cited the 120 deaths per 1000 as convincing argument against the safety of birth outside a hospital setting.

Finally, this confusion was scientifically broken down, and midwife-attended births are exonerated.

This study, and others soon to follow, becomes very helpful to me in clearing some of the misconceptions when testifying in states that are considering positive midwifery legislation. Concord Midwifery Service's personal statistics are still faultless and remain, over the years (knock on wood), as 1 per 1000. (This includes the suspect neonatal death that is on our record, which I still question to this day.) Our outcomes remain good, due in large part to the unfailing backup and consultation of Ken and Gerry Hamilton and to the generosity of Merrimack Valley Hospital.

THE COCKY APPRENTICE

There comes a time in all student midwives' training when they go through what I call the cocky phase. The student feels her skills have surpassed her mentor's, and she chaffs at the restrictions dictated by her teacher. This usually comes when the apprentice midwife has attended a good number of births and is becoming quite skilled. She begins to become arrogant, feeling she has an inside track to intuitive knowledge, and she disregards her more experienced teacher's advice. I know this phase only too well from personal experience, as I look back on some of the questionable decisions and unfounded risks I took in the earlier days of my practice. I realize the Ancient Mother definitely covered my overconfident butt on more than one occasion.

The apprentices with whom we work have all been dedicated, hardworking, and diverse, including two staunchly Catholic women who are religiously anti-choice. This is hard for Susie and me to swallow, but we all agree to disagree, so it very rarely becomes an issue. All in all, the women are compatible with us. We offer the traditional master/apprentice relationship of exchange, where the senior midwives trade their experience and knowledge in exchange for the apprentices' assistance and unfailing support, even when bone tired.

Most of the apprentices approach Susie and me deferentially, as they are soliciting us for our expertise and instruction. The exception is the new, young apprentice, Diana, whose strident and aggressive style I find refreshing and revitalizing ... in the beginning. Diana is tall and Amazonian, with long, dark hair and a great smile. She does not have children. She is very clear about her boundaries as far as work is concerned. She demands that she be on call and available only a few nights a week, which makes the other apprentices' mouths drop open in shock at her directiveness.

I find her powerful presence impressive for a while, until I begin to suspect that her lack of humility, rather than the subtle perceptions required for good midwifery, might not be a good fit. The combination of our personalities, two alpha bitches, is an even worse idea. We start to lock horns, although to her credit, she is careful never to challenge or contradict me in front of clients; she is not disruptive in the office.

After a year of working together, this amicable conflict culminates in Diana's demanding that I give her full charge of the birth for a woman with whom she has formed a bond prenatally. Diana is skilled but has yet to learn humbleness, and therefore, she needs to be restrained and supervised carefully until she recognizes her limits. I should have listened to my intuition—an immediate negative response to her request—but I don't. Instead, I agree to observe only and to let her fly. This decision is probably because I see so much of myself in her. Unfortunately, I don't see it as the adolescent rebellion that it really is.

Diana calls to summon me to the birth, late one evening. When I arrive at the farmhouse, which is quite a long way down a winding dirt road in the countryside, Diana announces that she has checked the woman and that she is five centimeters and is contracting well. Diana is labor coaching and helping the woman to breathe and stay focused. I congratulate everyone and wander off to find a bed where I can sleep for a while.

I wake once in the night and look in on the laborers. Diana says the woman is working hard, that the baby's heart rate is fine, and that she will wake me when things get imminent. I go downstairs to the kitchen and have a cup of tea with the grandmother. We chat about how dry our vegetable gardens are and discuss the best riddance for tomato hornworms; then I go back to sleep for what I assume will be just a short while.

I am surprised to wake in the morning to birds chirping and soft dawn light filtering through the leafy branches outside the window. I walk into the bedroom and see that the woman's behavior is pretty much unchanged, although now her breathing is half-hearted and she looks very tired. I ask Diana what is going on. She says the woman is still five, and the labor is flagging, although she is sure things will pick up now that morning is here. I say I need to check the woman myself, to see what the hang up is. Diana becomes very hostile, saying I am interfering with her birth.

I shoot her a look to stifle her mouth, as I am still ultimately responsible for the outcome.

She sits down.

What I find gives me the old "Oh, shit, here we go again" sinking feeling.

The woman isn't anywhere near five centimeters; in fact, she is only a fingertip and that is stretching it. The opening of the cervix is still high and posterior. The head is just now coming down into the mid-pelvis. *Shit!* I hate it when this happens! Then I begin to get angry, so angry, with Diana that I start to get an annoying twitch on my upper lip.

This means that the woman hasn't been in labor at all, or is just beginning, and instead of sleeping to conserve much-needed energy, Diana has had her up, huffing and puffing, all night! Now it is doubtful that the woman will have the stamina to go through another night of labor, especially when it's the real thing. This will become another long, drawn-out ordeal, ultimately resulting in transferring an exhausted woman to the hospital, all because she's been mismanaged! This is a classic setup for maternal fatigue.

Now I have to tell the woman that, in actuality, she is only two centimeters and has wasted an entire night. *Godammit!*

I take Diana outside in the backyard and ream her out in private.

"Jesus, Diana! What the hell did you think you were feeling in there? Five centimeters, my ass!"

She becomes very flip. "Well, I couldn't really reach her cervix, so I assumed she was five by the way she was acting. I've observed enough women in labor by now to know what I am doing."

My anger strangles in my throat.

"You *assumed?* You couldn't reach the cervix because it was too high and posterior to reach, because *she wasn't in labor!* You have to know to ask for help when you need it or to admit when you don't know what is going on; otherwise, you can be dangerous!" Damn, I am mad. "Now, in all probability, we'll be dragging a lunch-meat wiped-out woman to Concord, because we allowed her to become trashed! *This is not OK with me!* She's lost an entire night's sleep because you were guessing and were too proud to admit it!"

I yell at her until I feel some of my frustration subside. Diana stands her ground reasonably well.

I run out of gas. "Now, listen, if you want to redeem yourself, go back in there and use all of your skill to un-psyche that woman, and have her sleep for the morning as much as she possibly can. And no more cheerleading about her 'progress' until you can see hair on top of that baby's head!"

Miraculously, the woman is able to sleep fitfully, on and off, between contractions, for much of the late afternoon, which helps tremendously. She dilates steadily, although her progress is slow, due in part to exhaustion. She doesn't deliver until early the following morning. She does have her baby successfully at home, although she is so exhausted in second stage that she is weeping and barely has enough moxie to continue. We have to give her oxygen to keep her rallied enough to be able to push her child out.

Diana catches the baby and does a nice job of it, although I don't compliment her. She and I are barely speaking at this point. I am fairly certain that the family members are not aware of the depth of our altercation. Fortunately, everything comes out fine, so they are delighted with their birth experience. For this, I am thankful, but my relationship with Diana doesn't fare as well.

Later, I feel bad for riding roughshod over her, but she never apologizes, so neither do I. We are too much alike. Our power struggle with each other is never resolved. We are prickly with one another until she finally terminates her apprenticeship. She never does go on to become a midwife, and I feel guilty and partially responsible for this. She is one of our few failures. This is a woman with whom I worked closely for over a year, and I never see her again.

This makes me incredibly sad, but there was one alpha bitch too many, and one had to get out of Dodge.

In early spring of 1985, I travel to England to speak at the First International Childbirth Symposium in London. I take Milan with me, as this is at the same time as his tenth birthday. I have been asked to present a session on perineal massage and avoiding episiotomies, because many of the British midwives have been trained to do mediolateral episiotomies as a routine procedure. A mediolateral is an incision cut laterally, forty-five degrees off to one side of the perineal body, ostensibly to avoid possible extension through the anal sphincter and into the rectum.

The British midwives are expected to routinely perform these, even though they resist and object mightily to the practice. They ask me to address this problem, because by now, the sheer number of my good results means they are no longer considered anecdotal.

It is wonderful and heady to be surrounded by European midwives. I am particularly attracted to the Association of Radical Midwives (ARM) for their feisty and independent spirit. They are doing much to encourage the return of births in the UK to "domiciliary confinement," or home deliveries, with the use of an obstetric "flying squad" for unforeseen complications.

My lecture hall is packed. I walk to the podium wearing our Concord Midwifery Service bowling shirt that reads:

I SUPPORT PERINEUMS

This gets a good laugh. I talk about the sane and gentle use of perineal massage for relaxing and stretching the vaginal orifice, combined with a supported and controlled delivery of the head to prevent accidental tearing and damage to the pelvic floor. I present our techniques, which have resulted in very few significant lacerations or extensions of small tears.

To illustrate how traumatic and damaging episiotomies are, I use my bottom lip as a hypothetical perineum and stretch my mouth with my fingers, as though crowning with a baby's head, and then, at maximum stretch, when my bottom lip is blanched white with tension, I pick up a pair of scissors and pretend to cut through my bottom lip.

There is a lot of screeching and uncomfortable laughter and

squirming in distress, but my point is well made. Episiotomies are not only unnecessary in all but the rarest of cases, but they are also destructive and barbaric. Hopefully, a majority of the attendees will reconsider the next time they pick up a pair of scissors.

The English countryside is just beginning to green, and early spring bulbs are blooming. Milan and I are chafing to get out of London to explore Britain's rich and ancient historical sites. Milan is a devoted King Arthur fan. We rent a tiny little car and hit the road to follow in King Arthur's footsteps for two weeks. We have a blast, bombing around on the wrong side of the road. We don't have an itinerary or plan, but we retrace Arthur's legend and his travels, eating in pubs and sleeping in whatever accommodations we find along the way. At the end of our journey, Milan and I drive the bleak and desolate road through remote Cornish headlands to Tintagel by the sea, Arthur's birthplace.

We stay our last night in a bed-and-breakfast in the tiny town of Tintagel. It is too early in the season for the tourist trade, so we can find only an unheated room, and it is very cold. Milan and I stay snuggled together under a thin blanket for warmth. The next morning is his tenth birthday. I go into a slanting and crumbling ancient stone store in search of a birthday cake, but I can only find a chocolate ice cream cone. I also find one small candle.

We sit shivering in our tiny car. I light the little candle and stick it in his ice cream cone, and I sing "Happy Birthday" to him. I start to apologize for the ice cream when we are already freezing to death, but he laughs and says this is the best birthday of his life.

I watch as he smiles and closes his eyes to make a wish and blows out his candle. I wonder what he wishes for.

All these years later, I wonder if his wish came true.

MY COUSIN'S BIRTH

My mother was orphaned at a young age. After her two older brothers and their wives die in their later years, she reluctantly finds herself as matriarch of the whole family. With this position of honor in mind, my cousin Neal asks my mother, the grandaunt, if she would like to attend the birth of his second baby that I am intending to catch. She is delighted, for even after having four children herself, she regrets that she has never seen a baby born. Her telling the story of my birth, her oldest child, is always tinged with disappointment and anger.

My mother read Grantly Dick-Read's *Childbirth without Fear* in 1950, when she was pregnant with me. She felt confident in the process of birth and with herself. She requested that she be able to birth without medication. Her doctor patly said that this would be fine, and he never mentioned it again. Her labor was fast and easy, probably less than two hours total, although it's hard to know, because the doctor ignored my mother's request and knocked her out, colder than a mackerel.

She didn't learn the gender of her child until twenty-four hours later. She'd hoped to breast-feed her scrawny newborn daughter, but nursing was discouraged. She was told she didn't have enough milk to nourish her hungry baby. Her decision to breast-feed was not supported; she finally abandoned the idea out of frustration.

My mother, understandably, has a lot of ambivalence about childbirth.

My cousin Neal lives in western Massachusetts, which is an unusually long haul for me to commit to attending the birth, but I am very fond of this cousin. I agree to the drive. When their labor call comes in the night, it sounds like Neal's wife, Kerry, is more active than I would like when faced with a three-hour drive. I hurriedly pick up my mother on the way, and we race to the Berkshire Mountains.

I am driving pretty fast, but I am confident that we'll still make it with time to spare.

My mother says, "Honestly, Carol, do you really have to drive this fast?"

I reply, "Actually, Mom, yes, I think I do. Babies don't always wait for me, you know. I'm a really good driver; that's part of my job description. Why don't you close your eyes and try to nap until we get there?"

She closes her eyes and pretends to sleep, but I can see her knuckles are blanched white for the entire trip.

Neal and Kerry's birth is beautiful. Carston is born in the house that his dad has built by hand. At one point during transition, Kerry is fussing and carrying on in the usual fashion.

She says the classic line, "I can't do this!"

I say, "I wish I had a hundred dollars for every woman who has said this to me. I'd be independently wealthy."

My mother is very concerned. She leans over and whispers to me, "You call this natural birth *progress?* I think this is terrible!"

Kerry sits on the birthing stool and easily births Carston into my waiting hands. He hollers for a minute upon arrival and then commences to intently check out his surroundings and his new family. Then Kerry gets up and walks to her bed to begin nursing her son.

I look up to see that my mother is smiling, and her eyes are brimming with tears of joy. She finally understands the full impact and power of unfettered birth. Her face reflects pride and admiration for Kerry's strength. She delights in welcoming her new grandnephew.

On the drive home, which is at a much more relaxed pace, we actually carry on a conversation. My mother's elation turns to anger and then to deep pain as she talks about her own birth experiences. She has tremendous sadness that she was denied this kind of transformative experience four times. She was never permitted to be conscious or aware to greet any of her children's arrivals in this loving manner. She feels deprived of a very fundamental and rare moment in time. She is grieving for this loss.

My mother's description of her "confinements" reminds me of a teaching film I once saw of typical hospital births in the 1950s in New York City. I realize that my mother's deliveries were pretty standard for that time period; she might have even gotten off easy, compared to the poor brutalized women in the film. The film was meant to be a documentary that proudly presented state-of-the-art obstetrical care in the fifties, but it is a dead-on horror show.

This was the era of scopolamine, or "twilight sleep," an anesthesia that is a chemical cousin to LSD and was the childbirth drug-du-jour of the fifties. Scopolamine induces amnesia; the women still experience pain in childbirth but upon awakening, they remember nothing about their deliveries. The nightmare scene in the film that is forever burned in my memory is of a labor ward with perhaps a dozen laboring women, all strapped in beds with metal side rails. They are all "scoped" out of their minds, and they are all wearing football helmets. They are in varying stages of shrieking and grimacing insanely; they are flinging themselves around in desperation. It looks like a very bad acid trip.

The piece that physicians left out when touting this "wonder drug" was that it induces a horrendous psychosis in women, who then fight the nurses and scratch themselves. They all try to get up on their hands and knees to deliver. Because of this innate and unconscious knowledge in women to get up on all fours to birth, the doctors are forced to strap the women down in their beds. They put football helmets on the women to protect them from harming themselves on the metal side rails. I realize this must be the origins of my own bondage in labor, even though I had refused all drugs.

My mother's friends tell me that they believe they were scoped for their births, because upon regaining consciousness, they found themselves black-and-blue, with large bruises and cuts on their faces and terrible shiners on their eyes. They weren't sure if they had been abused by hospital personnel or even if their babies were truly their own! One woman tells me that she had laryngitis when she came to—and then realized she had become completely hoarse from screaming.

What a nightmare! I think wryly, *Yeah, right, just say No to drugs.*

I look at my mother, frowning in the passenger seat. As upsetting as her births were, she probably was spared the more brutal reality of the 1950s big-city teaching hospitals, being in Bangor, Maine. She is silent for the remainder of the trip until we pull into her driveway.

Finally, she says, "So, this is what you do for a living. What an intense job! I never realized. I know I raised you kids to believe you could do anything you put your minds to, but this—this is insane."

I grin as I watch her cross her porch and disappear into her house. What a character. She'll never say it—it's not her style—but this is the closest she'll ever come to saying she is proud of me.

Ken is pushing himself and working well beyond his limit. He is traveling to Boston weekly to learn state-of-the-art laparoscopic gynecologic laser surgery from a pioneer in the field. In turn, he is coaching Gerry Hamilton in cervical and vulvar CO_2 laser techniques and is supervising Gerry's OR laser cases. Ken's practice, Women's Health Care Associates, now employs three nurse-midwives, and they are out straight. He has made himself constantly available to all of his patients, which results in sleep deprivation and extreme exhaustion.

And with the exhaustion comes periods of severe depression, and his behavior becomes more and more erratic. He occasionally binge-drinks straight gin, which is never a good sign. His switching from wine to gin always signals a manic episode. He goes through periods of sullenness and total lack of communication with me.

His trips to the Tree for solace and comfort become more and more frequent. I am too blindly in love with my man to see how desperate these episodes really have become.

CHAPTER TWELVE

LION'S HEART, 1986

Ken and I have been married for five years, and the time has virtually flown by. We decide to honor our anniversary by throwing a party for our friends, to celebrate our being together for a decade. I make the invitations with old photos of Ken and me, circa mid-1950s, when Ken was a teenager and I was a little girl. In Ken's photo, he is posing proudly, with his arms crossed, and his hair is shaved in a thick Mohawk haircut. In my photo, I am dressed demurely as a bride, with a long white sheet for a veil, and I'm holding a bouquet of wilted dandelions.

I paste these photos together as one and dub it "The Bride and Don Eagle," as Don Eagle was the name of Ken's haircut at the time. Someone, inexplicably, had taken photos of the rear view of both of these poses, so the flipside of the invitation shows Ken, modeling the dark, stubbly-shaved backside of his Mohawk, and me, bending over with my veil flipped naughtily over my head, mooning and showing off the ruffles on my fancy new party panties. My friends say some things never change.

The party is a great success. I stand on the deck and watch Ken holding court with some friends on the back lawn. He pops open a bottle of Champagne out over the field. On this day, he seems very happy. I think that he really is aging gracefully. Despite his frenetic work schedule, at forty-seven he is as handsome as ever. He is still fit, and his hair is thick and black, although now it is tinged with a little white at the temples. He has a few tiny crow's feet around his eyes and some new laugh lines, but these only serve to make him look distinguished. He is a gorgeous, wonderful man. I love him more now after ten years than I did even in the beginning.

A BIRTH CENTER BIRTH

Dr. Gerry Hamilton and his wife, Christine, who is a nurse-midwife, have opened a free-standing Family Birthing Center in the lower level of their office building on the south side of Concord. Because Susie and I are now certified by the state, we are invited to use their facility and attend births at the center if we wish. I have remained something of a purist and a snob in my conviction that birthing in the comfort and familiar surroundings of one's own home is the way to go, but I soon find that the ease of the commute from my house to the center is a great luxury.

I am getting fried and downright crispy around the edges from driving around the New Hampshire countryside to some godforsaken little cabin, up a rutted, muddy, boulder-strewn, four-wheel drive logging road on the edge of a precipice somewhere, in the middle of the night—quaint though the cabin may be.

The birthing center has hired a full time, experienced labor-and-delivery nurse from Merrimack Valley; she is one of the riotous and seasoned old-guard night nurses of whom I am so fond. To have an assistant always available to monitor the first stage of labor until our clients get active is the nuts. It's not that I want to do perineal obstetrics—quite the contrary—but it's wonderful to have someone skilled to share the responsibility in the initial stages so I can get some rest. I am getting soft.

The first birth I attend at the birthing center is a Portuguese couple with the same surname as my mother's people. My mother's lineage is Portuguese from the Azores, until she dilutes it by marrying into Maine Irish fishermen, but they are seafaring people, all of them. This couple lives much too far away for us to assist, but because they have the name Gaspar, and they could be potential relatives, I agree to help them at the birth center. Emmanuel is a typical Mediterranean man in that he considers childbirth to be women's work. He has no intention of being present for the birth. This disappoints Sebastiana immensely, but she is resigned to his decision. I say I'll see what I can do.

I greet Manny and Sebastiana at the center when she is contracting every few minutes. They come with their whole family—grandmothers, sisters, aunts. The women stay out in the den/kitchen area, heating up food they have made for the nativity. It is very loud in the kitchen, but down the hall, where Sebastiana is laboring in the Jacuzzi, it is blissfully quiet, except for her labored breathing.

When she pushes and I can feel a tiny bit of head at the opening, she gets out of the water and lies on her side on the bed. Manny is nowhere to be seen, which starts to concern me. I genuinely don't want him to miss the opportunity to see his child come into this world. I begin to see bulging membranes, with the baby's head following close behind and some hair visible. I start to exclaim loudly how great Sebastiana is doing and how beautiful the baby looks.

I hear the relatives say excitedly to Manny, "Your baby is coming! The midwife can see its head!"

After a few more loud exclamations on my part, I can sense Manny standing just outside the door in the hall. I increase my enthusiasm and loud pronouncements until I see, out of the corner of my eye, that Manny is now standing in the doorway, watching. But I am blocking his view. I continue to carry on excessively. Sebastiana nods at me in between efforts; she knows that I've been baiting him, and now I am reeling him in.

He is caught, hook, line, and sinker. Before he knows it, he is at my elbow, sitting down gently next to me, completely mesmerized. He looks pale, but he is right in there with me. At this moment, at the peak of a push, Sebastiana's water breaks in a huge wave that soaks both our faces. I look at Manny in gleeful surprise, but he is not laughing. He looks like he is going to pass out.

He starts to bolt. I touch his arm and say, gently, "Please stay, Manny."

And he does.

As his baby's head begins to crown, there is a fair amount of molding, which causes a ridge of skin to form as the head presents.

Manny leans over and whispers, worriedly, "What's that? A piece of intestine?"

I laugh out loud. "God, no, Manny! At least we better hope not! I'm kidding. This is completely normal; the bones of the skull temporarily overlap to protect the brain as the head is being born. Relax—we're looking good."

I smile at how dear his concern is. I take his hands and place them on his baby's head as it is born completely, and Maria's face is freed.

Manny gasps, "This is the baby! Look! Look at the face—this is my baby's *face!*"

I am giggling a little bit now. I look up to see that his face is completely soaked with a combination of tears and amniotic fluid. Oh, how sweet!

Manny is all over this baby when she comes out. Sebastiana is trying to nurse Maria, but Manny is so goo-goo-gaw-gaw with his daughter that Sebastiana rolls her eyes and gives up for the moment. She hands Maria to her father. Maria starts to cry lustily when he takes her. Manny looks upset by this.

I say, "Take your shirt off, Manny. She needs to feel your skin. She needs to know she's safe."

Manny removes his shirt and leans back into the pillows, with Maria lying contentedly on his chest. Pretty soon, Maria finds Manny's little nipple, and she latches on.

Manny's eyes grow huge. He says, "Look! She likes me! She thinks I'm her mother!"

I look at Sebastiana, who is grinning. I say, "Good luck to you with all this, girl, is all I can say."

The relatives have created a huge feast for the occasion. The aroma of cooking is mouthwatering. They serve some of my favorites, like traditional molho cru, and shellfish cataplana with linguica, and they toast the baby many, many times with Vinho Verde. It must be my Portuguese blood that is responsible for my deep and abiding appreciation for cheap, shitty wine.

It is a wonderful celebration. As I am leaving the center, Sebastiana thanks me for getting Manny involved. She says the birth definitely wouldn't have been the same if I hadn't hooked him.

I say, "No problem. He was easy. We had some terrific bait."

⌐

As vice president of MANA, I do a lot of speaking engagements to further the profession of midwifery. One afternoon, Ken calls me in from mulching the vegetable garden to answer the phone. It is the *Today* show, asking if they can fly me down to New York City for the following day's live program with Jane Pauley, which is about natural childbirth. I say I'd be delighted, and I hop on the next plane to the Big Apple. I think this will be a lark. I meet up with a couple of midwife friends who work in the City and dine with them that night. We have a great time, compliments of the *Today* show. I am completely oblivious to what a slaughter this is about to be.

The next morning, the *Today* show's driver picks me up at the hotel to bring me to the studio. Seated in the limo is another woman, who is going to be on the show with me. We are chatting amicably when she mentions that the reason she has been asked to do the show is because she has written an article, published in *Mother Jones* magazine, titled "My Perfect Birth." In the article, she describes her birth as wonderful because she'd had an epidural, didn't feel a thing, and therefore, blissfully had her baby. My mouth drops open. I thought this was supposed to be a piece on natural childbirth, not on paralysis from the waist down. Uh-oh.

The more she talks, the more I get a queasy, uneasy feeling about the dynamics of this whole thing. I know from experience that epidurals majorly screw up the normal rhythm and progress of labor. I ask her more pointed questions about her "perfect" experience. She tells me that her labor did, in fact, stall in second stage and that she'd needed a forceps delivery to get the baby out because she couldn't push. Because of the forceps, she was on pain killers for three months in order to sit down comfortably, but since she hadn't felt anything, it was a great birth.

Right-o! Three months with a sore butt? How perfect can you get? I say, honestly, that I am shocked that *Mother Jones* would print a piece like this. I thought they were supposed to be a fairly radical rag and wouldn't buy into the co-opting of women's power in birth. She stops talking to me.

Unfortunately, it gets even worse at the TV station. We are herded into a holding area backstage as we await our turn. Bryant Gumbel is there, watching the TV monitors and making disparaging comments. Jane Pauley's smiling face is interviewing someone, and I suddenly realize that we're not going to have a little chat with Jane before we go on. We are going on cold. The atmosphere is highly charged, chaotic, and nerve-wracking. I start to get terrible stage fright; this isn't at all what I expected.

We are called during a station break and rush in to take our seats. Ms. Pauley casually mentions that she has just had twins. She developed toxemia and ended up with a section, thank God! She thinks natural childbirth is barbaric and cruel. She looks at me as though I have two heads. Oh, fucking great. I finally grasp the absolute reality of why I am here. I am to be the punching bag—and there's nothing I can do about it now.

The actual interview is blessedly short; it goes by in a blur for me. But it is long enough for Jane Pauley and the other guest to trounce me for being so backward, so uncivilized and crude, for torturing women by making them labor without the relief of pain medication. How could I be so irresponsible and uneducated?

I'm not prepared for confrontation, and the time is too short to address the real issues of the negative effects of medication on labor patterns and on the baby's well-being. The fact that our outcomes are consistently good is because we *don't* use any drugs; therefore, our babies are not narcotized and depressed when they are born. It is over before I can even begin to explain my motives. In short, it is carnage.

When I stumble offstage, Bryant Gumbel says very loudly, "What a masturbatory effort!"

Hey, thanks, Bry.

THE "MIRACLE BIRTH"

The apprentice, Raven, has completed her midwifery training and has moved to Montpelier, Vermont, with the intention of setting up a practice. I miss her greatly, and occasionally, there is a client who is geographically suited for the two of us to work together again. I enjoy this immensely.

This is one of the last births we are able to do together. Raven calls it the "miracle birth" and uses it as a shining example when talking about the role that intuition plays in everyday midwifery practice. In this particular case, I think we were flying by the seat of our pants and were bailed out at the last minute by divine intervention. On the other hand, Raven feels that I tapped into some deep, intuitive perception and maximum clarity that led to the cutting edge of my capability. Interesting—two interpretations, same case.

Wiggy is a vibrant and energetic young mother; hence, the nickname "Wiggy," I guess. She lives on the New Hampshire/ Vermont border. This pregnancy is her third. I have attended her other two babies, who arrived rather quickly and without a hitch, so I'm not anticipating anything out of the ordinary. Raven and I meet up at Wiggy's relatively swank condo when Wiggy is in early labor. Raven and I sit outside under the shade of some landscaped birch trees, catching up on the times, until Wiggy's husband summons us to come in.

Wiggy has dilated steadily and is progressing normally, but the one thing I don't like is the fact that there is nothing presenting yet in the pelvis. With a first baby, I'd be more alarmed, as that could signal that her pelvis is too snug a fit. But as this is her third bambino, it isn't as much of a concern as it is a possible malpresentation. But from everything I can tell externally, the head is down and all systems are "go." I believe that as soon as she gets really active and has some good, efficient contractions, the head will slam down in there.

I am wrong.

It is not a good feeling. When Wiggy gets to be seven centimeters and is really cooking, her membranes are bulging, but her cervix feels like an empty sleeve. What the hell is going on? By all rights, the head should have been down and filling the mid-pelvis way before now. The baby's heart rate is steady and clear. I haven't picked up even a hint of a deceleration at any time, so at least the baby is fine for now. I start to get very antsy. I don't like the feel of this one bit. My adrenaline is flooding, and my heart is pounding. I feel like I need to alert Ken, who is at the hospital doing surgery. I want to pick his knowledgeable brain.

I call him from a phone in another room to tell him what I'm *not* feeling and to hear his reassuring voice.

Instead, he says slowly, "Well, this doesn't sound good. I mean, it certainly isn't normal. Do you think the baby may be transverse?"

I realize I am almost panting, "No. I'm positive it's not. The head is clearly ballotable right over the pubes; it's just not descending. The placenta isn't there, either; that's the problem. I don't feel a thing in there."

He is quiet for a minute, then says, "Look, sweetie, I know from experience that you know better than anyone what's going on at this moment. I hesitate to make a recommendation because I'm not there, and I don't want to influence how you approach this."

I say, "That's just the problem; I *don't know* what's going on right now. I feel like I want to bring her in. I'm going to call the rescue squad to transport her. I'll call you back in a few minutes to let you know what's up."

Ken says, "Sounds good. I'm stuck here all day anyway."

Well, that helped a little.

I call the local rescue squad and tell them that I may need their help. I ask them if they will come and stand by.

They are on their way.

I walk into the bedroom. Raven frowns at me and says, "You look frantic."

She takes me out to a little balcony off the bedroom and sits me down. She puts her hands on my head. I close my eyes and try to still myself.

She says firmly, "Slow down, Carol. Take some deep breaths,

and focus your energy. That's better. Now, I want you to go to that place you have of your other knowing, that incredible reservoir you have that knows exactly what to do."

Such loving hands. Through her hands, I can feel all the jangled and jagged adrenaline drain out of me, and a sense of deep peace and well-being comes flooding in. I thank her for her art, and I approach this dilemma anew.

The rescue squad arrives, and they are very friendly, nervous, and excited. After we do introductions, I ask them to please just sit tight in the hall for a moment. Wiggy is really working with her body now. I don't want to break her concentration, but I need information from my fingers. I am desperately hoping I will feel a head. I don't. When I examine her this time, to my dismay, she is fully dilated, and the membranes are bulging tighter than a drum. I reach as far as I dare without risking rupturing the membranes. My fingertips find only emptiness. It feels like an enormous, vacant cavern. Damn!

I go back to the phone and call Ken.

This time he says, "OK, by now you've had time to sit and be with this. What do *you* think you should do?"

I say, so decisively it surprises me, "Nothing. I think I should do nothing. If I bring her in to the local hospital here, the first thing they'll do is break her water, and I think—no, I *know*—that will have disastrous results. I'm afraid of a cord prolapse. Nothing is presenting to prevent the cord from washing down the minute they snag that bag. I know this is way out of protocol, and I'm not sure *what* is going on, but the one thing I'm sure of now is that we're supposed to trust that Wiggy's body knows exactly what to do, and we should let her do it. And that's all I know."

"Good luck, kid," he says, "I'm glad it's you and not me. I don't have the patience."

I say sincerely, "Ken, thanks for being understanding. I feel confident in what Wiggy is doing now."

I can hear him smile. "Sweetie, you did all the talking."

I go back into the bedroom and lean on the side of the bed with Raven, observing.

Raven says, "The baby still sounds great. Since she's fully dilated, do you want me to start coaching her to get her pushing?"

"No. Definitely not. Whatever is going on, my guess is that we have less than thirty seconds to get that kid out once she starts bringing it down."

Raven smiles, "Oh, good, you're back. That was quite a little whirlwind you went on."

"Yeah, well, thanks for pulling me out of it. Anyway, why don't you get us set up for infant resuscitation, just in case I'm wrong and it takes longer than thirty seconds?"

While Raven is getting the resuscitation equipment attached and laid out, I say, "Wiggy, I want you to listen to your body very carefully. I don't want you to push until your body clearly tells you it's time, OK? Then I want you to tell me exactly what you're feeling."

The rescue squad folks are jammed in the doorway, watching wide-eyed and waiting breathlessly for a signal. We stay suspended in time like this for what seems like an eternity but is probably only a matter of minutes. Then Wiggy says, "I need to get up to go to the bathroom."

I tell her to go ahead, and then I whisper to Raven, "OK, here it comes. Get ready for the Mother Lode."

Wiggy has one foot on the floor and the other leg still in bed when she whips around, wild-eyed, and screams to me, "It's coming *now!*"

I crouch in front of Wiggy, with her legs straddling the bed, and I pray fervently: *Ancient and Holy Mother! Be with us now, and guide this baby quickly to the safety of this shore.*

It doesn't take thirty seconds; it is more like fifteen. In one push, the head is born and the cord is wrapped several times around the neck, so tightly that I can't budge it a millimeter. Raven slaps the scissors in my hand; the cord is cut, and it spins crazily, like a pinwheel, from the release of tension, spraying an arc of blood across the headboard and up the wall. The placenta follows immediately behind the baby's body. Raven is standing ready with an Ambu bag for the little guy, but he is absolutely fine, except his neck is blanched completely white.

He looks around as if to ask, "What's all the fuss? I made it in fine time, didn't I? Now relax and back off, ladies."

I am so happy to see him like this that I grab him and kiss his pale little neck. "Thanks, guy. That was a flamboyant entrance you made, but you did a great job!"

Raven rolls her eyes heavenward. "Lady, that was a close one."

Later, when I examine the placenta, I say to Raven, "Huh, here's our culprit."

The umbilical cord is *less than ten inches long*! In all the hundreds and hundreds of babies whose births I've attended, I have never seen anything like it. The poor child had been hung up in the womb by his own noose! Wiggy's body had been exquisitely fine-tuned to the potential danger in this situation and figured it out. This is the real miracle.

When the rescue squad people are leaving, they ask if we think it would be kosher to add a blue ribbon to their ambulance's collection, signifying a delivery they have done. I say absolutely. I appreciated their solid presence and was grateful for the confidence they gave me, just by being there. They leave, happy to add another ribbon to their trophy collection.

On the drive home, Raven and I stop by a small outdoor café for a much-appreciated glass of wine before we part company. Raven is grinning as she holds up her glass of wine, as if to toast or roast me; I'm not sure which.

She says, "Well, I have to say it once again. If it had been anybody else, her ass would have been grass. She would have screwed that up. If anyone had broken Wiggy's water and got her to push too soon, that baby would have strangled within minutes. But somehow, you knew to trust the process and to just sit it out. Jesus, that's a tough thing to do—nothing. You're crazy, Leonard, you really are. But that was a miracle, and it only happened that way because it was you."

———

Ken's practice is soaring. He has three nurse-midwives and two nurse practitioners working with him as a professional association, which is a profit-sharing plan as part of an incentive program. They are definitely the most popular show in town. Women like the type of care they receive, so the group is working to maximum capacity.

The downside to this popularity is that it generates a considerable amount of professional jealousy from Ken's colleagues and competitors who, in response to Ken's successfulness, begin to object by trying to limit the size of Ken's practice. His peers propose to the obstetrics department at Merrimack Valley Hospital that an obstetrician (i.e., Ken) can only provide adequate backup for *one* nurse-midwife, implying that the quality of care becomes diminished or irresponsible with the more midwives a physician has to supervise.

This proposal comes out of left field, in that Ken's practice's outcomes are not at issue. In fact, his number of cesarean sections has dropped radically with the use of nurse-midwives. The only basis for this restrictive edict is obvious: unmitigated envy. In addition to this, his colleagues refuse to back the midwives if there is an immediate emergency, and Ken or Gerry are not in-house.

These decisions are made, even though there have not been any inappropriate incidents involving the midwives. The obstetricians illogically state that they just "don't approve of this type of care." This is simply more of the continuing resentment and opposition to Ken's unwavering commitment to the midwifery model of care.

As transparent and as pathetic as this is, it throws Ken into the deepest, darkest depression I have experienced with him. At first, he is incredibly angry with his colleagues. He has a very violent reaction to their attempts to limit him.

He says (and I do quote exactly), "Those sons of bitches! Those fuckers! What the hell do they think they're trying to do? They're all warts on the asshole of mankind!"

He consults twice with an attorney. The proposal never goes anywhere, probably because it is so ludicrous, and he is willing to fight it. But the damage is done; he feels like he just keeps running into a wall with them. The bottom line is that Ken still craves support and admiration from his brothers in the medical profession, and this is not forthcoming. The more the conflict over midwifery escalates, the deeper Ken spirals downward.

Then, he just gives up. He becomes quiet and unnaturally withdrawn. It is very frightening. Ken's manic episodes are increasing to the point where I am gravely concerned, and I insist he get professional counseling. It is like a dark cloud has descended over our lives. Ken is finding it harder and harder to get motivated to even crawl out of bed in the morning.

He has switched from moderately drinking white wine at night to drinking straight gin—and lots of it. I am trying to take care of him the best I know how, but I am still pretty naïve as to the extent of his depression. And he is a first-class actor. Nobody knows how troubled he really is by this struggle, because he can cover his emotions flawlessly.

I become terribly afraid for him when I notice that the amber flecks of spirit are gone from his eyes. His eyes look dead and empty to me. He is like a man with a hole in his soul, and it is leaking.

For my benefit, he makes an appointment to see a therapist. He sees the therapist a few times, then reports that the well-meaning man has told Ken that he seems fine; he doesn't need to go back. I know Ken's brilliance has overwhelmed the therapist; he can really turn it on when he wants to.

"You bullshitted that poor guy, didn't you?" I ask.

"Yup" is all he says.

He never goes back.

Instead, to escape his demons temporarily, and as a last-minute surprise, he books us a flight to France to ski the glaciers in the French Alps. I am startled; this seems like running away to me, but if this is a way he can deal with his problems, then so be it. We take an overnight sleeper train from Paris to the snowy village of Chamonix, nestled in the majestic Alps along the Italian border. We stay in a stone chalet that is perched on the side of a mountain, and we eat obscene amounts of fabulous provincial food and drink even more amounts of local French wine.

We ski the glaciers of Mont Blanc at fifteen thousand feet with a French guide, who leads us safely down the steeps, avoiding avalanches and precipices. We put chairs in the snow in the blinding sun and nap like lazy cats, all the while gazing at impossibly craggy, snowcapped mountain ranges that loom as far as the eye can see.

On our last evening there, we walk in the village of Chamonix in search of authentic raclette. We pass a bearded man on a sleigh with wooden runners, which is pulled by two enormous gray workhorses whose colorful harnesses are covered with bells. The man teases us loudly to get in for a ride. Ken laughs and picks me up, and we get in the back. The bearded man covers us with a thick fur blanket, and we trot off down the snowy street. We pass enormous stone chateaus and ancient churches, with the imposing mountains as a backdrop.

I've always thought these horse-drawn rides would be corny,

but instead, it is incredibly romantic. I look to see that Ken has large white snowflakes in his black hair and on his eyelashes.

I ask, "Are you happy this moment?"

He smiles. "Yes. And you?"

I snuggle against him even closer. "Yes, of course."

As he leans to kiss me, I see that his green eyes are dancing with golden-amber flecks.

Maybe he *can* heal himself.

MY LITTLE SISTER'S BIRTH

My younger sister, Wendy, and her husband, Jim, have been trying to conceive a child for almost a year, when Milan has the great idea to make them a fertility box. I have no idea where he cooked this up, but we look in old herbal-folklore textbooks and find plants and related items that are considered fertility promoters. Milan gathers all these together and puts them in an ornately decorated wooden box. He is very much into the efficacy of his creation. He tells Wendy and Jim to sleep with the box under their bed. My sister is pregnant in one cycle.

During her pregnancy, Wendy is the vice president of a bank, and she goes to work in gorgeous caftans and pearls and pumps and a briefcase. I perceive her as being a serious professional businesswoman, so I spend a lot of time, prenatally, working with her to learn how to let go and surrender to the process. I am a little concerned that she might have what Susie and I call the "liberated woman syndrome," which is when powerful women try to dictate and direct how this physical process is going to go. This often results in calamity when their bodies rebel and refuse to cooperate with their plans. But despite my worrying, in the end, my sister surrenders to birth *and* directs how it goes.

At two o'clock one morning, right before Halloween, I wake up and know my sister has started labor. I lie awake, staring out the window at the stars, waiting for the phone to ring. I answer

"Hi, Wendy!" just to shock her. She has, in fact, started lightly contracting.

She putzes around like this until lunchtime, when I suggest we all go to our favorite local Mexican restaurant for some of their great, greasy, high-fat food. I tell Wendy that eating hot peppers will help put her into good labor. I am totally making this up, because I am hungry and I want to go there. I am torturing my kid sister, of course, but she still believes me. She eats a bunch of raw jalapenos, and damn if it doesn't work.

She starts breathing very heavily every few minutes—and not only from the heat of the peppers. Our waiter is eyeing her warily. He becomes very anxious every time she stops to loudly blow out her breath. He doesn't like this.

After one particular whopper contraction, he says, nervously, "Don't you people have somewhere you should be going?"

I say, "Nah, just boil some water, will you?"

Later that evening, I go to their house, which is across the road as the crow flies. Wendy is soaking in a tub and relaxing well. They have lit candles and burned some sage to create safe space, and they are playing soft Native American flute music. Jim has put a pillow in a plastic bag, and Wendy is leaning against it, almost asleep. Jim is sitting on the edge of the tub, rhythmically pouring warm water over Wendy's giant belly. She looks hypnotized, her eyelids fluttering as if in a trance. What a sweet scene.

I sit quietly on the bathroom floor, observing, until I almost fall asleep myself. When I rally, I check her and am astounded. She is almost completely dilated! I watch as Wendy begins to moan as she does the hardest work of opening up completely. I am so proud of her; she is really doing it.

I realize that birth is an initiation for women, an opening to our deeper powers. Women need to experience this part—the struggle my sister is in right at this moment—to understand the depth and unspoken commitment made at the summit of labor with her emerging child. Women innately know the importance of this work. They have made an unconscious decision at this point to freely die for their children to come safely through. This is the sacred contract. They will give their lives for their children's health and well-being; this is the pact a mother makes with her babe at the apogee of pain. And only now will the body open to release the child. My sister crosses that threshold somewhere deep in her soul, and she begins to bring her baby out.

When Wendy begins seriously pushing, she wants to be out of the water and in bed. Fanny's head becomes visible, and I am very excited as the potential new auntie. It is quite different, watching a new family member arrive. I get a little berserk. I am borderline hysterical with anticipation; I can hardly stand it.

I start babbling on and on about how great my sister is doing.

I exclaim, "Wow! This is awesome! You're doing such a good job! Everything looks great!" Fanny's head comes down a bunch more. "Wow! You're doing *fabulous!* This is so good!" Fanny's head is almost crowning. "Wow! Unbelievable! Whoo-weee! You've got tons of room!"

My sister finally snaps, "Will you shut up already? *Room?* What room? It feels like I'm pushing a square TV out of here! I thought this part was supposed to feel good? You just forget what this feels like, that's all. It's been too long for you to remember. *You* should have another kid!"

I think about Milan and how he is starting his teen-rebellion years prematurely.

I say, "Thanks, I'm all set."

I am aware of the other family members standing out in the hall—our mother, Jim's parents, and Wendy's two stepchildren are all anxiously waiting to be invited into the room to watch.

I ask Wendy if she wants them to be present for the birth.

She says, "Yes, but I don't want them to come in until after the head is born."

Okey dokey, that's pretty specific.

She pushes for about another ten minutes, and Fanny's head is easily (in my estimation) born. As Fanny hangs suspended, half in and half out, Wendy stops and looks around.

She says, "OK, they can come in now."

She waits until everyone is in and settled comfortably in front-row seats. Then, ever in control, she gives a little "ugh."

Fanny comes flying out, making a stellar debut amid the cheers and clapping of her admiring family. Fanny opens one eye and eyes me suspiciously.

I greet her. "Hey, there, little niece! Welcome to the family. I'm your favorite auntie!"

Fanny is a riot. She is the spitting image of her paternal grandfather, with blonde hair sticking up and intense blue eyes and freckles. I am tremendously relieved; everything has gone perfectly. Fanny is here, and she is adorable. A close pediatrician friend of mine says that he will make a house call to check her out in the morning.

Watching my sister nurse her newborn daughter fills me with so much love. Man, my sister has always been so much fun. She always does what I tell her to; she falls for it every time. I suppose now I should apologize for lying about that bogus hot peppers theory.

Instead, I kiss her good night. "I'm really proud of you, kid."

In November of 1986, I become the second president of MANA. I am elected to succeed Teddy Charvet when her term ends. I am installed as president in a ceremony during our annual convention in Wheeling, West Virginia. It is an incredible honor to know that the North American midwives have collectively asked me to represent and lead them; it also seems like a tremendous responsibility. It seems impossible that just a decade before, I was a young upstart, catching babies in the countryside as Dr. Brown's sidekick, unaware of the hundreds of other women across the nation who were doing exactly the same thing at the same time—these women who are now my sisters.

I am astounded and extremely flattered when the president of the ACNM, Judith Rooks, calls me "a midwife's midwife." I intend to live up to that label. I am a little bit shy when Teddy officially passes on the office to me, with the midwives present in West Virginia, celebrating and carrying on as only those women can do. I have reached the pinnacle of my career; it doesn't get any better than this!

Little do I know that I will reign as president of MANA for only a few short months.

As my career peaks, Ken is on a downward spiral, the depths of which I will never know. The night I am invested, he is in West Germany, learning the cutting-edge techniques of operative laser laparoscopy. He calls me from Germany to congratulate me, which I think is incredibly sweet. He sounds very excited and enthusiastic about his course. He is learning new techniques of CO_2 laser surgery through a laparoscope, for treating infertility and for removing adhesions and the tissue of endometriosis. He says it is "slick," as it saves women a lot of time spent recovering in the hospital.

I am proud of him. He is the first doctor in Concord trained to do this procedure. We have a great mutual-admiration conversation. He is so committed to the work that MANA is doing that he says he is going to set aside an entire clinic day at his office as a fund-raiser and donate the proceeds to MANA. What a wonderful man! All things considered, I feel like the most fortunate woman in the world.

~)(~

On Ken's forty-eighth birthday, he is speeding to an emergency at the hospital in the dark of predawn when an enormous stag leaps out in front of his car. There is nothing Ken can do to prevent a collision. He hits the huge stag broadside; it flies up over the hood, and its head smashes the windshield right in front of Ken's face.

Ken can't stop to look for the carcass until he is on his way home. He doesn't find a sign of the poor animal anywhere. When I see his smashed BMW in the morning, I gasp to see that the deer's fur that is stuck in the grill is pure white. Ken says it is the oddest thing—in the headlights, the stag appeared to be completely white.

My heart freezes. I know what this means in ancient Celtic legend—the killing of the white stag—but I refuse to believe it.

CHAPTER THIRTEEN

LION'S HEART, 1987

For our winter vacation, instead of skiing out West, we decide to go somewhere hot for a change. Ken has been working obsessively and is constantly complaining about being worn out. I have to admit that he is looking unusually drawn and haggard. We think that baking in the sun in a hot clime will do us good, and it does appear to be a miracle cure. We choose the tropical French island of Guadeloupe in the West Indies.

On the island, we do nothing but roast in the sun on the pristine white-sand beach, sleep in the shade of giant sea-grape bushes on the shore, and swim in the beautiful aquamarine waters of the Caribbean Sea. After a week of this, Ken looks restored and gorgeously tanned and healthy.

On the last day of our stay on Guadeloupe, a native entrepreneur working the beach asks me if I would like to have my hair corn-rowed and beaded. I think this will be a great 'do to wear home, so I have the enterprising young man braid my head with hundreds of long braids that end with lots of colorful beads.

I surprise Ken with my new look, which I think is incredibly sexy. I am flirting when I say, "Don't you think I look like Bo Derek in *10*?"

He pauses, then gets a naughty smile. "To be perfectly honest, sweetie, I was thinking you look more like Stevie Wonder."

When we return home, Ken is hit with a major medical-malpractice lawsuit. In 1985, a patient of his contracted the AIDS virus through a contaminated blood transfusion during a routine hysterectomy, and now she is HIV positive. This happens right on the cusp of the comprehension of the enormity of the epidemic, before blood banks screen their supplies. Ken's case becomes a nationally precedented case, because a physician has never before been sued for responsibility for transmittal of the disease. The outcome is being followed nationally with a critical eye.

Hospitals have been unsuccessfully sued, and the blood banks themselves have been exonerated for accidentally spreading the virus. Now, the attempt is to find the attending physician at fault, he being the captain of the ship, as it were.

The prosecution claims that a complication arose due to Ken's surgical technique that required a transfusion, when, in fact, a majority of gynecologists routinely use blood replacement therapy following hysterectomies, because the recovery time is greatly reduced. Many of Ken's colleagues testify to his skill and expertise as a surgeon, as well as to the routine use of blood transfusions necessitated by the large blood loss during this standard operation.

The defense states that while this situation is truly tragic, this occurred prior to a clear understanding of the extent and etiology of the AIDS virus; therefore, no one can be held accountable for that. Nevertheless, the case looms large and formidable and promises to be a long and horrendous court battle.

The woman is dying, and she has three young children who Ken had delivered, and he is fond of her. Understandably, the family wants to be compensated for her loss, although I don't feel it is appropriate for their lawyers to target Ken.

This is more than he can bear.

His whole life has been dedicated to healing and caring for his patients, and now the worst nightmare has come true. A woman is dying a horrible death because of something he inadvertently did. Ken retreats somewhere deep inside himself, and no amount of coaxing from me can make him come out.

Even though he is sweet and polite to me, he is no longer in his body—the pain is clear and obvious in his eyes. I can barely look at him. He is scaring me. I know my man is drowning. He is on a desperate slide this time, and there is nothing I can do about it. The depth of his grief is unfathomable. My heart is breaking, but I can no longer reach him nor follow him to where he has gone.

For once, I can't be there with him.

The full destruction of his depression hits with gale force one night early in February, when he sits on the edge of our bed with his head in his hands. He is crumpled as only a defeated man can be. I watch in horror as his sobbing grows to heart-stopping screams. *He is screaming in pain.* I try to comfort him by holding and rocking him, but he has unleashed the full fury of his demons now, and nothing is going to stop him. He is sobbing that he is sorry, that he is tired, that he can't do it anymore. I am kissing his eyes, his tears, trying in vain to take his pain away.

I know then that he is only peripherally aware of me. He has slipped away. I know, dully, that the damage of these events can never be undone, and that I have lost the battle. I have lost the man I love.

When he finally sleeps, I ski by moonlight to the Tree, where I collapse at the base of her enormous trunk, weeping uncontrollably. I can feel the violent destruction of the impending holocaust raging all around me. I pray desperately for it to be reversed. I cling to the Tree's rough bark for guidance. I get no sense of relief. The immutable laws of the universe have been set in motion.

Ken continues to go through the motions at work. In the midst of all this, Susie's father dies after a lengthy battle with congestive heart failure. Her father's funeral is on Sunday, and I sit with her family in their little church in Warner as their minister intones the words for the dead. I try to comfort Susie in her engulfing sadness for the passing of her beloved dad.

It is while we are at the funeral that Ken removes the twelve-gauge shotgun from the cellar.

I didn't even know it was functional.

I stop to see Ken in the office on my way home to ask if he wants to go to a movie with Milan and me that evening. He declines, saying he has a mountain of paperwork to catch up on. He actually seems quite chipper, and he isn't even drinking. He kisses me long and deep and tenderly as I sit on his desk.

I catch my breath and say, "Wow! I guess you're feeling a bit friskier!"

He gives me a huge grin and says he'll be home after the movie.

Instead, later that night he phones to say he's been called to labor-and-delivery to augment a woman, and he will probably be stuck there all night running a Pit drip. I am disappointed. I really feel a need to snuggle with him, to feel the warmth of his skin and to smell his scent, and I tell him this.

There is a long, silent pause.

Just before he hangs up, he says, uncharacteristically, "Carol, I love you more than you will ever know. I mean that with all my heart."

I think happily, *Jeesh, he must be getting better.*

He never makes it home.

I am awakened the next morning, alone in our bed, by the ringing of the phone. The call is from the midwives in the office, asking me where he is. They say they have patients waiting, and he hasn't arrived at the office yet. I am speechless. In over twenty years of practice, Ken has never missed a single day. So this is it; this is how it's all going to go down. I panic. I have never felt so alone. I call the Hopkinton police immediately to report my husband as missing.

The police come and talk to me and are very gentle and caring, but they ask if perhaps we've had a domestic dispute, that maybe Ken is just cooling off for a while. I respond no, that absolutely is not the case. I know my husband, and this is life-threatening. They are still very considerate, if a little patronizing, and they leave, assuring me that our marriage will survive to work out the kinks. Jesus.

The next day there is still no word. I keep Milan home from school, simply because I need him for strength. I can't stand the waiting; it is sheer torture. I am hoping against hope that Ken has gone somewhere to seek help, that perhaps he has taken his own best advice and has sought professional counseling. But I know, realistically, his past experience prevents this from being possible.

When the mail arrives in the afternoon, there is a letter from Ken. The letter, written in his scrawl, reads [in part]:

Dear Carol,

We have just hung up from talking on the phone. There are lots of things to say, and I hope the words will come. You have given me more than it's reasonable to ask any human being to give. You are the most caring and giving person I have ever known. Where you get the strength and reserve to draw on is a mystery to me. It is truly amazing. Any good that I've been able to do comes from your faith in me. But I don't have the confidence in myself to turn this awfulness around. I'm tired, Carol, too tired to struggle anymore. This decision has been a long time coming, and its time has come. Thank you for

your love, your caring, and your concern. I love you and will
always love you, as hard as this may be to understand.
Ken

The second page is a list of financial information, insurance policies, and investments.

In this single moment, my world shatters. I know this is not an empty threat. Ken is determined, and he will follow through. It is just a matter of time. I begin pacing the length of the sunroom, back and forth, my hysteria building quickly out of control. My head is roaring, and my sobs have turned to loud screams, screams coming from somewhere outside my body. The pain is unbearable. Oh, my god. I can't do this. The room is spinning. I am going to pass out.

Milan grabs my arms firmly and sits me down on the daybed.

He says clearly, "Mom! Mom! Look at me! Look in my eyes. Slow your breathing down. Way down. Slow it down *now*—that's it, gentle. In through your nose and out through your mouth. You know how to do it. Nice, there you go. Like that, slow and easy. Good."

I gaze in my son's intense brown eyes and follow his directions. I allow him to slow my hysteria down. Milan is coaching me as he has seen me do with hundreds of birthing women in the throes of their travail. My son is midwifing me through the worst pain I have ever known, and this is instinctual to him. I am profoundly grateful for his strength, his love. He is my rock in this storm.

This time when I call the police, they take the letter seriously. They put out a nationwide alert for Ken. If Ken uses his credit cards anywhere, they'll be picked up by computer and his location reported. The state police are combing the state for his vehicle. I later learn he has changed the plates on his car. I'm not surprised. I know he can outsmart everyone. I don't hold out much hope that he'll be apprehended.

The waiting is agony. It breaks my heart to think of his anguish in his flight. He must be in so much torment. My poor, sweet man—what can he possibly be thinking? How could I have made it better for him? What could I have done differently? My love has been so blind.

My mother comes to be with me to share the vigil. We sit silently for hours in the living room, waiting, waiting for the phone to ring; waiting for anything, any word.

Finally, I say to her, "He's not dead. Not yet, anyway. I will know because he will give me a sign. Of this I am certain. Ken and I are so intricately connected, I will know when he leaves me. He won't leave without finding a way to say good-bye."

My mother keeps knitting as huge tears roll silently down her cheeks.

KEN, FEBRUARY 11, 1987

When I wake the next morning, Ken's side of the bed is still empty and cold. I wander downstairs to the kitchen to make coffee. I am standing at the window, looking out over the back field. It is very bright, with the early morning sun reflecting off the snow, as only a February day can be. It is exceptionally still and silent in my kitchen.

All of a sudden there is a loud crash in the downstairs bathroom.

I run to the room, and I freeze when I see shards of shattered glass on the slate floor. A framed picture has fallen off the wall, and the glass has exploded everywhere. The picture is an old black-and-white photo of Ken, taken when he was a little boy, grinning in his wagon that is being pulled along by his pet goat, Billy Whiskers.

This is it.

Holy Mother, give me your wisdom to know what needs to be done now.

My mother comes running down the hall; she looks very upset when she sees what has fallen.

"I hope this isn't a bad sign," she says quietly.

"It is. Ken has died just now. I need to be alone. I need for you to leave now."

My mother walks in a daze over to a bowl of nuts and starts cracking them.

I say, "Mom!"

She looks startled. "Oh, right. Sorry." She hurries out the front door.

What happens next is somehow instinctive and somehow ancient. I take Ken's fallen picture with me, go upstairs, and very methodically remove all my clothes, and step out naked onto the balcony off our bedroom. I sit cross-legged in the sun. My grief comes welling up now. Ken's childhood picture is drenched with my tears. I kiss his little-boy face.

Even in my confusion, not truly understanding how he can leave like this, I know my joy and pain with him has come from the deepest wellspring of my love. I know that I will support him, even in this decision. He is through now with his struggle, and I respect his resolution, even though it is one I could never make.

I pray that his soul will fly to wherever he needs to be in a joyous, free-soaring flight of his sweet spirit, so when it comes my time, we can be united once again. This is my only hope, my one belief, that we will recognize and know each other again in some distant time, some far place ... and we will complete our dance together.

I still my breathing. I look out over the field where snow swirls are dancing down the path to the Tree. The sun is intensely bright and white and hypnotic. There is not a sound.

I am very, very calm.

I hear Ken now as clearly as if he is sitting next to me.

He says, "Carol, I'm OK."

I start to cry. "OK, Ken, I know."

I know what needs to be done. I take a deep breath.

"I love you, Ken ... and I let you go."

I feel him leave me now. I feel him kiss my neck as I cry. I feel him touch my hands in farewell. Then he is gone.

Forever.

Trembling, I walk to my bed and lie down to wait.

So, it ends.

EPILOGUE

The Health Center, where the seeds of my career were sown, continues to be a beehive of activity, even after thirty years of dedicated service to women. The name has changed from New Hampshire Women's Health Service to Concord Feminist Health Center. The women on the staff are smart and cheerful, compassionate and brave. They have survived arson and protesters and are ever committed to improving women's lives. They have gotten very sophisticated in their approach to women's health care. For further information, go to *www.feministhealth.org*.

Dr. Brown died peacefully in 1995. I believe he was happy in his elder years. He was always a fixture in Henniker, sitting on the bench in the middle of town in front of New England College, chatting with all the townspeople. After all, Francis delivered half of the town. He still had a bushy white beard and still looked for all the world like Santa Claus. I miss him still.

Susie ran the Concord Midwifery Service for years after I left. She worked by herself for over a decade, doing what she loved, until she got sick of not making any money at it. She went back to school and became a registered nurse. Now she is a high-octane OB-nurse at the "Big House," which is what I call Dartmouth Hitchcock Medical Center in Lebanon. They get the train wrecks from all over the state. She is still midwifing the women, only now it's the high-risk women. She has aged gracefully; she is having fun in her "old lady" years. She sea kayaks in the summer, skis in the winter, and trains for marathons. Now she is *Susan Bartlett, RN.*

Ken's practice, Women's Health Care Associates, PA, continued on for a year before they closed. The nurse-midwives were committed to attending all the mothers who were enrolled with them at the time of Ken's death. Gerry Hamilton, MD, very generously agreed to be their backup for that year. The midwives had zero cesarean sections for the year. Gerry is retired now. He still is encrusted with turquoise-and-silver jewelry, still wears cowboy boots. He is still supporting women through his work as a board member of the CFHC. A lot of his spare time is spent raising orchids—or bugging me.

The apprentice, Raven, lives in Montpelier, Vermont. She had another child, a boy this time. She is still with her young man. She never did go on to become a midwife. Instead, she became an incredible healer, doing intense cranial-sacral work. She still has magic hands. She is the one I go to when I have a mystery ailment. She is a beautiful, loving woman.

The New Hampshire midwives were forced to re-do their legislation in 1999 to evolve to a licensing process. Out of a potentially scary situation came a wonderful development. The legislature created for the state's midwives the New Hampshire Midwifery Council, which is a completely autonomous regulatory board and state agency governing midwifery practice. It was the first independent Board of Midwifery in the United States. For further information, go to *www.NHmidwives.org.*

The Midwives Alliance of North America is still going strong; it withstood the tests of time. I read excerpts from this book at MANA's twenty-fifth anniversary celebration. It is still an umbrella professional organization for midwives in the United States, Canada, and Mexico. For further information, go to *www. MANA.org.*

My mother was married to Ken's father for several years

before Mac died at age eighty-six. My mom is in her mid-eighties now, and she is a pistol. She is a snowbird, living in Florida in the winter and in my backyard in Maine in the summer. She is independent and runs around with all her girlfriends. She hasn't slowed down one bit.

Milan is a grown man. He is smart and funny and is extremely handsome. He is a talented musician and lives in Maine.

And I ... I lost my mind for quite some time. I knew I had to stop working before I hurt someone. My grief was much too raw for me to be able to take care of others. I had to heal myself. I built a lodge out of woven saplings at the base of the Tree, where Ken died. I covered the saplings with tarps and made a fire pit in the center. I stayed there for the better part of a year without speaking much.

Looking back on this, it seems a little insane, but I had the support of my family and friends. It was a painful time but also a time of intense healing, living in the beauty of the forest. The Tree and the deer and the pileated woodpeckers and the coydog all healed me. I began to recover.

I had a spiritual decade, where I delved deeply into women's spirituality and the blood mysteries. I went back into midwifery practice in the late nineties. I opened my birth center, Longmeadow Farm Birthing Home, and attended births at my home.

I'm OK; I made it through. I'm happy now. I am married to a wild French Canadian redneck builder, Tom Lajoie. Tom is eighteen years my junior. Actually, Tom and his family lived across the street from Ken and me when we lived in the little farmhouse in Concord. Little Tommy was my "handyboy" when he was young; he stacked my wood. He says he's been in love with me since he was eleven.

Tom and I have a four-hundred-acre parcel of land in Ellsworth, Maine, that we are making into a tree farm. We are doing sustainable harvesting, and Tom has a sawmill there. We have named the land Bad Beaver Farm.

And Ken ... Ken lives on forever in the hearts and minds of the lives he touched with his loving hands and his gentle way. He will never be forgotten.

GLOSSARY
OF
MIDWIFERY TERMS

Abortifacients. Herbs used to cause abortion.

Aftercoming head. The fetal head (coming after the trunk) in a breech delivery.

AIDS virus. Acquired immunodeficiency syndrome, usually fatal. (1982)

Amniotomy. Artificial rupture of the amniotic sac or membranes.

Anencephaly. A gross congenital malformation in which the cranial vault and the cerebral hemispheres fail to develop.

Apgar score. A system devised to assess the condition of a baby during its first few minutes after birth, so that severe neonatal asphyxia can be diagnosed and treated immediately. It is based on five criteria: heart rate, respiratory effort, muscle tone, response to stimulation, and color.

Arborescent. Branching like a tree.

Aseptic. Free from pathogenic bacteria.

Aspirator. An apparatus for drawing fluid from a cavity of the body by suction.

Asynclitic. A parietal presentation of the fetal head (i.e., coming down sideways).

Atony. Lack of muscle tone.

Auscultation. Listening to the fetal heart sounds.

Autistic. Withdrawn. A term describing a child who has great difficulty in making personal relationships. (see **Vaccines**)

Autoclave. A strongly built and hermetically sealed machine for raising the temperature of steam for the purpose of sterilization.

Bag of waters. The amnion and chorion which contain the amniotic fluid surrounding the fetus.

Ballotment. Bouncing. Tapping the fetus in the amniotic fluid in such a way that it rebounds against the examining fingers.

Bandl's ring. Extreme thickening of the retraction ring of the uterus which occurs when labor is obstructed; it is a sign of imminent rupture of the uterus.

Bimanual compression of the uterus. A maneuver to arrest severe postpartum hemorrhage after the third stage of labor when the uterus is atonic. It is exhausting, but should be maintained until the uterus recovers its tone and remains contracted.

Blood transfusion. The introduction of blood from a donor to the circulation of a recipient.

Breech. The buttocks.

Cesarean section. An obstetric operation where the fetus is extracted from the uterus through an incision made in the abdominal and uterine walls; major abdominal surgery.

Calipers. (Dr. Brown's favorite tool.) Compass for measuring pelvic diameters and curved surfaces, to ascertain pelvimetry.

Cannula. A metal or plastic tube for insertion into a cavity or blood vessel.

Caput. An edematous swelling formed on the head of the baby by pressure onto the dilating cervical os.

Cardinal movements. Rotation of the baby's head through the pelvis during labor and birth.

Castor oil. A purgative used by midwives for the induction of labor. By stimulating peristalsis, it reflexly stimulates uterine contractions.

Caul. The amnion which occasionally does not rupture but envelops the infant's head at birth (considered good luck).

Cephalopelvic disproportion. This refers to disparity between the fetal head and the particular pelvis through which it is to pass.

Cerclage. A purse-string suture placed around the internal os in women with a history of cervical incompetence.

Cervix. In obstetrics, pertaining to the *cervix uteri* or neck of the uterus; it is about 1 inch long and opens into the vagina.

Circumcision. Excision of the prepuce (foreskin) of the penis.

Clitoris. In women, a small sensitive organ consisting of erectile tissue, situated at the junction of the labia minora. It is a complex and wonderful organ that is designed for one specific purpose—*pleasure.*

Colostrum. The fluid secreted by the breasts in the last few weeks of pregnancy and for the first 3 or 4 days after birth, until lactation begins. In humans it is an important source of antibodies.

Compound presentation. Presentation of more than one part of the fetus, e.g., head and hand. A rare complication of labor.

Congenital. Born with. Used to describe a condition, generally a malformation, present at birth.

Contracted pelvis. A pelvis in which any diameter of the brim, cavity or outlet is so shortened as to interfere with the progress of labor.

Contraction. A temporary shortening of muscle fiber, which returns to its original length during relaxation. During labor this may, and generally does, become painful and is accompanied by retraction of the uterus.

Cord. In midwifery, the umbilical cord.

Cotyledon. A division or lobe of the placenta.

Crowning. The moment during birth when the baby's head is distending the vulval ring and no longer recedes between contractions.

Cyanosis. Blueness of the skin and mucous membranes due to deficiency of oxygen.

Descent. A downward movement, e.g., of the fetus. During labor, the baby must descend through the brim, cavity and outlet of the pelvis in order to be born.

Dilation. A natural stretching of an orifice, as in the cervical os, in the first stage of labor.

Domiciliary midwifery. The "confinement" of a woman in her own home where she is attended by a midwife. (Old English)

Down syndrome. A chromosomal abnormality, the commonest type having 47 instead of 46 chromosomes. These children are often affectionate and friendly and benefit from special education.

Dystocia. A term sometimes used to describe a labor which is prolonged or complicated by mechanical difficulty.

Episiotomy. A surgical incision made into the thinned-out perineal body to enlarge the vaginal orifice.

Exsanguinate. To deprive of blood, as after a severe hemorrhage.

External version. A maneuver designed to convert a breech presentation to a vertex presentation. The manipulation is carried out by massaging through the abdominal wall.

Face to pubes. Persistent occipito-posterior position (or "sunny-side up".)

Fallopian tubes. The uterine tubes or oviducts.

Febrile. Feverish.

Fertility. The ability to conceive.

First stage of labor. The period from the onset of labor until complete or full dilation of the cervix.

Flaccid. Limp, without tone. The condition of a baby suffering from severe asphysia. Occasionally, a penis.

Friable. Easily torn, broken or crumpled.

Fundus. The top of the uterus—the part farthest from the cervix.

Genitalia. The organs of reproduction.

Grandmultip. A woman of high parity, usually who has borne 4 or more children.

HIV. Human Immunodeficiency Virus.

Hydrocephaly. A congenital malformation with an increased amount of cerebrospinal fluid distending the ventricles of the brain, severe degrees of which are incompatible with life.

Intrauterine demise. Death of the fetus in utero, generally used to refer to death during pregnancy rather than one during labor.

Introitus. The entrance to the vagina.

Laceration. Perineal tear.

Laparoscope. An instrument for the examination of the peritoneal cavity.

Lithotomy position. The patient lies flat on her back with thighs abducted and legs flexed and held in place with lithotomy stirrups.

Malpresentation. Any presentation of the fetus other than vertex (head down).

Meconium. The greenish-black material present in the newborn's intestinal tract, which is passed via the rectum during the first few days of life.

Oxytocin. Term applied to any drug which stimulates contractions of the uterus in order to induce labor or in the third stage.

Palpation. Examination by touch.

Parietal plate. One of two thin flat bones forming the major part of the vault of the skull.

Perineum. Anatomically, the area extending from the pubic arch to the coccyx, with the underlying tissues.

Pfannenstiel's incision. A transverse abdominal incision just above the symphysis pubis.

Pitocin. Proprietary name for a preparation of synthetic oxytocin.

Placenta. The afterbirth. The placenta transmits oxygen and nutrients from the maternal blood to the fetus and excretes carbon dioxide and other waste products of metabolism from the fetus to the mother.

Pudenda. The external female genitalia.

Quickening. The first perceptible fetal movements felt by the mother at approximately the 16th to 18th week.

Scopolamine. Hyoscine.

Second stage of labor. The expulsion stage, lasting from full dilation of the cervix to complete birth of the child.

Souffle. (Maternal) A soft blowing sound heard on auscultation that is due to the blood passing through the uterine arteries of the mother, particularly over the placental site. It is synchronous with the maternal pulse.

Speculum. A metal or plastic instrument used to open up the vagina to view the hidden, adorable cervix. (A speculum looks like a duck-bill).

Sterile technique. Free from micro-organisms.

Subarachnoid hemorrhage. A hemorrhage into the space below the middle covering of the brain where the cerebrospinal fluid circulates.

Sudden infant death syndrome (SID). A few babies die mysteriously in their beds during the first few months of life. (see **Vaccines**)

Surfactant. A lecithin found in the lungs which helps the alveoli to remain open. Babies who are born pre-term and suffer from respiratory distress syndrome do not have enough of this substance in their lungs.

Third stage of labor. The period from the birth of the baby to the complete expulsion of the placenta and membranes.

Ultrasound. An echo picture obtained from using ultrasonography.

Umbilical cord. The cord which connects the fetus and the placenta. It is usually 20 to 24 inches long and has a spiral twist. It consists of two umbilical arteries carrying deoxygenated blood and one umbilical vein carrying oxygenated blood; this is surrounded by connective tissue and is covered by amnion.

Uterine inertia. Sluggishness. Better termed hypotonic uterine inaction. Inability of the uterine muscle to contract efficiently. A common cause of prolonged labor and postpartum hemorrhage.

Uterus. The womb: a powerful, pear-shaped orbed, muscular organ situated in the pelvic cavity between the bladder and the rectum. It is by far the most amazing organ of any creation of the Universe.

Vaccinate. To inoculate with a virus or bacteria in order to procure immunity to a disease.

Vaccine. A suspension of killed organisms in normal saline; one prepared from living organisms which have lost their virulence; an attenuated bacteria or strain of live virus.

Vernix. The greasy substance, secreted from the sebaceous glands, that covers the fetus *in utero* to protet the skin.

Yoni. Yoni is an East Indian word for the female genitalia and was the primary object of Tantric worship. The Yoni represents the Great Mother, the source of all life, and is my favorite—non medical—name for the beautiful pudenda.

About the Author

Carol Leonard, a "foremother of the modern midwifery movement," is a New Hampshire certified midwife who has been practicing for the last three decades. She is co-founder of the Midwives Alliance of North America (MANA), which represents all midwives in the United States, Canada, and Mexico, and served one term as its president. Her work to improve maternity care in Moscow, Russia, was featured on *20/20* and was written into the Congressional Record. She is currently building a four-hundred-acre farm in Ellsworth, Maine, named Bad Beaver Farm.

FINIS

Printed in the United States
213894BV00004B/14/P